The Influence of Faith

The Influence of Faith

Religious Groups and U.S. Foreign Policy

Edited by
Elliott Abrams

Copublished with the
Ethics and Public Policy Center

ROWMAN & LITTLEFIELD PUBLISHERS, INC.
Lanham • Boulder • New York • Oxford

ROWMAN & LITTLEFIELD PUBLISHERS, INC.

Published in the United States of America
by Rowman & Littlefield Publishers, Inc.
4720 Boston Way, Lanham, Maryland 20706
www.rowmanlittlefield.com

12 Hid's Copse Road
Cumnor Hill, Oxford OX2 9JJ, England

British Library Cataloguing in Publication Information Available

Library of Congress Cataloging-in-Publication Data

The influence of faith : religious groups and U.S. foreign policy / edited by Elliott
Abrams.
    p. cm.
    Includes bibliographical references and index.
    ISBN 0-7425-0762-9 (alk. paper) — ISBN 0-7425-0763-7 (pbk. : alk. paper)
    1. United States—Foreign relations—Moral and ethical aspects. 2. Religion and
politics—United States. 3. Lobbying—United States. I. Abrams, Elliott, 1948–

JZ1480 .I54 2001
327.73—dc21   2001019020

Printed in the United States of America

♾™ The paper used in this publication meets the minimum requirements of
American National Standard for Information Sciences—Permanence of Paper for
Printed Library Materials, ANSI/NISO Z39.48-1992.

Contents

Introduction

Elliott Abrams

Realists have long argued that the international system, and our own foreign policy, must be based on hard calculations of power and interest. Yet it is undeniable that religion has become an increasingly important influence upon this realm in recent years, especially since the end of the Cold War. Why has the salience of religion for world politics and U.S. foreign policy grown so greatly? Why does the persecution of Christians in Sudan or China, or religious conflict in the Balkans, or the murder of priests in India or East Timor, now quickly become a matter of concern in foreign ministries and parliaments across the globe? How does religion, and how do religious groups, affect the formulation and implementation of U.S. foreign policy?

These are the kinds of questions that engage the contributors to *The Influence of Faith*. The book grows out of two conferences held by the Ethics and Public Policy Center in 1998. The first addressed the role of religion in international politics and foreign policy, while the second looked more specifically at the influence of faith-based organizations—such as missionary groups and humanitarian aid organizations—upon American foreign policy. The papers written for those conferences have been revised and updated for this volume.

It has been an article of faith—secular faith, to be sure—since the Enlightenment that religion was bound to decline in importance. Most children of the Enlightenment agreed that religious conflicts were outmoded. In the modern age—the new age of liberty, the new age of science—there would be religious freedom in place of persecution. But the real reason why religious wars would end was not that religious freedom would prevail: it was that religious faith would disappear. As one of America's leading students of religion, Martin Marty of the University of Chicago, has written, "It was consistently assumed that as Enlightenment reason and science spread, something else must decline. That something included the sense of the sacred and transcendent. . . . Religion, in most of its forms, would lose significance and power."

But precisely the opposite appears to be happening. Nowadays we hear more and more often about religious faith and attempts to suppress it. Why is the denial of religious freedom a daily occurrence throughout the world? Why do some governments perceive religious faith as threatening? Why are religious minorities ill treated, or forcibly converted, or even tortured and killed? No one has explained this phenomenon better than Samuel Huntington, who says in this book,

> Religious persecution has become an issue because the power and salience of religion have increased. The renaissance of religion throughout the world has made freedom of religion and religious persecution key issues. . . . Religion has become a potent factor in the lives of people and in the politics of nations.

Huntington's argument that "religious persecution is the price of religious power" suggests that religious freedom will be a continuing challenge in this new century, not least for U.S. foreign policy.

A connection between religion and America's foreign relations is not a recent development, Leo Ribuffo of George Washington University makes clear in his chapter. Ribuffo calls attention to some striking and little known episodes in American history. For example, President Franklin Pierce considered establishing diplomatic relations with the Papal States, but Archbishop Gaetano Bedini, sent by the Pope to discuss the issue, was driven from the country by mobs in 1854. Pierce's predecessor had also felt the power of religion-related protest. In the 1850s a commercial treaty with Switzerland conceded the right of individual cantons to exclude Jews; but when an American Jewish merchant was expelled, American Jews launched a campaign of protest, enlisted support from Henry Clay and other politicians, and forced the Fillmore administration to renegotiate the treaty.

The most effective action has often been connected with an ethnic faith, the efforts of Jews and Greeks being prime examples. During the Russo-Japanese War, American Jews were pro-Japanese because of tsarist anti-Semitism; they were able to block loans to the tsarist regime while they lobbied Washington about cases of anti-Semitism and helped Japan raise funds. For decades there has been pressure from the American Greek Orthodox community to protect the rights of the Ecumenical Patriarch in Istanbul. Another of the questions discussed in this volume is, *Without* an ethnic church will American Christians be able to organize themselves effectively to protest the persecution of foreign Christians? Jews and Greeks felt that those people over there were brothers, or cousins; do American Christians feel a similar connection with, say, Sudanese Christians?

The influence of such "ethnic churches" can be overstated, as can the role of religion more generally, but the contributors to this book do not exaggerate the impact of religion on foreign policy. Professor Ribuffo, for example, states flatly that "a strong republican sense of mission thrived apart from the legacies of Reformation-era Protestantism. In the absence of these Protestant influences, the United States would still have risen to world power and probably would have justified the rise with ideological claims akin to the French 'mission to civilize.'" He argues, moreover, that no *major* foreign-policy decision has turned on religious issues alone.

The broad focus and activities of America's myriad religious groups serve to undermine—for better or for worse—their efforts to affect foreign policy. As Allen Hertzke points out, the major denominations are at any given time pushing an agenda that may include everything from campaign finance reform, food stamps, child care, health care, and Haitian refugees to the landmine ban, trade with Cuba, and the Earned Income tax credit. "The Catholic Church," Hertzke says, "as the operator of the largest parochial school system, has huge interests to defend and extend, and is heavily invested in the abortion controversy." For both Catholics and Protestants, this broad agenda makes it difficult to keep foreign policy in focus.

And then there are the divisions among religious groups on foreign-policy issues, producing a cacophony that is likely to do little to impress lawmakers. Should they listen to Catholic bishops pushing a nuclear freeze or evangelicals opposing it? To the National Council of Churches' criticism of Israel or the American Jewish Committee's support of that nation?

Finally, issues of competence reduce religious influence. As Mark Amstutz of Wheaton College notes,

Mainline Protestant policy statements on the nuclear dilemma and the Strategic Defense Initiative in the mid-1980s, the Middle East peace process in the late 1980s and early 1990s, and the Persian Gulf conflict in 1991 had little impact on the decision-making process. Indeed, such documents may have hurt the churches themselves, as informed parishioners called into question the theological and technical competence of the professional staffs who had written them.

One lesson of these pages is that it may be futile to search for direct cause-and-effect relationships between religion and foreign policy. Whatever its measurable and direct impact, the larger role of religion may be found elsewhere. Amstutz concludes that religious groups do "have a legitimate role to play in the democratic development of policy," but that role is "modest and indirect." Their main contribution to international affairs, he says, is not political but ethical:

> As moral teachers and the bearers of ethical traditions, religious communities can help to structure debate and illluminate relevant moral norms. . . . They help to develop and sustain political morality by promoting moral reasoning and by exemplifying values and behaviors that are conducive to human dignity.

The vast scope of churches and religiously based nongovernmental organizations (NGOs) as actors on the international scene is made apparent in the latter chapters of this book. At the more abstract end of the spectrum, they contribute to the conceptualization of national interests and the formulation of foreign-policy objectives. At the concrete end, they provide a huge amount of humanitarian aid and other social services in poor countries, helping to advance U.S. national interests by ameliorating hunger and poverty in the Third World. They engage the services of tens of thousands of Americans living at home and overseas, and offer a perspective far removed from that of the businessmen, academics, diplomats, spies, and soldiers who traditionally make up our foreign-policy elites.

The passage of the International Religious Freedom Act of 1998 made it evident that the role of religion will not soon diminish. "It shall be the policy of the United States," the statute states, "to condemn violations of religious freedom, and to promote, and to assist other governments in the promotion of, the fundamental right to freedom of religion." It characterizes U.S. policy as "standing for liberty and standing with the persecuted." Realists may shudder, but being realists they will also recognize that religion is now one of the organizing principles behind American policy. The excellent papers in this volume help explain why, and what to expect, and they make a signal contribution to understanding U.S. foreign policy in the post–Cold War period.

The intersection of religion and world politics has often been a bloody crossroads. If tomorrow it is to become the locus of a principled struggle for freedom and human dignity, we will require imaginative thinking and careful research. We are grateful to the authors of these chapters, who provide both. We are grateful as well to the Smith Richardson Foundation for supporting the conferences that made this book possible.

CHAPTER ONE

❦

Religion in the History of U.S. Foreign Policy

Leo P. Ribuffo

Congressional consideration of the Freedom from Religious Persecution bill introduced in 1997 by Representative Frank Wolf and Senator Arlen Specter precipitated a small-scale debate about a little studied subject, the connection between American religion and foreign relations. The resulting International Religious Freedom Act (IRFA), signed by President Bill Clinton in October 1998, is an official embodiment of the concern many Americans have long had about religious freedom abroad. American officials have intermittently protested against persecution since the early days of the republic.

Four aspects of the historical connection between American religion and foreign relations will engage our attention in this essay. First, in what ways have religious beliefs contributed to the widely shared assumption that the United States is an exceptional nation with a unique role in the world? Second, to what extent have religious "interest groups" at home and religious issues abroad affected U.S. foreign policies? Third, how much influence have serious religious ideas—including esoteric theological doctrines—had upon those interest groups and upon important international-relations theorists

Leo P. Ribuffo is Society of the Cincinnati George Washington Distinguished Professor of History at George Washington University in Washington, D.C. Among his writings are *The Old Christian Right: The Protestant Far Right from the Great Depression to the Cold War* and *Right Center Left: Essays in American History*. An earlier version of this paper, prepared for a 1998 conference of the Ethics and Public Policy Center, was published in the summer 1998 issue of *The National Interest*. The author wants to thank Tyler Anbinder, Justus Doenecke, Donald Jacobs, Edward McCord, Linda Levy Peck, Jeremiah Riemer, Howard Sachar, Ronald Spector, and Dewey Wallace for their helpful suggestions.

and policy makers? Finally, to what extent have foreign involvements affected the domestic religious scene?

The recent debate over the U.S. role in combatting religious persecution draws attention to religion per se rather than to the related and much more frequently studied phenomenon of ethnic influences on U.S. foreign relations. In this historical retrospective we can leave aside, for example, the "Irish question." But religion itself is complicated enough. Not the least of our conceptual problems is that everyone involved in the contemporary "culture war" homogenizes this country's religious history in one way or another. Whereas the left tends to view white Protestants as an undifferentiated mass, the center and right optimistically postulate an ecumenical "Judeo-Christian tradition." That term itself began to enter our lexicon in the 1940s, when many citizens still routinely referred to "Christian Americanism" or even "Protestant Americanism." Similarly, the label "fundamentalist," now applied promiscuously to groups from Tulsa to Tehran, was coined by a Baptist editor in 1920 to describe *one branch* of theologically conservative Protestantism.[1]

Although Jimmy Carter and Ronald Reagan liked to underscore American uniqueness by citing Puritan John Winthrop's admonition to build a "city upon the hill," the relationship between Reformation-era Protestantism and the American sense of mission has never been simple.[2] Almost all white residents of the thirteen colonies on the eve of independence thought Protestantism superior to Catholicism. But within Protestantism, such differing groups as Congregationalists and Quakers defined their worldly missions very differently. The large German pietist population paid slight attention to inspiring the wider world, while a small Enlightenment elite spoke of "virtue"—rather than salvation—in an idiom both cosmopolitan and classical. From the outset some Americans defined their country's international mission as *leading the world by moral example*, while others favored *direct intervention to spread virtuous American ways*.

The actions of what we now call religious interest groups can be deemed legitimate by reason of longevity. They were involved in the first and foremost foreign-policy decision: whether or not to create an independent country. The rebellious colonists believed—mistakenly—that the British planned to reduce them to "slavery," and one sure sign for Congregationalists and Presbyterians was the lingering threat of a resident Anglican bishop. From the Quebec Act of 1774, which granted special privileges to French Canadian Catholics, the heirs to Puritanism and the first Great Awakening inferred that the tyrannical Crown was consorting with tyrannical popery. At the same time, most of the 25,000 Catholics in the thirteen colonies supported independence because they thought, quite rightly as things turned out, that the new republic would grant them greater rights. Quakers and Mennonites who refused to serve in the Revolutionary army were subject to fines, confiscation of property, and imprisonment.[3]

The victorious revolutionary coalition began to crack almost immediately, and some of the fissures occurred along religious lines. An incongruous alliance of deists and dissident Protestants ensured that there would be no religious test for federal office and began the process of disestablishing state churches, a process that continued until the 1830s. By the 1790s, no more than 10 percent of the population formally belonged to churches.[4]

Disagreements about both religion and foreign affairs shaped the first party system in the 1790s. The Jeffersonian Republicans, ancestors of today's Democrats, were religiously more diverse, tolerant, and (in terms of government policy) neutral than the Federalists. Such sins (in the eyes of the Federalists) were compounded by the Jeffersonian tilt toward revolutionary France and against Great Britain, a country the Federalists admired for attempting to spread pure—that is, Protestant—Christianity around the world. These issues came to a head when the United States and Britain went to war in 1812.

The causes of the war, which are still hard to rank in order of importance, were essentially secular and psychological: the issue of free trade in wartime, British impressment of American sailors, and a craving for territory in the West. Once the conflict began, however, rival religious factions offered their own distinctive interpretations of events. Federalist Congregationalists and Presbyterians reiterated their admiration for British Protestantism, damned Napoleon as an autocratic ally of Pope Pius VI, and characterized impressed sailors as runaway Irish Catholics unworthy of sympathy. Even President James Madison's proclamations of national fast days were deemed theologically deficient because he recommended but did not *require* participation. Pro-war Baptists and Methodists denounced the autocratic Church of England, hailed Madison as a friend of religious liberty, and noted that the Pope was allied with Britain and imprisoned by Napoleon. Although no Protestant spoke well of the Pope, there were few denunciations of American Catholics, in part because they already served disproportionately in the armed forces.[5]

The Expansionist Consensus: Manifest Destiny

These political and religious battles occurred within a larger consensus that the United States should expand its territory, trade, and power. In his patriotic *American Geography*, published in 1789, the Rev. Jedidiah Morse looked forward to the "largest empire that ever existed," to include "millions of souls

. . . west of the Mississippi." Even before such expansion, the Rev. Ezra Stiles said in 1783, the *example* of the United States would spread the "empire of reason" and thus hasten the establishment of God's kingdom on earth. But George Washington, less conventionally devout than these Congregational-ists, had the precedent of ancient Rome in mind when he predicted that the American "infant empire" would soon grow and mature.[6]

Although the War of 1812 ended in a draw, and the British burning of the White House might have given pause, Americans came out of the conflict with a heightened sense of mission. Between the 1810s and the 1850s, most wanted to expand the country's boundaries. With the exception of Quakers, Mennonites, and some Unitarians, they expressed few qualms about using force to do so.

The Democratic publisher and diplomat John O'Sullivan caught the pre-vailing mood when he coined a famous phrase in 1845. The American claim to Oregon was, he said, "by right of our manifest destiny to overspread and possess the whole of the continent which Providence has given us for the great experiment of liberative and federative self-government entrusted to us." "Manifest Destiny" coincided with a second Great Awakening that en-ergized Protestantism, precipitated numerous theological disputes, and pro-duced new faiths such as Seventh-day Adventism and the Church of Jesus Christ of Latter-Day Saints.

Yet theology per se had slight impact on the expansionist consensus. As O'Sullivan's declaration suggests, the rhetoric of manifest destiny exuded more Enlightenment republicanism than religious beliefs. Claims to the con-tinent were based on what historian Norman Graebner calls "geographic pre-destination." Within the expansionist consensus, debate centered on geopo-litical and racial questions. Did the Rocky Mountains or the Pacific Ocean represent the "natural limits" of the United States? Would the great bay at San Francisco facilitate trade with Asia? Would Canada ultimately throw off British "slavery" and join the United States? Could the republic absorb the "mongrel race" of Mexicans? And most important, would the new territory be slave or free soil?[7]

Yet religious concerns related to foreign policy remained. In addition to the second Great Awakening, the pre–Civil War expansion coincided with a surge of non-Protestant immigration, a strong nativist response, and the creation of a second party system that arrayed Jacksonian Democrats against the culturally more conservative Whigs. In this context, Democratic expan-sionists attributed manifest destiny to an ecumenical Providence partly be-cause the bulk of Catholic and Jewish immigrants supported their party. On the other hand, the Rev. Lyman Beecher, prominent Whig nativist, issued a famous "plea" to save the American West from the "slavery and debasement" of Catholicism. Despite nativist fears that they would aid the papist enemy, Catholic soldiers, including at least two generals, helped to defeat Mexico in the 1840s. Democratic President Franklin Pierce considered establishing diplomatic relations with the Papal States. Unfortunately, Archbishop Gaetano Bedini, sent by the Pope to discuss the issue, was driven from the country by mobs in 1854; some of his assailants were nativists, but many others were anticlerical immigrants who resented Bedini's role in suppressing the Italian republican movement in 1848.[8]

Religious Alliances and Animosities

As the population became religiously more diverse, so too did diplomatic personnel, foreign-policy issues, and domestic political pressures. Mordecai Noah, a Jew, began his long political career in 1813 as consul in Tunis, where he negotiated the release of several Americans held captive. In 1840, the United States joined European governments in protesting the imprisonment of Syrian Jews for allegedly committing a ritual murder. Ten years later, a commercial treaty with Switzerland conceded the right of individual cantons to exclude Jews, and in at least one instance an American Jewish merchant was expelled. After American Jews protested, with support from such prominent gentiles as Henry Clay and Lewis Cass, the Fillmore administration renegotiated the treaty. But the changes were cosmetic, and both protests and quiet diplomacy continued until Switzerland adopted a new constitution in 1874.[9]

The imbroglio over the Swiss treaty provides an early illustration of the complicated religious alliances and animosities that persisted despite the widely shared belief that the United States was an exceptional nation with a unique role in the world. Many Protestants supported the Jewish protests, not only because they valued the republican principle of equal treatment for all white Americans, but also because they wanted to set a precedent for receiving equal treatment in Catholic countries. Conversely, Catholic Archbishop John Hughes ridiculed the notion that sovereign states should change their policies whenever a U.S. citizen arrived "with a full measure of American atmosphere, American sunbeams, and American religion."

Catholics and Jews also clashed over the Mortara affair in the late 1850s. Edgaro Mortara, a Jewish child in Bologna, was secretly baptized by a servant and then removed from his family by the Church on the grounds that since the boy was now a Catholic, he should not be raised by Jews. Protests against the Church's action were widespread in Europe and the United States, but President James Buchanan, caught between Catholic and Jewish constituents, refused to join them. It was "neither the right nor the duty" of the American government to "express a moral censorship over the conduct of other independent governments," Buchanan said, "and to rebuke them for acts which we may deem arbitrary and unjust toward their own citizens or subjects."[10]

The most significant intersection between religion and foreign relations in the nineteenth century was the extraordinary burst of Protestant missionary activity initially spurred by the second Great Awakening. Indeed, some missionaries became what we would now call lobbyists, and their "interest group" often allied with less devout expansionists. On this continent, they promoted the settlement of Oregon and urged President James K. Polk to stand firm against British claims. Across the Pacific, where the most important missionary activities occurred, conversion, commerce, condescension, and the promotion of Protestant American values usually went hand in hand. An American diplomat in China named Charles Denby called the missionaries "pioneers of trade and commerce." Horace Allen, who arrived in Korea as a Presbyterian medical missionary, later became the U.S. government representative, actively promoted American investment, and established himself as the most influential foreigner in the country. In Hawaii, however, missionaries were criticized for warning the king about sharp American business practices.[11]

There were other controversies, too. Unitarians questioned the propriety of converting any country from its ancient religion. When a treaty signed in 1858—composed in part by missionaries—protected the religious activities of Protestants and Catholics in China (including Chinese believers), some Jewish leaders protested again that Christianity was being written into the law of the land.[12]

The religious disorder of the late nineteenth century was no less consequential in its sphere than the better remembered social upheaval. Sometimes social and religious issues were intimately related, as in the case of a large "new immigration" of Catholics and Jews from eastern and southern Europe. Protestants were confronted not only by these immigrants but also by the intellectual challenges of Darwinism and biblical "higher criticism." Some responded by becoming theological liberals; they accepted evolution, denied original sin, doubted biblical miracles, and emphasized Jesus' ethical teachings. A minority of these theological liberals also became advocates of a politically liberal or radical "social gospel." New faiths emerged, notably Christian Science, several Pentecostal Protestant groups, and the International Bible Students' Association (known as Jehovah's Witnesses since the early 1930s).[13]

A Pious Pair: McKinley and Bryan

Not surprisingly, the election of 1896 produced the most devout pair of presidential nominees in American history, William Jennings Bryan and William McKinley. Nor is it surprising that the amalgam of ideas sanctioning the next phase of "manifest destiny" (a phrase President McKinley still used) contained a larger religious component than its pre–Civil War counterpart. Congregationalist minister Josiah Strong became a major ideologist of expansion with the publication of *Our Country* in 1886. Mixing geographic determinism, missionary zeal, and a sense of "Anglo-Saxon" superiority, Strong concluded that the United States would be the "elect nation for the age to come"—but only if non-Protestant immigrants were successfully Americanized. For most expansionists, new concerns seemed at least as pressing as the old sense of mission. They sought foreign markets as a solution to the depression of the 1890s, cheered military adventure as an antidote to national softness, and argued that the "closed" frontier would produce a domestic social explosion unless energies were diverted abroad.[14]

The most dramatic foreign-policy event of the late nineteenth century, the Spanish–American War, was rooted in sympathy for Cuban rebels fighting for independence. Attempting to achieve that goal without war, McKinley halfheartedly pursued papal mediation and used Archbishop John Ireland as an intermediary with the Vatican. Most Catholic spokesmen favored this approach and criticized "bloodthirsty" Protestants for demanding quick military action. No Protestant denomination showed greater enthusiasm for war than McKinley's own, the Methodist Episcopal Church. Intervention in Cuba, McKinley finally told Congress in April 1898, would fulfill American aspirations as a "Christian, peace-loving people." In subsequent proclamations, he thanked the "Divine Master" for granting victory with few casualties.[15]

Debate about the peace treaty centered on the acquisition of the Philippines from Spain. In a famous interview with Methodist leaders, McKinley said that after prayer and reflection he had concluded that the United States must "uplift and civilize and Christianize [the Filipinos], and by God's grace do the very best we could by them, as our fellow-men for whom Christ also died." The debate about ratification turned on secular issues: the propriety of a republican empire, the threat posed by a nonwhite colony, and the perennial dream of the great China market. Most Quakers and Unitarians opposed acquisition, but Catholic bishops and Protestant social gospelers, like the country at large, were divided. The prospect of a new missionary field influenced some proponents of the treaty.[16]

An empire in Asia proved more troublesome than anticipated. The squalid little war to suppress the Filipino independence movement kept alive secular and religious opposition to annexation. Meanwhile, religious groups carried their American conflicts to the Philippines. While Protestants assailed "greedy friars" with large land holdings, Catholics complained about desecration of church property and pointed out that most Filipinos were already Christians. Meanwhile, in the face of rising nationalist opposition and grassroots assaults, missionaries extended their enterprise into the Chinese interior and became increasingly involved in Chinese affairs; the United States ultimately joined in Western gunboat diplomacy to protect them. In the worst confrontation, the Boxers highlighted their animosity to foreign influence by killing almost two hundred missionaries and thousands of Chinese Christians.[17]

The Progressives: Theodore Roosevelt, Wilson, Taft

The foremost presidents of the Progressive era, Theodore Roosevelt and Woodrow Wilson, were more complicated than can be inferred from their place in international-relations courses as exemplars of, respectively, "realism" and "idealism." Roosevelt expounded often on "righteousness," and his eagerness to enter World War I was hardly based on a sober evaluation of reality. A pro forma member of the Dutch Reformed Church who may have doubted the existence of God and an afterlife, TR showed that a strong sense of American mission needed no theological underpinning. As for Wilson: H. L. Mencken, President Victoriano Huerta of Mexico, and countless scholars to the contrary, he is not usefully interpreted as a latter-day Puritan. A theologically liberal Presbyterian like his minister father, Wilson paid scant attention to doctrinal disputes, easily accepted evolution and higher criticism, and almost never discerned God acting directly in history (Wilson's explanation of his own election was an exception to this generalization). Certainly theology did not shape Wilson's version of the venerable belief that the United States was an exceptional nation with a unique role in the world.[18]

Although less enthusiastic than Roosevelt about the military ethic as an antidote to national softness, Wilson proved no less willing to use force abroad. Despite these similarities, however, their successors in the White House are more aptly called Wilsonians than Rooseveltians. From Washington's baptism of an "infant empire" to TR's celebration of the onward march of civilization, presidents had often spoken candidly about pursuing American interests at the cost of somebody else's interests. After Wilson, they were much more likely to stress that what was good for the United States was also good for the rest of the world.

Although the third president of the Progressive era, William Howard Taft, is rarely cited as an exemplar of anything other than girth, his administration was marked by perhaps the most successful instance of lobbying by a religious interest group in U.S. history. A grassroots campaign conceived by prominent Jews forced the abrogation of a commercial treaty with imperial Russia in 1912. This campaign capped a long series of protests against the czarist regime for discriminating against American Jews and persecuting Russian Jews, and anti-Semites have long cited the abrogation as evidence of a powerful "international Zionist conspiracy." But Taft could be prodded into action only because the issue intersected with broad American republican principles. Consequently, Jewish protesters were able to win support from influential Christian clergy, publishers, and politicians.[19]

Religion and World War I

When World War I began in 1914, both the American president, Woodrow Wilson, and his secretary of state, William Jennings Bryan, were Presbyterians convinced that the United States had a special mission in the world. Their divergent responses illustrate the inadequacy of glib generalizations about the connection between religious dispositions and specific foreign policies. Although susceptible to intermittent military enthusiasms, Bryan regarded the pursuit of international peace as his Christian duty. He negotiated more than two dozen "cooling off" treaties, and commemorated some of them by having swords melted down and recast as tiny plowshares. Bryan resigned in 1915 because he thought Wilson was forsaking neutrality. But he also placed his resignation in a broader context. The United States had always "sought to aid the world by example," he said. Participation in European power politics would represent "descent" from this morally superior position. "Our mission is to implant hope in the breast of humanity and substitute higher ideals for the ideals which have led nations into armed conflicts."[20]

Bryan supported the war effort after American entry, but a substantial minority of Americans did not. Among religious dissidents, Quakers and Mennonites received better treatment than the more adamant and less familiar Jehovah's Witnesses, who typically went to jail. On the other hand, evangelist Billy Sunday hailed American soldiers as "God's grenadiers." Amid a sordid debate about the bayonet's legitimacy as a Christian weapon, Unitarian Albert Dieffenbach affirmed that Jesus himself would use it against the Germans. Not everyone spoke so zealously. Yet even prominent clergy who had opposed intervention before 1917, including Rabbi Stephen Wise and the Rev. John R. Mott, rallied to the cause. The major denominations organized to provide services for their men in uniform. Under the leadership of James Cardinal Gibbons, an interfaith League of National Unity promoted the war across denominational lines.[21]

Even among supporters of the war, however, there was more disagreement than ecumenicism. When Pope Benedict XV offered a peace plan in mid-1917, Protestants thought the proposal too "Austrian"; though more favorably inclined, the Catholic hierarchy nonetheless recognized the futility of urging the plan on President Wilson. Ultimately religion influenced the war effort less than the war affected the domestic religious scene. Adding denunciations of German American brewers to their stock arguments, Protestants secured the enactment of Prohibition in the face of Catholic and Jewish opposition. And theological conservatives attuned to a form of Bible prophecy called "premillennial dispensationalism" interpreted the British promise of a Jewish homeland in Palestine as evidence of Jesus' imminent return.[22]

The Interwar Years and Anti-Interventionism

Above all, the high emotions generated by the war turned the nation's cultural splits into cultural chasms. Accordingly, as the United States entered the twenties, not only were Protestants increasingly arrayed against Catholics, but also Protestant theological liberals and conservatives were increasingly arrayed against each other. Yet religious leaders were no more "isolationist" than businessmen or bohemian intellectuals. Missionary agencies saw the rising tide of Chinese nationalism, and, partly as a means of self-defense, most responded by urging the United States to surrender extraterritoriality and special protection for Christians. Prominent Catholics and—to a lesser extent—Protestants shared the widespread enthusiasm for Benito Mussolini. While Catholics credited Il Duce with Italy's "resurrection," Protestants appreciated his anticlericalism. The Mussolini vogue simultaneously highlights both the persistent belief in American exceptionalism and the restraints this belief imposes on Wilsonian aspirations to reform the rest of the world. Although inappropriate for the United States, "Mussolini methods" suited Italians, the Catholic journal *Commonweal* editorialized. Meanwhile, Protestant fundamentalists studied Scripture and world affairs to determine whether or not Mussolini was the Antichrist predicted in the Book of Revelation.[23]

The Soviet Union attracted at least as much attention during the twenties as Mussolini's Italy. All along the religious spectrum the Soviet regime was denounced for promoting atheism and murdering believers. Even so, a significant minority of Protestant theological liberals expressed cautious interest in the "Soviet experiment." Interest grew and caution diminished after the Crash, and in the mid-thirties, some social gospelers actively participated in the Popular Front.[24]

What is usually mischaracterized as interwar isolationism was the pervasive belief that the United States must remain aloof from any European war.

With varying sophistication, scholars, pundits, and public figures attributed entry into World War I to economic entanglement with the Allies, machinations by arms manufacturers, and British propaganda. The diverse peace movement that developed in this context contained a large religious element, including many clergy. Some of these activists were full-fledged pacifists, such as the members of the Fellowship of Reconciliation (FOR), the War Resisters League, and the Catholic Worker group. Yet many more simply regretted "presenting arms" in 1917–1918.[25]

From the outset, foreign-policy issues related to religion threatened Franklin D. Roosevelt's eclectic coalition. In 1933 Roosevelt tried to minimize opposition to recognition of the Soviet Union by charming prominent anticommunists (including the legendary Father Edmund Walsh of the Georgetown University School of Foreign Service) and extracting a Soviet promise to respect the religious freedom of resident Americans. The next year, Catholic criticism precipitated the first major test of the Good Neighbor Policy. The Mexican government's insistence on breaking the political and economic power of the Church sometimes went beyond anticlericalism to outright persecution. In 1934, when Ambassador Josephus Daniels praised the creation of secular schools, American bishops charged the Roosevelt administration with indifference to the plight of Mexican Catholics; 10,000 letters to the State Department echoed the same theme, and 250 members of Congress requested an investigation. While FDR quietly urged the Mexicans to moderate their anticlericalism, the Democratic Party pointedly urged Ambassador Daniels to stay out of the United States during the 1936 campaign.[26]

When the Spanish Civil War erupted in 1936, Congress passed (with one dissenting vote) a ban on arms sales to the republic. The action was unusual in that recognized governments were traditionally allowed to buy weapons in the midst of insurrections. Roosevelt signed the bill primarily because he wanted to coordinate policy with the British and French, feared the spread of war beyond Spain, and at this point shared the anti-interventionist sentiments of his fellow citizens. Nevertheless, the administration derailed efforts to lift the arms embargo even after FDR edged toward a policy of quarantining international aggressors.

The president's perception of Catholic opinion was an important though not necessarily decisive factor. According to a Gallup poll in late 1938, 42 percent of Catholics favored the republic while 58 percent supported General Francisco Franco's rebels. Yet Catholic clergy at all levels were virtually unanimous in hailing Franco as the savior of sovietized Spain and, frequently, as the Spanish George Washington. Most Protestants disagreed, and the resulting conflicts were sometimes vehement. When 150 prominent

Protestants signed an open letter criticizing the Spanish Church for supporting Franco, Catholic leaders accused them of fostering a "species of religious war" in the United States.[27]

Religion and World War II

The acrimonious debate in 1939–1941 about aiding the nations fighting
Germany centered on three questions. Noninterventionists doubted the ability of these countries to hold out, expected unneutral acts to draw the United
States into the conflict, and warned that any war to save or spread freedom
abroad would destroy freedom at home. Roosevelt had faith in the military
capacity of the British and the Soviets, believed that an Axis victory would
threaten freedom everywhere, and was willing to risk war. These divergent
analyses were rarely discussed dispassionately. Indeed, the whole debate was
wrapped up in ideological, ethnic, and religious loyalties and animosities.

In Roosevelt's view, religious freedom was one aspect of civilization under
threat. In January 1939 he declared, "The defense of religion, of democracy,
and of good faith among nations is all the same fight." He also understood
the political potency of religious references. In October 1941, justifying further expansion of the undeclared naval war against German submarines,
Roosevelt denounced the Nazi plan "to abolish all existing religions—
Catholic, Protestant, Mohammedan, Hindu, Buddhist, and Jewish alike."[28]

As in previous crises, the relationship between faith and foreign policy remained complicated in the country at large. Catholics were less interventionist than Protestants. Many Irish American and German American
Catholics viewed Britain skeptically, some Italian Americans still admired
Mussolini, and all Catholics loathed the prospect of a de facto alliance with
the Soviets. At the same time, few Catholics were pacifists in principle. Episcopalians tended to rally behind Great Britain, but there were numerous exceptions, including young Gerald Ford, an early supporter of the America
First Committee. The anti-interventionist camp included both social gospelers at the liberal Protestant journal *The Christian Century* and the anti-
Semitic fundamentalists of the old Christian right. The clearest trend was
the reduction of pacifist ranks to a devout remnant. Prominent among the
defectors was "Christian realist" theologian Reinhold Niebuhr, who moved
from the chairmanship of the pacifist Fellowship of Reconciliation in the
early 1930s to advocacy of war against Nazi Germany in 1941.[29]

After Pearl Harbor, FDR continued to ask God's blessings on the war effort. Most denominations rallied to the cause, though less zealously than during World War I. Despite their wariness of internationalism, Catholics again
served disproportionately in the armed services. They also remained aloof

from the widespread but evanescent enthusiasm for the Soviet Union. The pro-Soviet vogue owed less to agitation by radical social gospelers than to a popular inclination to think well of an ally, as well as to continuing doubts about the likelihood of perfecting foreigners. According to a wartime poll, 46 percent of Americans thought the Soviet Union had a government "as good as she could have for her people." In portrayals of the enemy, the Japanese seemed less human than the Germans not only because they were Asians, but also because Shintoism and emperor worship looked pagan.[30]

Probably no foreign-policy issue associated with religion has produced greater controversy than the question whether more European Jews could have been saved from the Holocaust. American Jews denounced the Nazi regime immediately after Hitler came to power. As on many previous occasions, they enlisted non-Jewish allies and appealed to generic American values. These appeals fell flat during the 1930s, however, when anti-Semitism was widespread and even tolerant Americans feared losing their jobs to refugees. As reports of genocide reached the United States in 1942 and 1943, American Jews sought government action. But U.S. entry into the war in December 1941 had focused attention on the threat to American lives, and the Roosevelt administration took no effective action to aid European Jewry until the War Refugee Board was created in January 1944.[31]

The retrospective judgment that little more could have been done is simply wrong, and those who make it often rest their case on a narrow strategic determinism. Supposedly policy makers subordinated all such secondary issues to the greater good of beating the Axis as quickly as possible. In fact, the United States engaged in numerous actions of dubious military merit in order to achieve nonmilitary ends. For example, the Doolittle bombing raid on Japan sought to raise American morale, the invasion of North Africa conciliated the British, and the Philippines-centered strategy in the Pacific fulfilled a popular general's pledge to return. If the fate of European Jewry had elicited comparable concern, more denunciations of the "final solution" would have been forthcoming from officials, more ransom would have been paid in wavering German satellites, more visas would have been issued to refugees, and more military ingenuity would have been devoted to disrupting the Holocaust.

The Postwar Period

Among the many extraordinary changes brought by the war, two stand out for any consideration of religion and foreign relations. First, with "isolationism" thoroughly discredited, debate about the postwar world centered on the *kind* of internationalism the United States should pursue. Prominent internationalists ranged from publisher Henry Luce, the son of missionaries in China, who envisioned an "American century," to former Vice President Henry A. Wallace, an unconventional social gospeler and early Cold War dove, who promoted a "century of the common man."[32]

Second, the war sparked a religious revival that significantly affected the style of the Cold War at home and abroad. Among theologically conservative Protestants, there was renewed interest in foreign missions. Christian Cold War realist Reinhold Niebuhr became, in the judgment of historian Walter LaFeber, the most influential American theologian since Jonathan Edwards. George F. Kennan, the conceptualizer of containment, saw himself as a Niebuhrian. Dwight Eisenhower echoed millions of Americans in his repudiation of "Godless Communism." Eisenhower's dour Presbyterian secretary of state, John Foster Dulles, seemed to personify the Cold War as an unambiguous struggle between good and evil.[33]

Nevertheless, this "fifth great awakening" barely affected the *substance* of the Cold War. This generalization certainly holds true for the impact of Christian realist theology. The sense of tragedy and irony intrinsic to Protestant neo-orthodoxy is compatible with a wide variety of positions on specific diplomatic issues, and during their long careers Niebuhr and Kennan seem to have taken most of them. By the early 1950s, Kennan was complaining that his theory of containment had been misconstrued, and Niebuhr was denying that the Cold War could be reduced to a conflict "between a god-fearing and a godless civilization." Dulles, like the president he served at the Versailles conference and like his own minister father, was a theological liberal. After regaining his faith in the late 1930s, he seems to have felt a heightened sense of American mission. But his definition of that mission changed significantly during the next two decades. Dulles was in turn a noninterventionist, bipartisan internationalist, a partisan proponent of "liberation," and a more flexible secretary of state in private than he appeared in public.[34]

Not religious ideas but religious interest groups helped to shape the early Cold War. As Communists advanced in China, some missionaries advocated assistance to Chiang Kai-shek in the vain hope of winning a military victory, while others edged away from Chiang in the vain hope of establishing decent relations with Mao Tse-tung. Among missionaries who became major public figures, Walter Judd, a leader of the congressional China bloc, held the former position, and J. Leighton Stuart, U.S. ambassador to the last Nationalist government on the mainland, held the latter. As Eastern Europe fell under Soviet control, Catholics took the lead in highlighting the suppression of religion and abuse of priests. During the late 1950s, the American hierarchy depicted President Ngo Dinh Diem of the Republic of Vietnam as a Catholic hero. Truth mixed with hyperbole in Clark Clifford's advice to Harry Truman that anticommunism was the decisive factor in the Catholic vote.[35]

The quick de facto recognition accorded to Israel in 1948 represented a victory for one of the great grassroots lobbying efforts in American history. President Truman took this action in the face of opposition from his senior diplomatic and military advisers—as well as from oil companies and some prominent Reform Jews. Certainly he would not have moved so quickly if few Jews had been registered to vote. Yet Truman also acted to minimize Soviet influence in Israel. Moreover, in this instance Zionists were able to find powerful Christian allies. Not only was there widespread sympathy for victims of Nazism, but there was also support for Zionism among nativists who feared that these victims might come to the United States. To many fundamentalists, the "regathering" of Jews in the Holy Land fulfilled Bible prophecy. Although no group worked harder to infer God's will from the Bible itself, fundamentalists were not immune to world events. In the wake of the Holocaust, they began to reinterpret Scripture in philo-Semitic fashion and concluded that the regathering of Jews did not advance the interests of the Antichrist.[36]

We must beware of exaggerating both the consensus on foreign policy and the level of religious comity during the fifties. Although anti-Semitism steadily declined, tensions rose between Catholics and Protestants, and the Cold War was one of the reasons. Unlike Protestant social gospelers, virtually no practicing Catholics had drifted into the Popular Front or avidly celebrated the Soviet Union. On the contrary, according to a quip often attributed to Daniel Patrick Moynihan, Fordham graduates in the FBI investigated Harvard graduates in the State Department. Many Catholics, including the formidable Francis Cardinal Spellman, pointedly asked why their patriotism went unappreciated by the Protestant elite. The answer, some members of the Protestant elite responded, was that Catholic patriotism was too crude, and they cited Senator Joseph McCarthy as a case in point. In the long run, however, both World War II and the Cold War served Catholic interests well. Without PT 109 and the country's post-Sputnik fear of falling behind the Soviets, John F. Kennedy would have lost to Richard Nixon in 1960.[37]

Religion and Vietnam

Opposition to the Vietnam War contained a large religious component. An interdenominational network of doves called Clergy and Laymen Concerned About Vietnam (CALCAV) was founded in late 1965. Protestant theological conservatives were typically more hawkish than theological liberals. Some evangelical hawks pointed to Indochina as a fertile field for missionaries.

Pacifists like A. J. Muste, working in obscurity since Pearl Harbor, reemerged as national figures. The Rev. Martin Luther King, Jr., and Senator George McGovern found sanction for antiwar activism in their own versions of the social gospel. Making his latest foreign-policy turn within the framework of neo-orthodoxy, Niebuhr praised the "heroic" divinity students who burned their draft cards. None of this was surprising.[38]

What was surprising—indeed, what would have been virtually inconceivable fifteen years earlier—was significant Catholic opposition to a war against Communism. From 1966 onward, the bishops grew steadily more critical of the Vietnam conflict, and in 1972 they endorsed amnesty for draft evaders. Clerical and lay participants in nonviolent resistance attracted national attention; some served prison terms. As Garry Wills noted, the Catholic Church now produced both FBI agents and radical priests, occasionally in the same families. Polls in the late sixties revealed that Catholics were less likely than Protestants to favor military escalation. Ironically, after loyal service in the Cold War and in five hot wars since the 1840s had incrementally legitimated Catholics, opposition to the Vietnam War now brought them further into the American mainstream. When Eugene McCarthy ran for president in 1968, almost nobody worried about his religion even though he discerned a connection between his Catholic faith and his opposition to the war.[39]

After more than a decade of domestic turmoil, the major political parties in 1976 nominated Gerald Ford and Jimmy Carter, the most devout pair of presidential candidates since McKinley and Bryan eighty years earlier. In their efforts to preserve détente, promote human rights abroad, and mediate a Middle East peace, there was considerable continuity between Ford's and Carter's administrations. Yet Carter was distinctive in his calls for American humility, emphasis on world leadership through moral example, wariness of military intervention, and respect for poor and nonwhite nations. In his own mind, he was applying to world politics Niebuhr's admonitions against national egotism (much to the distress of both Cold War Niebuhrians, who thought he missed the larger point, and many of his fellow southern evangelicals, who celebrated a more interventionist version of American mission). Carter was a Wilsonian, but a Wilsonian with large doses of Bryanism.[40]

Religious interest groups continued to influence foreign policy in the post-Vietnam era. The most important development—virtually inconceivable fifteen years earlier—was the move rightward by a significant minority of Jews. An important landmark along the road was the Jackson-Vanik Amendment to a trade treaty, introduced by Senator Henry Jackson and Representative

Charles Vanik to pressure the Soviets into increasing Jewish emigration. At first, Jewish leaders approached the measure cautiously, but most ultimately came around. As was the case with abrogation of the commercial treaty in 1912, a "Jewish" concern attracted widespread support from non-Jews appalled by Russian autocracy. Indeed, the emigration issue provided ample ammunition for critics of détente during the Nixon, Ford, and Carter administrations. Carter himself received the smallest percentage of the Jewish vote of any Democratic presidential nominee since the 1920s.[41]

For members of Ronald Reagan's coalition, Carter's diplomatic and military humility was part of the international problem rather than part of the solution. As Jeane Kirkpatrick argued, Carter's soft Christianity led him to repudiate friendly authoritarian regimes whose virtues included acceptance of "traditional gods and . . . traditional taboos." In his first substantive meeting with the Soviet ambassador, Reagan himself raised the issue of Russian Pentecostals who, denied permission to emigrate, had been granted asylum at the American embassy in Moscow; they were subsequently allowed to emigrate. Most important, following almost two decades of détente in fact if not in name, Reagan himself resumed the presidential practice of bluntly denouncing the Soviet Union as the source of atheistic evil. Presidential aides raised in the pre–Vatican II world of Catholic anticommunism worked with Pope John Paul II to crack open the East bloc. In 1984 Reagan sent an ambassador to the Vatican and encountered only minimal grumbling from the new Christian right. In addition to evangelicals and fundamentalists, Reagan's remarkable religious coalition included working-class Catholics, neoconservative Jews, and even a few apostate CALCAV doves.[42]

Ironically, a religious bond, real or imagined, facilitated relations between President Reagan and Soviet leader Mikhail Gorbachev as they negotiated the end of the Cold War in the late 1980s. Gorbachev's passing references to God and prayers for peace convinced Reagan that he was a Christian beneath a Communist veneer. Whatever his personal beliefs, Gorbachev sensed Reagan's positive response and increased his religious references in their conversations.[43]

After the Cold War

The rituals of civil religion as they relate to foreign policy remained intact after the Cold War. President George Bush invited Billy Graham to spend the night at the White House on the eve of the Gulf War in 1991. Yet these rituals became increasingly complicated as immigration altered the American religious scene. In the midst of his confrontation with the Ayatollah Ruhollah Khomeini, President Carter took pains to commemorate Islamic holidays and distinguish Muslim friends from Muslim foes. The religious complications were not confined to the home front. President Bush's invocations of God prompted some Muslims to complain that he was leading a religious war against Islam itself rather than a limited effort to roll back the Iraqi invasion of Kuwait. Meanwhile, military personnel deployed to Saudi Arabia were barred from wearing religious insignia, discouraged from receiving Christmas cards, and obliged to camouflage New Testaments.[44]

Avid Wilsonians who wanted the United States to organize and lead international posses faced an especially difficult problem following the Cold War. After winning the great ideological conflict of this century, Americans across the political and religious spectrums began reverting to their visceral Bryanism. They preferred to lead the world by example, if at all.

This problem was particularly acute for Wilsonian Republicans. Theologically conservative Protestants joined the Reagan coalition primarily because they considered the Democrats too liberal on such issues as abortion, gay rights, and school prayer. Aside from a theologically based commitment to Israel, rank-and-file fundamentalists and Pentecostals showed only a routine patriotic interest in foreign affairs, even during the Cold War. Both Wilsonian Republicans and Pat Buchanan, who finds his diplomatic usable past in the America First Committee, consider this constituency up for grabs. The International Religious Freedom Act may help to keep theologically conservative Protestants in the Republican and internationalist fold.[45]

Yet enthusiasm for the IRFA is hardly confined to conservatives. The bill passed the Senate unanimously and cleared the House of Representatives on a voice vote. The main provisions established "three new entities to investigate religious freedom violations around the world." A bipartisan Commission on International Religious Freedom was created to monitor religious persecution abroad. An ambassador-at-large for International Religious Freedom serves as the president's "principal adviser" on religious freedom, and an analogous Special Adviser on Religious Persecution was mandated for the National Security Council. Taking their advice into account, the president must submit to Congress an annual report on international religious freedom. In addition, the IRFA offered a "menu of sanctions" to be applied "against *any* government which engages in or tolerates any violation of the internationally recognized right to religious freedom." These sanctions, ranging from public condemnation to prohibitions on aid and trade, can be waived at the president's discretion.[46]

The first *Annual Report on International Religious Freedom*, which was issued by the State Department in September 1999, not only defined "persecution and discrimination" broadly but also criticized friendly governments as well as adversaries. The clearest examples were violent actions by "totalitarian or authoritarian regimes" to suppress unapproved religious movements, often those of ethnic or cultural minorities. For instance, the Taliban in Afghanistan murdered Shiite Muslims and Iran suppressed the Baha'i faith. The People's Republic of China (PRC) cracked down on the mystical movement Falun Gong and continued to assault Tibetan Buddhism; it also pressed tolerated religions to register with the government and arrested leaders of groups that refused to comply, including many Catholic and Protestant clergy. Some regimes used less forceful means to foster an "atmosphere of religious intolerance." As part of a concerted campaign against so-called Muslim fundamentalism, Turkey expanded enforcement of a ban on Islamic-style head garments in government offices and some other state-run facilities. In Saudi Arabia, public worship by non-Muslims and attempts to convert Muslims were criminal offenses. Other governments placed minority religions at a "disadvantage" or stigmatized them with pejorative labels. Austria, Belgium, France, and Germany issued reports or appointed commissions to guard against "sects" or "cults," including the Church of Scientology. India and Egypt endorsed religious freedom in principle but failed to act "with vigor" against abuses by local officials and nongovernmental entities. Indeed, the State Department's country-by-country account reveals countless examples of persecution and discrimination by ordinary citizens. According to the *Annual Report*, these critical judgments were based on "international standards" such as the Universal Declaration on Human Rights.[47]

The *Annual Report* also surveyed actions taken by American officials to promote international religious freedom. President Clinton and Secretary of State Madeleine Albright were credited with setting the tone. At a summit conference with Chinese leader Jiang Zemin in October 1997, the president arranged a meeting for the following February between American religious leaders and their Chinese counterparts. Speaking in Moscow in June 1999, Secretary Albright condemned anti-Semitism and urged Russians to build a society in which "all are free to worship God in whatever way they choose." The Office of International Religious Freedom publicly condemned religious persecution and discrimination in countries where the United States had little or no official presence, such as Iran, Iraq, and Cuba. It also worked to sensitize foreign-service officers to the issue in countries where they served. American diplomats observed trials, inquired about missing religious dissidents, contacted harassed religious leaders, and explained the heightened American interest in religious freedom abroad. Robert Seiple, the ambassador-at-large for international religious freedom, traveled widely to spread the message. The most productive work was often done behind the scenes, especially by junior or midlevel officials.

The first *Annual Report* elicited almost predictable responses. Many Muslims protested—sometimes in anti-Semitic terms—that the United States was meddling in the internal affairs of their countries and trying to disrupt Islamic unity. Some international religious-rights activists thought the report was too soft on the PRC, which the Clinton administration was seeking to grant permanent normal trading relations (PNTR). What is most striking, however, is how little coverage the *Annual Report*—and the diplomatic initiatives noted in it—received compared to earlier discussion of the Wolf-Specter bill. As often happens, news media and much of the public tend to assume that a problem has been solved once legislation is passed, and thus there is scant interest in subsequent implementation or nonimplementation.[48]

At this writing in early May 2000, religious persecution in China has played only a small role in the debate over that country's trade status. Representative Wolf, who opposes PNTR, has highlighted the issue, but even he gives at least equal weight to the PRC's alleged threat to American security. Repeating a familiar historical pattern, men and women united in their belief that the United States must support religious freedom abroad disagree about the impact of a specific policy. Convinced that Chinese suppression of religion has "increased markedly" in the past year, the Commission on International Religious Freedom opposes PNTR. Ambassador Seiple, whose post was also created by the IRFA, counters that continuing the current practice of annual congressional votes on normal trade relations "will not advance the cause of religious freedom in China and will not improve the circumstances of any of the religious adherents about whom we are all deeply concerned." Former President Carter goes even further, declaring that congressional rejection of PNTR would be a "major defeat" for human rights generally in China.[49]

Concluding Observations

Amidst current interest in the relationship between religion and foreign policy, what generalizations can we make about the American experience? First, *a strong republican sense of mission thrived apart from the legacies of Reformation-era Protestantism.* In the absence of these Protestant influences, the United States would still have risen to world power and probably would have justified the rise with ideological claims akin to the French "mission to civilize."[50] Moreover, the American sense of mission has been complicated by the Catholic and Jewish presence, by divisions and shifts within Protestantism itself, and above all by secular concerns about economic advantage, national security, and race. Rigorous fundamentalists aside, even the Protestant theological conservatives who still regard the United States as a "city upon the hill" are less likely than their forebears who lived in less affluent times to expect much retribution for personal or national sins. Thus, instead of trembling before divine judgment, they tend to expect God to bless the United States as a matter of course.

Second, although religious interest groups at home and religious issues abroad have affected foreign policy, *no major diplomatic decision has turned on religious issues alone.* For example, Eisenhower would have aided Diem in the fifties without the Catholic Church's urging. On the other hand, religious interest groups *have* significantly affected subsidiary foreign policies. FDR hesitated to help the Spanish Republic partly because most American Catholics supported Franco; Truman recognized Israel partly to woo Jewish voters. In such instances, however, religious interest groups have been most effective when they found allies outside their own communities and invoked widely shared American values.

Third, *serious religious ideas have had at most an indirect impact on policy makers*—far less, for example, than strategic, economic, or political considerations, perceptions of public opinion, and the constraints of office. George Kennan's Niebuhrian doubts about human perfectibility rendered him more prudent than many of his fellow cold warriors, yet he expressed more caution in retirement than he had shown as a State Department employee. Similarly, Jimmy Carter was able to advocate international human rights with greater consistency as an ex-president than as president. Equally important, not only can divergent policy prescriptions be inferred from the Bible and other sacred texts, but also even the theories of interpretation have multiplied as the religious scene has become increasingly complex. Carter joked in 1980 that unlike his critic, dispensationalist Jerry Falwell, he found no passage in Scripture determining whether or not "you should have a B-1 bomber or the air-launched cruise missile."[51]

Fourth, *major foreign policies have significantly affected the domestic religious scene,* sometimes in ways that no one anticipated. A war for independence won during the Enlightenment brought about the separation of church and state, which in turn facilitated a vigorous competition among legally equal denominations. American expansion on this continent fueled Protestant nativist fears that the West might be conquered again—by Catholics and Mormons. World War I ushered in a decade of religious conflict unparalleled in this century. The war against Nazism helped to banish anti-Semitism from public life. Vigorous Catholic patriotism both legitimated Catholicism and distressed some of the Protestant elite. From the mid-1960s until the end of the Cold War, fundamentalists and social gospelers clashed over Vietnam and détente as well as Darwinism and biblical criticism.

These general trends will probably persist for the foreseeable future. In addition, the International Religious Freedom Act may complicate foreign—and perhaps domestic—policy in ways that no one has thought through. The IRFA now requires the U.S. government to decide what constitutes legitimate religious practices in nations with experiences, traditions, and collective memories very different from our own. For instance, when many Americans remember missionaries in China, they think of their denominational heroes and heroines, but when Chinese remember those same missionaries, they think of the "unequal treaties" imposed on their country. As the first *Annual Report* shows, the United States must also decide what constitutes "persecution and discrimination." Murder, torture, rape, abduction, forced relocation, and arbitrary arrest or imprisonment obviously qualify. Yet these actions deserve denunciation whether or not there is an antireligious motive.

Certainly there are gray areas in the definition of legitimate religious practices on the one hand and persecution and discrimination on the other. These areas of contention may multiply as religious interest groups exert pressure in the venerable American fashion. Furthermore, while the *Annual Report* repeatedly invokes common "international standards," its actual standards often derive from our own recently achieved high level of tolerance. This seems to be especially true in evaluating problematical cases of discrimination.

While seeking to enhance religious freedom abroad, Americans in and out of government should recall the long and sometimes bloody road to our current level of civil though sometimes contentious pluralism. As late as 1948, when the United Nations General Assembly adopted the Universal Declaration of Human Rights, the U.S. Supreme Court had only recently decided that a Jehovah's Witness who refused to salute the flag could nonetheless attend public school and ruled unenforceable real estate covenants that banned the sale of houses to Catholics and Jews. A national survey akin to the *Annual Report* would have recorded numerous examples of religious persecution and discrimination by local officials, nongovernmental entities, and ordinary citizens. Some religions remained—or remain—"at a disadvantage" (to recall the *Annual Report*'s term) two generations later. Until recently the Internal Revenue Service shared the opinion of several current European governments that Scientology was less legitimate than older, more popular religions. In 1993, assaults on the Branch Davidian compound near Waco, Texas, by agents of the Bureau of Alcohol, Tobacco, and Firearms and the Federal Bureau of Investigation left eighty Davidians dead, a disaster that might have been avoided if officials had bothered to learn about Davidian beliefs instead of acting precipitously. President Clinton dismissed the tragedy as a case of "religious fanatics [who] murdered themselves." Indeed, from U.S. cavalry attacks on Mormons in the 1850s to the Waco siege, Americans have often justified religious persecution and discrimination in ways now dismissed when invoked by foreign leaders: prevailing values must be respected, new faiths are delusions or rackets, "cults" threaten the family, and national unity is at stake.[52]

Given our history, many Americans understandably feel a special calling to promote religious freedom abroad. But also given our history, we should do so without self-righteousness.

Notes

1. Mark Silk, *Spiritual Politics: Religion and America since World War II* (New York: Simon and Schuster, 1988), 40–53. George M. Marsden, *Fundamentalism and American Culture: The Shaping of Twentieth Century Evangelicalism 1870–1925* (New York: Oxford University Press, 1980), 107.

2. John Winthrop, "A Modell of Christian Charity," in Conrad Cherry, *God's New Israel: Religious Interpretations of American Destiny* (Englewood: Prentice-Hall, 1971), 39–43.

3. Bernard Bailyn, *The Ideological Origins of the American Revolution* (Cambridge: Harvard University Press, 1967).

4. Mark A. Noll, *A History of Christianity in the United States and Canada* (Grand Rapids, Mich.: Eerdmans, 1992), 119–21.

5. William Gribbin, *The Churches Militant: The War of 1812 and American Religion* (New Haven, Conn.: Yale University Press, 1973).

6. Ezra Stiles, "The United States Elevated to Glory and Honour," in Cherry, *God's New Israel*, 82–92. Richard W. Van Alstyne, *The Rising American Empire* (Chicago: Quadrangle, 1965), 69.

7. O'Sullivan quoted in Frederick Merk, *Manifest Destiny and Mission in American History: A Reinterpretation* (New York: Vintage, 1963), 31–32. Norman Graebner, ed., *Manifest Destiny* (Indianapolis: Bobbs-Merrill, 1963), xix.

8. James Hennessey, *American Catholics: A History of the Roman Catholic Community in the United States* (New York: Oxford University Press, 1981), 117–25. John Tracy Ellis, *American Catholicism* (Chicago: University of Chicago Press, 1963), 60–70. Tyler Anbinder, *Nativism and Slavery: The Northern Know Nothings and the Politics of the 1850s* (New York: Oxford University Press, 1992), 27–29.

9. Howard M. Sachar, *A History of the Jews in America* (New York: Knopf, 1992), 39, 45–48, 83. Morton Borden, *Jews, Turks, and Infidels* (Chapel Hill: University of North Carolina Press, 1984), 82–94.

10. Borden, *Jews, Turks, and Infidels*, 54–56, 87–89. Sachar, *History of the Jews*, 82. David I. Kertzer, *The Kidnapping of Edgaro Mortara* (New York: Knopf, 1997), 122.

11. Sydney E. Ahlstrom, *A Religious History of the American People* (New Haven, Conn.: Yale University Press, 1972), 862. Martin E. Marty, *Pilgrims in Their Own Land:*

500 Years of Religion in America (New York: Penguin, 1985), 182–84. Richard W. Van Alstyne, The United States and East Asia (New York: Norton, 1973), 69, 72. Thomas J. McCormick, China Market: America's Quest for Informal Empire 1893–1901 (Chicago: Quadrangle, 1967), 66. Michael H. Hunt, The Making of a Special Relationship: The United States and China to 1914 (New York: Columbia University Press, 1983), 24–39. Warren I. Cohen, America's Response to China: An Interpretive History of Sino-American Relations (New York: Wiley, 1973), 12–24.

12. Marty, Pilgrims, 184. Cohen, America's Response, 28. Borden, Jews, Turks, and Infidels, 79–82.

13. The scholarly literature on these religious developments is enormous, but for a brief overview, see Ahlstrom, Religious History, chaps. 44–51.

14. Richard V. Pierard and Robert D. Linder, Civil Religion and the Presidency (Grand Rapids, Mich.: Academie, 1988), 114–17. Josiah Strong, Our Country (1886; reprint, Cambridge: Harvard University Press, 1963), 254.

15. Pierard and Linder, Civil Religion, 122–29. Ernest R. May, Imperial Democracy: The Emergence of America as a Great Power (New York: Harper Torchbooks, 1961), 154–55. Julius W. Pratt, Expansionists of 1898 (Chicago: Quadrangle, 1964), 279–316.

16. Pierard and Linder, Civil Religion, 131. May, Imperial Democracy, 243–62. Richard E. Welch Jr., Response to Imperialism: The United States and the Philippine-American War 1899–1902 (Chapel Hill: University of North Carolina Press, 1979), 88–90, 93–99.

17. Welch, Response to Imperialism, 90–92, 97. Hunt, Making of a Special Relationship, 154–68, 286–88.

18. Pierard and Linder, Civil Religion, 136–60. John Milton Cooper Jr., The Warrior and the Priest: Woodrow Wilson and Theodore Roosevelt (Cambridge: Harvard University Press, 1983), 18–19, 88. William Harbaugh, The Life and Times of Theodore Roosevelt (New York: Collier, 1966), 213–16. Theodore Roosevelt, "Warlike Power—The Prerequisite for the Preservation of Social Values," in William Harbaugh, ed., The Writings of Theodore Roosevelt (Indianapolis: Bobbs-Merrill, 1967), 353–64. For the conventional interpretation of Wilson's religion, see Arthur S. Link, Woodrow Wilson: Revolution, War, and Peace (Arlington Heights: AHM, 1979), 4–5.

19. Sachar, History of the Jews, 221–34.

20. Richard Challener, "William Jennings Bryan," in Norman A. Graebner, An Uncertain Tradition: American Secretaries of State in the Twentieth Century (New York: McGraw-Hill, 1961), 94–95. Lawrence W. Levine, Defender of the Faith: William Jennings Bryan: The Last Decade, 1915–1925 (New York: Oxford University Press, 1965), 29–30.

21. Marty, Pilgrims, 361–71. Ray H. Abrams, Preachers Present Arms (New York: Round Table, 1933), 53–54, 68. Roger A. Bruns, Preacher: Billy Sunday and Big-Time American Evangelism (New York: Norton, 1992), 210. Hennessey, American Catholics, 225. See also John F. Piper Jr., The American Churches in World War I (Athens: Ohio University Press, 1985).

22. Abrams, Preachers Present Arms, 130. William Vance Trollinger Jr., God's Empire: William Bell Riley and Midwestern Fundamentalism (Madison: University of Wisconsin Press, 1990), 33–61. For the essentials of premillennial dispensationalism, tune in Jerry

Falwell, Pat Robertson, or Jack Van Impe on cable television. A more detached explanation can be found in Paul Boyer, *When Time Shall Be No More: Prophecy Belief in Modern American Culture* (Cambridge: Harvard University Press, 1992).

23. Dorothy Borg, *American Policy and the Chinese Revolution 1925–1928* (New York: East Asia Institute, 1968), 68–94. Yu-ming Shaw, *An American Missionary in China: John Leighton Stuart and Chinese–American Relations* (Cambridge: Harvard University Press, 1992), 92–100. John P. Diggins, *Mussolini and Fascism: The View from America* (Princeton: Princeton University Press, 1972), 182–203. Boyer, *When Time Shall Be No More*, 108–9.

24. Peter G. Filene, *Americans and the Soviet Experiment, 1917–1933* (Cambridge: Harvard University Press, 1967), 83–88, 246–51. Robert Moats Miller, *American Protestantism and Social Issues 1919–1939* (Chapel Hill: University of North Carolina Press, 1958), 40–44, 68–71.

25. Lawrence S. Wittner, *Rebels against War: The American Peace Movement 1933–1983* (Philadelphia: Temple University Press, 1984), 5–13. Abrams, *Preachers Present Arms*, 3, 234–39.

26. Robert Dallek, *Franklin D. Roosevelt and American Foreign Policy, 1932–1935* (New York: Oxford University Press, 1979), 79–81. E. David Cronon, *Josephus Daniels in Mexico* (Madison: University of Wisconsin Press, 1960), 82–111. Karl M. Schmitt, *Mexico and the United States 1821–1973: Conflict and Coexistence* (New York: Wiley, 1974), 171–73.

27. Dallek, *Roosevelt and American Foreign Policy*, 136, 141–42, 179–80. Hennessey, *American Catholics*, 272–74. David J. O'Brien, *American Catholics and Social Reform: The New Deal Years* (New York: Oxford University Press, 1968), 86–87. "American Catholics Reply," in Allen Guttmann, *American Neutrality and the Spanish Civil War* (Boston: Heath, 1963), 61.

28. Pierard and Linder, *Civil Religion*, 178–79.

29. Alfred O. Hero Jr., *American Religious Groups View Foreign Policy: Trends in Rank-and-File Opinion, 1937–1969* (Durham: Duke University Press, 1973), 21, 23. Diggins, *Mussolini and Fascism*, 346–47. Justus D. Doenecke, *In Danger Undaunted: The Anti-Interventionist Movement of 1940–1941 As Revealed in the Papers of the America First Committee* (Stanford: Hoover Institution Press, 1990), 7–8. Leo P. Ribuffo, *The Old Christian Right: The Protestant Far Right from the Great Depression to the Cold War* (Philadelphia: Temple University Press, 1983). Wittner, *Rebels against War*, 15–16, 22, 43, 158, 189. Richard Fox, *Reinhold Niebuhr: A Biography* (New York: Pantheon, 1985), 193–200.

30. Pierard and Linder, *Civil Religion*, 161, 181. Hero, *American Religious Groups*, 33, 40–41. John Lewis Gaddis, *The United States and the Origins of the Cold War 1941–1947* (New York: Columbia University Press, 1972), 43–56. Wittner, *Rebels against War*, 115–19. John Dower, *War without Mercy: Race and Power in the Pacific War* (New York: Pantheon, 1986), 20, 141, 162.

31. The scholarly literature on this issue continues to grow, but the most important books remain Henry L. Feingold, *The Politics of Rescue: The Roosevelt Administration and the Holocaust, 1938–1945* (New Brunswick, N.J.: Rutgers University Press, 1970), and David S. Wyman, *The Abandonment of the Jews: America and the Holocaust, 1941–1945* (New York: Pantheon, 1985). For a balanced overview, see Sachar, *History of the Jews*, 483–501, 533–53. For the Protestant response, see Joel A. Carpenter, *Revive Us Again:*

The Reawakening of American Fundamentalism (New York: Oxford University Press, 1997), 98–105, and Robert Ross, So It Was True: The American Protestant Press and the Nazi Persecution of the Jews (Minneapolis: University of Minnesota Press, 1980).

32. Henry R. Luce, "The American Century," reprinted in Warren Susman, ed., Culture and Commitment 1929–1945 (New York: Braziller, 1973), 319–26. John Morton Blum, ed., The Price of Vision: The Diary of Henry A. Wallace (Boston: Houghton Mifflin, 1973), 13–15.

33. Pierard and Linder, Civil Religion, 198. Carpenter, Revive Us Again, 167–71, 177–86. Walter LaFeber, America, Russia, and the Cold War, 1945–1966 (New York: Wiley, 1967), 40. For a sound overview of the religious revival, see James Hudnut-Beumler, Looking for God in the Suburbs: The Religion of the American Dream and Its Critics, 1945–1965 (New Brunswick, N.J.: Rutgers University Press, 1994).

34. Walter L. Hixson, George F. Kennan: Cold War Iconoclast (New York: Columbia University Press, 1989). Reinhold Niebuhr, The Irony of American History (New York: Scribner's, 1962), 173. Townsend Hoopes, The Devil and John Foster Dulles (Boston: Little Brown, 1973). Mark G. Toulouse, The Transformation of John Foster Dulles: From Prophet of Realism to Prophet of Nationalism (Macon, Ga.: Mercer University Press, 1985).

35. Hennessey, American Catholics, 281, 289–90. Shaw, American Missionary in China, 152–269. Foster Rhea Dulles, American Foreign Policy toward Communist China, 1949–1969 (New York: Crowell, 1972), 74.

36. Sachar, History of the Jews, 572–619. Thomas A. Kolsky, Jews against Zionism: The American Council for Judaism, 1942–1948 (Philadelphia: Temple University Press, 1990). Boyer, When Time Shall Be No More, 187.

37. Donald F. Crosby, God, Church, and Flag: Senator Joseph R. McCarthy and the Catholic Church, 1950–1957 (Chapel Hill: University of North Carolina Press, 1978). James Terence Fisher, The Catholic Counterculture in America, 1933–1962 (Chapel Hill: University of North Carolina Press, 1989), 152–66.

38. Wittner, Rebels against War, 279–89. Mitchell K. Hall, Because of Their Faith: CALCAV and Religious Opposition to the Vietnam War (New York: Columbia University Press, 1990). Anne C. Loveland, American Evangelicals and the U.S. Military, 1942–1993 (Baton Rouge: Louisiana State University Press, 1996), 118–64. David J. Garrow, Bearing the Cross: Martin Luther King Jr. and the Southern Christian Leadership Conference (New York: Morrow, 1986), 543, 551–52. George S. McGovern, Grassroots: The Autobiography of George McGovern (New York: Random House, 1977). Fox, Niebuhr, 288.

39. Hennessey, American Catholics, 318–21. Garry Wills, Bare Ruined Choirs: Doubt, Prophecy, and Radical Religion (Garden City, N.Y.: Doubleday, 1972), 232.

40. Leo P. Ribuffo, "God and Jimmy Carter," in Ribuffo, Right Center Left: Essays in American History (New Brunswick: Rutgers University Press, 1992).

41. J. J. Goldberg, Jewish Power: Inside the American Jewish Establishment (Reading: Addison-Wesley, 1996), 167–76. John Ehrman, The Rise of Neoconservatism: Intellectuals and Foreign Affairs, 1945–1994 (New Haven, Conn.: Yale University Press, 1995).

42. Jeane Kirkpatrick, "Dictatorships and Double Standards," reprinted in Marvin E. Gettleman et al., eds., El Salvador: Central America in the New Cold War (New York: Grove, 1981), 15–39. Raymond Garthoff, The Great Transition: American–Soviet Relations

and the End of the Cold War (Washington, D.C.: Brookings Institution, 1994), 103, 109. Carl Bernstein and Marco Politi, His Holiness: John Paul II and the History of Our Time (New York: Penguin, 1996), 237–389, 449–83.

43. Edmund Morris, Dutch: A Memoir of Ronald Reagan (New York: Random House, 1999), 519, 561, 569, 634, 823.

44. Samuel P. Huntington, The Clash of Civilizations and the Remaking of World Order (New York: Simon and Schuster, 229). Loveland, American Evangelicals and the U.S. Military, 320–21.

45. James L. Guth, ed., The Bully Pulpit: The Politics of Protestant Clergy (Lawrence: University Press of Kansas, 1997), chaps. 5–6. Jeffrey Goldberg, "Washington Discovers Christian Persecution," New York Times Magazine, December 21, 1997, 46–52, 60, 64–65.

46. The "International Religious Freedom Act" is available from Representative Wolf's office at www.house.gov/wolf/free/nicsum.htm.

47. U.S. Department of State, Annual Report on International Religious Freedom for 1999, available at www.state.gov/www/global/human_rights/irf/irf/_rpt/1999.

48. "Religious Freedom Report Released," Christianity Today, October 25, 1999; "America Legislates for the World! (Part 1 of 2)," Christianity Today, November 19, 1999, available at www.christianityonline.com/ct.

49. Frank R. Wolf, "The Chinese Gulags," Washington Post, April 29, 2000. "Religious Group Urges Rejection of China Bill," Washington Post, May 2, 2000. "Permanent Normal Trade Relations with China," C-SPAN, May 10, 2000.

50. Mort Rosenblum, Mission to Civilize: The French Way (New York: Anchor, 1988).

51. Ribuffo, "God and Jimmy Carter," 246.

52. James D. Tabor and Eugene V. Gallagher, Why Waco? Cults and the Battle for Religious Freedom in America (Berkeley: University of California Press, 1995), 159.

~

Comment by Nathan Tarcov

Professor Ribuffo presents a rich and nuanced account of the various roles that religion and religious groups have played in U.S. foreign policy, from the Declaration of Independence to the present. Asking first, "In what ways have religious beliefs contributed to the widely shared assumption that the United States is an exceptional nation with a unique role in the world?" he answers that a strong republican sense of *mission* thrived apart from the legacies of Reformation Protestantism, and that without those religious legacies the United States would have justified its rise to world power with other ideological claims.

I would like to distinguish more emphatically between two notions that appear in his account: (1) American exceptionalism and (2) America's sense of mission, whether purely exemplary or crusading and interventionist. A truly exceptional nation cannot reasonably be considered a universal model for others, nor can it rightly crusade to recreate others in its own image. American exceptionalism in its purer forms points in another direction: toward withdrawal from a very foreign world that cannot share in its distinctive blessings and that, should we become involved with it, threatens to corrupt those blessings. A sense of mission, in contrast, whether affected by force of example or by examples of force, presumes that the nation is not truly exceptional but merely *first* and ultimately universal.

Neither of these powerful notions, American exceptionalism and American mission, is necessarily religious; both have secular forms as well. Amer-

Nathan Tarcov is a professor in the Committee on Social Thought and the Department of Political Science at the University of Chicago.

ican exceptionalism can take the form of the withdrawal of a virtuous republican people from a corrupt monarchical or aristocratic Old World, as
well as the form of separation of the saints from the damned. American mission can be either the spread of republicanism and human rights or the conversion of the heathen. Nonetheless, it might be true that American exceptionalism and withdrawal derive more decisive sustenance from the legacies
of Reformation Protestantism than does the American sense of mission. If so,
then those of us who prefer the sense of active mission (whether purely exemplary, crusading and interventionist, or some combination) to the sense of
exceptionalist withdrawal may not simply welcome a resurgence of the role
of religion in U.S. foreign policy.

Among other interesting points, Professor Ribuffo says that no major
foreign-policy decisions have turned on religious issues *alone* and that religious groups have significantly affected only "second level" foreign policies,
and then only by finding other allies and invoking more widely shared American principles. These are trends that he expects to continue. Although I am
not inclined to argue with those points, I would note that what he calls "second level" foreign policies, such as those toward the Spanish Civil War or toward the state of Israel, are assuredly not unimportant, even if they are out-
weighed by such matters as U.S. participation in World War II or the Cold
War. And besides, perhaps it is best to understand our present post–Cold War
international outlook as *nothing but* "second level" foreign policies.

Why has the role of religion in U.S. foreign policy been so limited? Americans have a majority religion, Christianity, and polls and church attendance
figures indicate that they are one of the most religious peoples on earth. For
those who call themselves "realists" this seeming discrepancy poses no problem: according to their theory, every country's foreign policy is dictated solely
by its geostrategic situation, not by religious or ideological views. But that
simply is not so. Who can believe that, for example, the foreign policy of the
Islamic Republic of Iran would be the same in the absence of Shiite Islam?

I would note three obvious factors that explain why the United States
doesn't have as religiously influenced a foreign policy as, say, Iran. First,
Christianity is much too diverse a religion to support a consensus on foreign
policy, as Professor Ribuffo's account indicates. It is divided not only into
Catholics and Protestants but into many denominations and theological tendencies, differing not only in their sympathies for particular groups abroad
but in fundamental beliefs that shape their outlook on foreign policy, beliefs
about such matters as the human capability for improvement, the morality of
the use of force, and the imminence of apocalypse. Ribuffo observes that
even among Christians of the same denomination or theological inclination

there is no uniformity on foreign policy. But let me add that the mere fact that there is no observable correlation between the religious convictions of American Christians and their foreign-policy positions does not necessarily mean that those religious convictions are unimportant to their thinking about foreign policy.

Second, our constitutional disestablishment of religion—now enforced by minorities of Jews, Muslims, Hindus, and above all secular humanists—prevents the establishment of an emphatically *Christian* foreign policy. And third, our founders established a tradition of foreign-policy conduct and rhetoric independent of Christianity.

On the basis of his historical survey, Professor Ribuffo offers some cautions about an enhanced role of religion in foreign policy. He warns of difficult matters of definition and vexatious "gray areas." I agree that if we make it a policy to protect the rights of American missionaries to spread their religious beliefs in every unwelcome environment abroad, rather than protecting the rights of existing indigenous religious groups in other countries to be free from blatant persecution, we are asking for trouble both at home and abroad.

I would also add that we must not judge religious freedom abroad by the standards of the unique American separation of church and state. Practically every other state I can think of either establishes one religion (at least in some symbolic ways, as in the U.K.), positively aids a range of recognized religions while refusing to aid others (Germany), or, conversely, acts to enforce secularism (Turkey). Our own First Amendment distinguishes religious freedom from nonestablishment, and we would do well not to confuse the two in any attempt to promote religious freedom abroad. The need to distinguish universal principles from American particularities and to respect the particularities of others is present in any foreign policy concerned with human rights.

∾

CHAPTER TWO

Religious Freedom and U.S. Foreign Policy: Categories and Choices

J. Bryan Hehir

Violations of religious freedom, of which religious persecution is the extreme example, are both visible and pervasive in world politics. How should U.S. policy respond to them? The cornerstone of an effective policy must begin with an understanding of religious freedom itself. The idea, now firmly enshrined in the Universal Declaration of Human Rights and in the constitutions of most states, has deep roots in the political history of the West. The modern formulation, the right to religious freedom, is the most recent and the most philosophically precise expression of the concept, but it has an extended history in Western political thought. The origin of the story is linked to the emergence of the Christian Church in the midst of the Roman Empire. In classical Greco-Roman polity and philosophy, religion did not have independent status or standing; religious authority was clearly subservient to political authority, and religion itself was understood as a component element of the polis.

Christianity—the personal faith of believers, the doctrine that expressed the faith, and the institutional structure that arose from the faith—set out to redefine the relationship of religion and politics. It did this in two distinct but complementary ways.[1] First, the conscience of the believers was shaped by the conviction that they must respond to an independent source

J. Bryan Hehir is professor of the practice in religion and society and chair of the Executive Committee at Harvard Divinity School. He also serves as counselor to Catholic Relief Services in Baltimore and is a faculty associate of Harvard University Weatherhead Center for International Affairs. From 1973 to 1992 Father Hehir served in Washington at the U.S. Catholic Conference of Bishops and at Georgetown University.

of religious–moral authority, distinct from the state and of greater weight than the state could ever possess. Second, complementing this internal standard of moral authority (i.e., conscience), the early church took shape as an independent institution that established a claim to social space in the empire. The classic text explicating the claim was Pope Gelasius's letter to the Emperor Anastasius, *Duo Sunt*, in which he set forth the Christian conception of the origin and nature of political and religious authority. To state it synthetically, all authority resides in God, who has given "two swords" to human rulers: political authority is given to the state and religious authority is given to the pope. In principle each authority is allocated a sphere of activity (the secular and sacred spheres), but the two should collaborate in the service of human society. This sparse structural account of how authority is legitimized and how it should be exercised became a classic text in the history of both church and state, and it framed the struggle of the two powers for much of the next 1,500 years.

This double statement of independence from the state—a claim of personal conscience and of a social institution within which conscience was schooled and its exercise protected from state power—was the basis from which the different but related modern right of religious freedom developed. The process of development had its own inner tensions and contradictions. While the primary historical struggle about the right took place between the two "perfect societies" (church and state), there was always a subtheme about claims of freedom of conscience within the Church itself.[2] Neither of these complex stories can be told adequately here, nor is that necessary for the purposes of this essay. But two principal moments in the history of religious freedom should be identified.

After the Protestant Reformation and the religious wars that consumed Europe for a century, church and state forged a practical formula in pursuit of civil peace. Expressed in the dictum *cujus regio, ejus religio*, it designated each of the major European states as Catholic or Protestant, established a religion of the state according to the religion of the prince, and privileged the religious rights of one community within the state. A corollary to the institution of the "religion of the state" was the concept of "religious toleration" (quite different from the modern concept of religious freedom), which sought to provide limited protection for religious minorities within a state. The concept of toleration embodied two elements: first, no one should be coerced to believe or accept a religious truth that was not held from inner conviction and choice; second, religious minorities were severely limited in any public profession of faith, especially in any effort to share their faith with others.[3]

This mix of "establishment and toleration" held sway as the dominant pattern of religion and politics until the eighteenth-century democratic rev-

olutions brought a competing order into existence. The new order constituted the second phase of the development of religious liberty. As one dimension of the modern conception of democratic liberties, the right of each
person to religious freedom and its extension to the right of religious communities to function freely in society were affirmed in civil law. The affirmation of these rights in turn was tied to drawing a distinction between church
and state (reflective of *Duo Sunt* but more explicit in detail and structure).
These developments did not necessarily rule out the institution of a state
church, for instance, in England, but they set new limits on state power in
the realm of conscience and faith.

The basic lines of the eighteenth-century innovations regarding religion
and politics were maintained in a process of development through the twentieth century, finding expression in the UN's 1948 Universal Declaration of
Human Rights. In a sense the current policy debate over religious freedom is
a product of the inclusion of that freedom in the Universal Declaration. The
presence of religious freedom in the panoply of basic human rights creates an
important political-legal presumption: that states are to be held to standards
on the protection of the right to religious freedom, and that states have obligations to respond to the violation of that right, particularly when it as-
sumes the proportion of religious persecution. Claims made in the Universal
Declaration require both defining the obligations of states to act on behalf of
rights and formulating policies that will effectively implement those obligations. This has been a halting process for religious freedom; other rights have
received more policy attention. But the new activism around issues of religious persecution and in defense of religious freedom is having its effect, and
to some degree it can benefit from the lessons and legacy of the last half-cen-
tury of human rights advocacy.

In light of this conviction, I can summarize the argument of this chapter
as follows. First, I will argue that the appropriate policy response to religious
persecution or lesser violations of religious freedom is to locate the protection of religious rights within an activist human rights policy. Second, I will
assess whether such a view pays adequate attention to the character of the
right of religious freedom. Third, I will propose a mix of strategy and tactics
for a U.S. policy committed to the defense of religious freedom.

Religious Freedom and U.S. Human Rights Policy

In December 1997 the *New York Times Magazine* published an article by Jeffrey
Goldberg with the creatively provocative title "Washington Discovers Christian Persecution."[4] Provocation was the appropriate literary style, because

Goldberg sought to depict an eruption both in the normal foreign-policy debate in the United States and in the standard human rights advocacy that itself had been a provocative element in the 1970s and 1980s. Goldberg's emphasis was on the new—even alien—character of human rights discourse that focused on the right of religious freedom, or its denial and repression. Describing the diverse coalition pressing the religious-freedom agenda, he wrote: "These unlikely partners are united by their desire to remoralize American foreign policy. Within the past year, they have seized an issue, Christian persecution, that existed on the margins of the human rights agenda and yanked it to the center of America's foreign policy debate."[5] By 1999, the coalition had a victory in the passage of the International Religious Freedom Act, but Goldberg's article remains useful because he sought to emphasize not simply the legislative objective of the coalition but its potential to recast broad themes in the debate about religion, human rights, and U.S. foreign policy.

In pursuit of his theme Goldberg had some undeniable facts on his side. While the right of religious freedom had not been denied by standard human rights advocacy in the past thirty years, it had hardly been emphasized; to press this right is to alter the human rights equation. Moreover, the catalyst for change had arisen outside the community that since the 1970s had creatively and effectively pushed human rights as a dimension of U.S. foreign policy. Again, while the human rights standard-bearers had not conspired to ignore religious freedom, it was difficult to dispute Goldberg's description that it remained at "the margin" of the policy debate. Finally, the inclusion of this right as a central rather than a marginal dimension of the foreign-policy process inevitably opened the larger question of the role of religion in world politics.

The assertion that all these factors converged to create something novel on the human rights agenda and in broader policy debates was not difficult to sustain. But the proposition should not be argued from a position of historical innocence. Religion has not been absent from the U.S. policy debates of the last fifty years. In a recurring pattern, religious convictions and concerns surfaced throughout the Cold War era: from Soviet repression of religious personalities and communities in Central and Eastern Europe in the 1940s and 1950s to the campaigns in support of Jews and Baptists in the Soviet Union in the 1970s to the intense conflicts generated in U.S. politics by the religion-laden issues of Central America in the 1980s, U.S. politics and policies were permeated by religious themes. A balanced view will do justice to the historical record while acknowledging the distinctive qualities of the positions taken by those whom Goldberg calls "the new activists" on religious freedom.

The new activists have a definite position on how the human rights agenda should address religious freedom: they want this right to be understood and pursued as an independent variable in the policy equation. From Sudan to China to the Middle East, the new activists seek to redress the previous marginalization of religious freedom by giving it unique status in the policy process. There are normative and empirical reasons that can be legitimately adduced in support of this position, some of which will be examined below. But it is a position that does not rest easily within policy discourse, nor does it accord with the specific positions most representative of mainline human rights advocates over the last thirty years. Goldberg's article, written just before the congressional debate that produced the International Religious Freedom Act, captures some of the tension created by the new issues and new actors:

> Still many in the human rights community are less than enthusiastic about the Christian Right's newfound interest in human rights. This might be the result . . . of cultural distaste. But there are other reasons as well. Many human rights activists cringe at the possibility of a Government-run office to monitor religious persecution, for other movements would surely demand the same treatment and create a bureaucratic morass.[6]

Relating the Old and the New

How should the old and new human rights causes be analyzed and engaged? The difference in approaches could fracture the human rights community, which is neither large enough nor successful enough to withstand this kind of civil strife. A second *New York Times Magazine* essay, written by David Rieff two years after Goldberg's, clearly illustrates the stakes of such conflict. Rieff acknowledges the real accomplishments of human rights advocates over the last three decades but tempers this accolade with a sober assessment of the challenge facing them:

> Yet paradoxically, at the very moment when its ideas have become mainstream, the human rights movement seems adrift. . . . For all its influence in elite circles, the human rights constituency is a tiny fraction of that commanded by grassroots organizations of either the right or the left. Without a broad base of support, it may have reached the limits of its effectiveness. Whether its leaders know it or not, the human rights movement is in trouble.[7]

The new activists represent, in part, a grassroots style of politics; an important sector of their constituency is the recently emergent communities of evangelical Protestants, decidedly Christian and decisively conservative. But to analyze the new emphasis on religious freedom only in these terms would be excessively narrow. There are Christian evangelicals who are not politically conservative, and there are other Christians who are neither evangelical in style nor conventionally conservative in social policy but are both serious and persistent in their support of religious freedom.

In addition, determining how to relate the old and new human rights voices requires a move beyond constituencies and policy proposals, a move to the policy framework needed for effective impact in the complex setting of world politics at the start of a new century. To summarize the position advocated here, I would agree that the pursuit of religious freedom (and resistance to religious persecution) must be located within the broader context of an activist human rights policy. Because this approach situates the right of religious freedom in the broader fabric of rights discourse, I will then have to address claims that such an approach does not do justice to the unique character of religious freedom. In conclusion I will need to return to the policy question of strategy and tactics, testing how either old or new activists must compete for influence and leverage in a foreign-policy debate that is not solely focused on human rights of any kind.

While I agree with the new activists on the need for greater systematic attention to the right of religious freedom in human rights policy, I do not agree with their analysis of why religious freedom has not received sufficient attention in the past. Some of the new activists describe this in conspiratorial terms that I find both unconvincing and not essential to their central point.

A more substantive difference between my position in this essay and theirs centers on how to redress the balance of human rights advocacy. The new activists, in my view, seek to give priority to religious freedom by separating it from the range of other rights and developing a strategy uniquely designed to protect and promote "religious rights." My position here is that the protection and promotion of religious freedom is best understood philosophically and best pursued politically as an essential dimension of an activist human rights policy. In my view, the systematic elaboration of an activist human rights policy capable of addressing the changed character of world politics today is as urgent an objective as attending to the role of religious freedom within such a policy. I do not believe a unilateral policy style in pursuit of religious freedom or in response to religious oppression is either sound or effective. The better approach, in my view, is to press both the broader objectives of human rights strategy and the specific role of religious freedom within such a policy.

Three Stages of Human Rights Development

Defining an activist human rights policy requires a sense of the history of the human rights regime now in place. In other settings I have distinguished three stages in this development, reaching from 1945 to 2000.[8] While there are different ways of characterizing these stages, the most useful for our purposes here is to see them as a systemic phase, a state-centric phase, and a transnational phase.

1. *The systemic phase.* Stage one is the period from 1945 through the 1960s, when new texts and foundational documents established the basis for the human rights regime in world politics. The term "systemic" is meant to highlight the change introduced in the conception of world politics through the human rights initiatives of the United Nations.

The systemic phase had both a philosophical and a juridical character. On the philosophical side, the 1948 UN Universal Declaration of Human Rights, while not the first UN document to invoke human rights (the 1945 UN Charter holds this distinction), is the foundational text for all human rights advocacy. The Declaration is not a tidy philosophical essay; it draws upon diverse philosophical positions, particularly the natural-law and natural-rights traditions, to weave an eclectic but ultimately coherent statement of the place of human rights in international politics. In conjunction with statements found in the UN Charter, the Declaration ties the role of the United Nations to the protection and promotion of human rights in a substantial fashion. The linkage is at the level of philosophical concepts and moral principles; it has none of the structural architecture that is associated with the concept of a regime in the contemporary study of world politics.[9]

On the juridical side, the philosophical statement did have a bearing upon the role of the United Nations and the responsibility of states. Prior to the founding of the United Nations, the phrase "human rights" had moral content but little political consequence. The crucial constraint on human rights policy was the concept of domestic jurisdiction, which effectively ruled out of order any significant responsibility of outside actors for the internal policies pursued by states. To put it differently, states, on the whole, were immune from being acted upon by outsiders because of the way they treated their citizens.[10] The two kinds of activity that created exceptions to this policy of virtually absolute state sovereignty were the crime of genocide and the mistreatment of another state's citizens. Either of these opened the door—narrowly—to some form of response by outside actors.

The systemic shift introduced by the UN texts involved the affirmation in principle of a political-legal responsibility of states and of the United Nations to address human rights violations within other states. Taken as a whole, within the context of the UN system, the obligation of states or the UN itself was carefully constrained. The combined concepts of state sovereignty and nonintervention took precedence in the UN system, but the inclusion of human rights as an objective of the system relativized both of these notions. The systemic articulation of how human rights were to be promoted and protected continued in stage one through the adoption of the UN Covenants and the slow growth of juridical structures designed to implement the philosophical ideas of this period.

2. *The state-centric phase*. Given the strength and significance of the philosophical-juridical breakthrough of stage one, it is surprising how marginal a role human rights played in world politics from the 1940s through the 1960s. Stage two, the period of the 1970s and 1980s, signifies the move from principle to policy formulation. In both stages U.S. policy can serve as an example of the changing role of human rights.[11]

Although the United States was a primary contributor to and catalyst for the Universal Declaration of Human Rights, during the next twenty-five years there was no systematic effort to move from declaratory statements to an effective policy. The declaratory policy was systemic in focus and intent—to establish standards that would influence all states. But the United Nations as an organization did not fundamentally change the "state-centric logic" of world politics; without vigorous action by states the declaratory policy floated above interstate relations, with little influence upon them. In the 1970s the United States showed what could happen once a state began to address human rights as a goal of foreign policy. I do not want to overstate the degree of change introduced in stage two of the human rights narrative, but only to indicate how even modest state attention to rights can influence the ebb and flow of world affairs.

The shift toward an activist human rights policy was driven primarily by an internal struggle in the U.S. policy process. By the 1970s, an increasingly frustrated Congress was in search of effective leverage on the Executive branch in the area of foreign policy. The center of the struggle was (as it had been for a decade) Vietnam policy, but the dominance over foreign policy of Secretary Kissinger and his classic style of *realpolitik* had frustrated both conservatives concerned about human rights in the Soviet Union and liberals concerned about U.S. policy in the Southern Hemisphere.

The twenty-fifth anniversary of the UN Declaration in 1973 provided the opportunity for a coalition of the Congress to address systematically the relationship of human rights and U.S. foreign policy. Through a combination of well-publicized hearings, calls for reform in the State Department policy process, and legislation (the ultimate influence), the Congress initiated an era of debate and decision making on human rights. The policy product over the next twenty years was neither regularly successful nor consistently coherent, but it demonstrated both the potential and the complexity of seeking to pursue human rights as a dimension of a broader range of foreign-policy goals. This second stage of development, while driven by state policy, catalyzed new writing and research on human rights, helped to create new institutions, and was partly responsible for the rise of nongovernmental organizations (NGOs) dedicated to an activist human rights policy.

A defining characteristic of stage two in the human rights narrative is that it was played out in the vise of Cold War politics. Introducing human rights into the policy equation meant bringing it into constant tension with security objectives that were the defining categories of superpower politics. Conservatives in the United States often believed that arms-control policies ignored human rights issues within the Soviet Union (the voice of Senator Henry Jackson), while liberals believed the United States ignored human rights violations of regimes regarded as important strategic allies (the voice of Senator Tom Harkin). Like much else in international relations, the context of the human rights agenda was decisively altered by the end of the Cold War.

3. *A transnational phase.* The third stage of human rights advocacy, while not wholly the product of post–Cold War politics, coincides with the last decade and can be expected to extend into the foreseeable future. This stage is transnational in two senses: first, the transnational activity of NGOs, whether they are explicitly human rights organizations or simply drawn into human rights policy by their work in relief and development or their role in conflict resolution, continues to expand in size and scope; and second, the transnational character of the global economy, a mix of private corporations, state policy, and international institutions, has become at least as important as security issues as a context for human rights policy. In stage three the contested human rights choices often bear upon issues of trade, foreign investment in countries with no child-labor standards, and the role of human rights and international institutions. Stage three, when compared with the first two stages, presents a different range of issues and actors for both the United Nations and states to address. It is in this context that the debate about religious freedom as a human right has arisen.

Formulating an Activist Policy

The dominant foreign-policy matter of U.S. relations with China raises classical security and arms-control issues, questions of economic policy, and the grim reality of religious repression. The China case provides a very good illustration of what an activist human rights policy requires and how the role of religion is located in it. Such a policy is one in which the support of human rights permeates the state's foreign policy, both in its conception and in complex policy choices. Human rights in this formulation is not an "add on" to policy, nor is it a desirable but dispensable element of policy. Shaping an activist policy requires that the definition of basic policy interests include human rights objectives. It then requires a recognition that the complexity of world politics means that human rights will always be a *dimension* of foreign policy, not its sole defining category. An NGO dedicated to enhancing human rights around the globe can pursue a policy in which rights are the controlling factor in policy conception and choice, but a major state will never be able to see its policy obligations or objectives through the single lens of human rights.

Carrying this point forward, some would then want to define the policy problem as one of relating policy interests (hard objectives) to moral obligations (soft objectives), but such a conception prejudices the possibilities of sustaining the role of rights in policy formulation. A preferable construct is one in which the protection and promotion of human rights (to which the United States is committed through its UN membership) is regarded from the outset of policy as an "interest" of the state. In the face of realist objections that the human rights of others do not fit in the tight circle of vital interests that a state must defend lest it jeopardize its very existence, I would draw a distinction between "vital interests" and "national interests." The former have the "hard" quality of security and economic concerns; the latter include these objectives but also extend to the values, traditions, and sense of national identity that define a state's and a people's understanding of their role in the world.

If human rights should permeate policy but cannot exhaust its content, then an activist policy will inevitably have to weigh rights causes against other policy objectives. To weigh human rights proposals, balance them against other interests or goals, or rank them in some order of priority often elicits the charge of inconsistency or moral failure. The criticism can emerge from different sources; for the realist, it is often an element in a critique that says the inclusion of human rights will inevitably lead to confusion or hypocrisy in the world of foreign policy; for the committed human rights activist, such a process of defining a specific but limited role for rights inevitably means trampling upon them. Such responses fail to address the role of moral reasoning in complex policy choices. They beg the question of what consistency requires, or they ignore the fact that moral choice is seldom linear—it frequently involves ranking goods, making choices about limiting evils, defining the possible as well as the desirable. Maintaining a commitment to human rights throughout the policy process does not require that rights always trump other policy objectives. Arms-control measures involve moral objectives also; to use human rights claims as a veto on such agreements with a major power like China can be defective moral reasoning.

Sound moral reasoning requires the clarification of inherently moral objectives like human rights as a standard for policy making; but it also involves an assessment of means and choices that can effectively achieve the objectives. The more ancient policy ethic of war is instructive on this point: it affirms broadly defined "just causes" for which force can be used, but it also includes criteria like "last resort," "possibility of success," and "proportionality" as ethical guides for pursuing policies in the midst of competing moral norms. An activist human rights policy will be formulated in terms of the declaratory goals of the UN human rights texts; but it will pursue those goals in a matrix of multiple state objectives. The essence of skillful policy entails a willingness to test a state's policy at any time against human rights claims and then to sustain those claims against the pressure of the traditional foreign-policy necessities of security and economics.

Given this maze of principle and power, of absolute moral claims and limited policy choices, one can understand the desire of the new activists to insulate the unique role of religion from such an uncertain fate and compromising process, and to favor a distinctive—perhaps unique—approach to protecting religious rights. The reaction is understandable, but the strategic vision, in my view, is ultimately detrimental to human rights and the protection of religious convictions and communities. Human rights will always be an endangered species in the anarchic arena of world politics; an effective strategy of support for them requires a definition of core rights and the consistent pursuit of them.

How to define the core is always a contentious philosophical and political question. The UN Declaration itself has too broad a spectrum to be pursued seriously and effectively. There are solid, persuasive reasons to say that any core should include the right to religious freedom. The energies of those committed to this right should be focused not on isolating it but on securing it a permanent place among the priority rights that the policy of a state is bound to respect and defend. Such an approach not only reduces the chance that rights advocates will be set against one another but also diminishes the possibility that religious rights will be seen as "sectarian" concerns over against the universal objectives of human rights advocacy.

Such an inclusive approach seeks to respond to the dictates of good strategy and the need to combine objectives in coherent policy making. But do these prudential policy criteria simply relativize the status and meaning of religious freedom as a distinct human right? To answer this question, the analysis must shift from the world of policy to the content of this particular right.

Religious Freedom and Other Human Rights

To examine the intrinsic meaning of religious freedom, I will draw upon a tradition that has been a source for human rights discourse at the United Nations, namely, the natural-law ethic as it has been developed within the Catholic tradition. From the French philosopher Jacques Maritain, who participated in the drafting of the UN Declaration, to the major addresses on human rights given by John Paul II to the UN General Assembly in 1979 and 1995, this normative tradition has been a dimension of the UN conversation. It is also the case that the Catholic tradition had a long public struggle within its ranks about the meaning and weight of the right to religious freedom, a struggle that culminated in the Second Vatican Council's *Declaration on Religious Freedom* (1965). This authoritative statement owed its appearance in part to Catholicism's learning experience in dialogue with twentieth-century reflection on human rights. While issuing from a specific religious tradition, the statement articulated the meaning of religious freedom in universal terms.[12]

The Basis and Scope of Religious Freedom

The basis of the right of religious freedom is not a religious claim as such, but a philosophical claim rooted in the dignity of the human person. The dignity of the person demands that the search for truth, including religious truth, be freely conducted, pursued without constraint or coercion. More specifically, the right to religious freedom involves a double immunity or protection. First, no one should be coerced or constrained to believe; assent to religious truth should arise freely from the distinguishing dimensions of human dignity, intelligence, and free will. Second, no one should be prohibited or prevented from publicly affirming his/her faith, or from seeking to share it with others so long as the methods of sharing are free of all coercion. This right, rooted in dignity, is universal, applying to all persons, and it should find expression in civil law.[13]

While expressed as a right of the person, religious freedom is both personal and social, a protection of individual believers and of the community to which they belong. Often it is the social dimension of the right that comes into conflict with the claims of states. The social meaning of religious freedom involves the right of a religious community to teach, to celebrate worship, and to create institutions to fulfill its ministry to others (schools, hospitals, charitable organizations). Religious communities occupy social space, and so they can come in conflict with, or be seen as a competitor to, the state and its institutions or policies.

The possibility of conflict with the state or with other groups in a society raises this question: are there limits on the exercise of religious freedom, as there are with other human rights? The answer is that a definable limit exists that in principle does not violate the right itself. Religious freedom can be limited in its expression if it can be shown that it constitutes a threat to "public order." Because this phrase is so broad in its potential meaning, it is open to abuse, but some agreed content exists for it. Public order comprises three goods: public peace, justice (understood as the protection of the rights of others), and public morality (a phrase that in turn requires further specification). The point to be made here is that even this most personal human right—the search for ultimate truth—does have to yield to well-defined restrictions made in the name of protecting the rights of others and the essential requirements of social life.[14]

Is Religious Freedom a Unique Right?

Here we reach the heart of the argument over whether the nature of this right as just defined means that it cannot simply be classified as one right among many. To illustrate the argument I will use three positions.

First, the UN Universal Declaration of Human Rights presents religious freedom as *a right like any other*. In the context of the UN text, religious freedom, based on human dignity, has a secure place.[15] While the new activists may be able to complain that the human rights advocates have not attended to this right, they cannot fault the United Nations itself for ignoring or omitting it. But religious freedom is given neither special attention nor any special priority in the UN panoply of rights. The right to religious freedom is located within the cluster of rights known as political-civil rights in the UN regime. It is understood as an immunity or protection. While there is no specific articulation of its content such as one finds in the text from Vatican II, the usual characteristics that accompany political and civil rights are assumed to belong to religious freedom. The immunity is first a protection against the power of the state, but it then extends to other groups in society, private and public, restraining them from invading the social space of individuals or their communities as they seek to find religious truth and to express and share it.

The second position is the one that best accords with that of John Courtney Murray, S.J., an American Jesuit whose scholarship was uniquely important in leading the Catholic Church to its modern position on religious freedom. Murray's position may be expressed this way: religious freedom is *a right analogous to other rights*.[16] In his work at Vatican II, Murray argued against the church's using primarily religious or theological arguments to express its position on religious freedom. He sought to locate the defense of the right within the range of other philosophical and juridical arguments made for religious freedom.[17] Murray decisively influenced the Vatican II teaching set forth in the

Declaration on Religious Freedom. After the council he went on to produce commentaries on the text that sought to defend the uniqueness of religious freedom while maintaining its relationship with other human rights arguments.

Technically, the Murray position is best expressed as an analogous relationship between religious freedom and other political and civil rights. Analogy seeks to compare two realities that are somewhat the same, yet distinctively different. The two realities overlap in a limited way, yet they can never be identified with each other. For Murray, the totally different dimension of religious freedom is that the object of the right is the reality of God; unlike other rights, whose pursuit is worked out in a human context, religious freedom seeks to relate the person to some transcendent reality, however it is defined. While this relationship takes the person beyond daily human relationships, the similarity or overlap with other rights lies in the fact that the purpose of the right is to provide the social space needed to pursue one's religious convictions. The Murray position is more explicit about the uniqueness of the right than the UN documents are, but it does not set this right apart from others, nor does it necessarily yield a view that religious freedom should have priority among rights in the policy process.

Third, the position of Pope John Paul II teaches *the primacy of religious freedom*. John Paul II was deeply involved at Vatican II in developing the *Declaration on Religious Freedom*; in that sense his position and Murray's share common ground. But in his twenty years in the papacy, the Pope has developed a series of arguments that give priority to this right over others. A statement that is representative of the position the Pope has developed is this: "The civil and social right to religious freedom, inasmuch as it touches the most intimate sphere of the spirit, is a point of reference of the other fundamental rights and in some way becomes a measure of them."[18] The emphasis in this statement is on the distinctive spiritual relationship that a link to the transcendent implies. It seeks to distinguish this relationship from the multiple other ties that bind persons in social relationships.

Understandably, the UN texts make no reference to this idea. Murray's position recognizes it but does not make the explicit transition to an argument for primacy. John Paul's position moves from the theological distinctiveness of the divine–human relationship to a moral hierarchy of rights with religious freedom "a measure" of other rights.

It is also the case that the Pope's extensive engagement in protecting religious freedom at the practical level, both as a bishop of Poland and as pope of the universal church, seems to have reinforced his theoretical argument with a policy position. Essentially it is that religious freedom is a test case for other rights: if a state moves against religious freedom, John Paul II is convinced it will move against the wider range of personal and social rights. It is a reasonable inference that the combination of theological-philosophical conviction and concrete experience with authoritarian regimes of left and right has produced a papal policy of making religious freedom the test case for encounters with state power. From Poland to Chile to Cuba and the Sudan, John Paul II has advocated the primacy of "religious rights" as the leading edge of his defense of human rights.[19]

Does Distinctiveness Require a Distinction?

How do these diverse positions on the nature of religious freedom relate to the practical policy discussion that has been set off in the United States by the new activists? The starting point of the assessment should be a recognition that intrinsically there is a distinctive difference about the right of religious freedom, based on its term or object; ultimately the exercise of this right seeks to relate its possessor to a different realm of reality than all other rights. If a religious relationship is possible, it is about connecting the human to the divine (however the latter is defined). This transcendent possibility has a different character than the quest for political freedom or economic well-being, or even the intellectual pursuit of truth in teaching, research, and publishing. It is clearly understandable that the UN documents do not seek to articulate this distinctive character of religious freedom, and it is to be expected that in scholarly literature and legal commentary many who would respect the right would not be convinced by arguments about its intrinsic character. There is an analogy within the U.S. constitutional system: in one sense religious freedom is defined and treated like other rights, but in decisions of the Supreme Court and in the debates surrounding them, there is an added dimension of complexity that bears upon how religious claims are related to American public life.

The crucial policy question, however, is whether the intrinsic distinctiveness of religious freedom should translate into a moral distinction that in turn would demand a different approach to religious rights than to other human rights, either within the UN regime or in U.S. policy. Clearly the new activists are convinced that violations of religious freedom either have been overlooked or have been overridden by other concerns in the policy process. But one could address these two criticisms through reform of both private advocacy and public policy without concluding that a specific hierarchy of rights exists with religious freedom in a unique position of primacy. To be clear, the statement of John Paul II cited previously does not *necessarily* entail such an ordering of rights in the policy process. On the other hand, one could espouse the position I have taken—that religious freedom should be located within a core set of rights—and nonetheless argue that religious freedom should rank first in the core and in the shaping of human rights policy.

In my view, the unique character of religious freedom does not generate a moral claim of primacy in the policy process. Violations of religious freedom, in their lesser forms or in religious persecution, demand a response on moral and political grounds. Moreover, the power of religious claims to generate broad and sustained public response will often reinforce the moral demand. But weighing how to respond either through international institutions or in the policy of a state should reflect a policy consistent with the pursuit of other human rights claims. Hence the question, what does consistent policy look like in this policy area?

Religious Freedom and U.S. Foreign Policy

The theme the new activists want to stress, the role of religion in foreign policy, is not often a welcome or familiar topic in the world where international relations is studied or where foreign policy is made. Neither the standard study of world politics nor the conventions of professional diplomacy has made room in any explicit, systematic fashion for addressing religious ideas or institutions. It is possible to identify historical and intellectual traditions that produce this black-box approach to religion in international relations. First, the origins of the modern state system are associated with the end of the religious wars in Europe in the sixteenth and seventeenth centuries. One dimension of the Westphalian legacy was the effort to take religion out of the realm of interstate politics, or at least to prevent the appeal to religion as a justification for war. This initial impulse was, in my view, then reinforced in the eighteenth-century democratic revolutions, which greatly influenced the modern conception of the individual's right to religious freedom, but also contributed, implicitly at least, to the conviction that religious freedom for the individual flourished best if the realm of conviction and belief were confined to the private aspects of life, insulated as much as possible from public policy.

Second, the historical record above and beyond the Westphalian era illustrates the fact that religion inherently has a bivalent potential in the life of a society or between states. Religious conviction can help individuals and groups transcend their particular perspectives, conceive of the human community as a family, and inculcate a strong sense of responsibility for others; but the same convictions can be joined to other ethnic, racial, and nationalist themes to separate societies, intensify the secular issues that cause tension among states, and provide reasons to suppress others or make war on them. Faced with this potentiality of religion to unite or divide, to be a force of reconciliation or the driving power of conflict, some scholars, politicians, and diplomats see the safer course as the attempt to secularize world politics, thereby sealing off the negative potential of religious conviction.

Finally, in the setting of the United States, there is an almost instinctive reaction that addressing religious issues as an explicit part of foreign policy will inevitably raise constitutional problems of church and state.

These reasons and others like them are deeply rooted in the minds and institutions that directly affect foreign-policy calculations. In essence they converge on a conclusion that it is best to stay clear of religious ideas and communities in trying to address the always complex and conflicted world of international politics. The problem with that position in the contemporary context is that it cannot confront the actual role that religion is playing—positively and negatively—throughout the international system. From the Middle East to Central Europe and the Balkans, from South Africa to Latin America, from the Philippines to Russia and the United States, religious traditions, ideas, and communities are intricately woven through the public choices being made about war and peace, economics and culture, law and policy.

Because religious forces are at work throughout the world, and because they appeal to and feed back into U.S. public life, an approach that defines religion as private and simply tries to stay clear of it will be inadequate as a framework for U.S. policy choices. The more satisfactory approach, both for religious leaders and for political leaders, is to recognize the inherent ambiguity of religion's impact on politics and to attempt to direct it toward positive objectives.

Recommendations for a U.S. Policy Framework

How does this very general proposition relate to proposals for strategy and tactics regarding religious freedom as an objective of U.S. foreign policy? My purpose here is not to comment on the International Religious Freedom Act, which has served over the last two years as the focus of debate on religious freedom and foreign policy. Some of the recommendations that follow have already been incorporated into the Act as it moved through the Congress; they remain important criteria for determining policy in light of the new legislation.

First, as a basic principle U.S. policy should be grounded in the conviction that since the right to religious freedom is universal, U.S. policy cannot be focused on the plight of one or two particular religious traditions. The impetus behind congressional activism on religious freedom (or responses to religious persecution) has been rooted in conservative Christian churches, aided by some powerful voices outside those churches. But the debate within Congress and the influence of other religious communities, often in support of the goals of the legislation, have broadened the focus to a universal scope. Such a broad-gauged approach is necessary if the policy is to have moral credibility.

Second, the judgment that religious freedom has not received adequate systematic attention in the past has merit; the argument that this has been due to a kind of cultural conspiracy that disdains religious convictions and those who hold them is much less convincing. It is also a difficult premise from which to build some consensus on human rights policy. The objective reasons—however inadequate and misguided—articulated above can explain the marginalization of religious issues in the foreign-policy debate. In a liberal, secular culture and polity, it would not be surprising to find these customary ways of thinking intersecting with subjective bias against religion, but it is the former that should be the focus of policy reform.

Third, as I have argued throughout this chapter, increased attention to religious freedom should not isolate it but give it secure standing in the core group of rights that the United States is committed to pursue and protect. This linkage of rights has been proposed above in the name of strategic coherence and moral consistency. But there is another major reason why the analysis of religious persecution or even lesser violations should be pursued in connection with other human rights. It is that in most conflict situations where religion is the object of repression, other human rights are at stake also, and the political, socioeconomic, and cultural conflicts in the society are virtually inextricable from religious tensions. I would be hesitant to argue this point as a universal proposition, but I believe it can be sustained as a general proposition cutting across diverse parts of the globe. In brief, adequate analysis of "religious conflicts" requires a broad social-science perspective, and effective redress of religious discrimination or persecution will require a comprehensive human rights strategy.

Fourth, activism is called for in defense of religious freedom, but crusades are neither appropriate nor defensible. The distinction bears upon the general tone or style of the policy, the means and methods used, and the calculation of consequences that guides policy choices. Religion has deep and powerful connections to individuals and groups; to prevent crusading mentalities, attention must be given not only to the specifics of policy choice but also to the broader messages that are communicated in a society about the sources of religious conflict and the measures being used to address it.

Fifth, in the analysis of situations of religious repression, the definition of what constitutes a violation of religious freedom should be both personal and social. Often governments will note that freedom of worship is constitutionally guaranteed or that "the churches are open," but such claims do not address the public or social dimensions of the right of religious freedom. These aspects of the life of religious communities bear upon their role in society, their critique of socioeconomic policy, their relationships to unions, their rights to publish journals or support a newspaper. Here again one is drawn back to the value of linking religion and other sectors of the society.

Both the passage of the International Religious Freedom Act in the United States and broader trends in global politics that have placed emphasis on intrastate conflicts cutting across ethnic, religious, and national lines guarantee that the role of religion, while always deeply personal, will hardly be purely private. The new activists have pressed the boundaries of the standard human rights and foreign-policy debate; one does not have to agree with all their conclusions to note the timeliness of their protest. The challenge for them and for those who dissent from some of their analysis is to shape a policy perspective adequate to a time when religion is both a public and a powerful force in world politics.

Notes

1. For a sense of the history see Ernst Troeltsch, *The Social Teaching of the Christian Churches* (New York: Harper and Row, 1960), vol. 1; and J. Bryan Hehir, "Social Values and Public Policy: A Contribution from a Religious Tradition," in Milton M. Carrow, Robert Paul Churchill, and Joseph J. Cordes, eds., *Democracy, Social Values and Public Policy* (Westport, Conn.: Praeger, 1998), 57–58.

2. John Noonan, "Development in Moral Doctrine," *Theological Studies* 54 (1993), 662–77.

3. John Courtney Murray, "The Human Right to Religious Freedom," in Leon Hooper, ed., *Religious Liberty: Catholic Struggles with Pluralism* (Louisville, Ky.: Westminster/John Knox Press, 1993), 231–32, 235–36.

4. Jeffrey Goldberg, "Washington Discovers Christian Persecution," *New York Times Magazine*, December 21, 1997, 46ff.

5. Goldberg, "Washington Discovers Christian Persecution," 46.

6. Goldberg, "Washington Discovers Christian Persecution," 67.

7. David Rieff, "The Precarious Triumph of Human Rights," *New York Times Magazine*, August 8, 1999, 37–38.

8. J. Bryan Hehir, "The Ministry of Human Rights and Catholic Higher Education," in *Vincentian Chair of Social Justice—1996 Presentations* (Jamaica, N.Y.: St. John's University, 1996), 3–6; also J. Bryan Hehir, "United States and Global Human Rights," in *Human Rights at Harvard: Interdisciplinary Faculty Perspectives on the Human Rights Movement* (Cambridge, Mass.: The President and Fellows of Harvard College, 1995), 14–17. (Both are transcriptions of lectures.)

9. Stephen H. Krasner, "Structural Causes and Regime Consequences: Regimes as Intervening Variables," in Stephen H. Krasner, ed., *International Regimes* (Ithaca, N.Y.: Cornell University Press, 1983), 1–21.

10. R. J. Vincent, *Human Rights and International Relations* (Cambridge: Cambridge University Press, 1986), 111–52.

11. The literature on U.S. human rights policy is now enormous; for examples, see Arthur Schlesinger, "Human Rights and the American Tradition," *Foreign Affairs* 57 (1979), 503–26; Tamar Jacoby Reagan, "Turnaround on Human Rights," *Foreign Affairs* 64 (1986), 1066–86; David P. Newsom, ed., *The Diplomacy of Human Rights* (Lanham, Md.: University Press of America, 1986); J. Bryan Hehir, "The United States and Human Rights: Policy for the 1990s in Light of the Past," in Kenneth A. Oye, Robert J. Lieber, and Donald Rothchild, eds., *Eagle in a New World: American Grand Strategy in the Post–Cold War Era* (New York: Harper Collins, 1992), 233–55; and Rieff, "The Precarious Triumph."

12. Vatican II, "Declaration on Religious Freedom," in Walter Abbott, ed., *The Documents of Vatican II* (New York: Guild Press, 1966), 675–96.

13. Vatican II, "Declaration on Religious Freedom," para. 2, 678; for an elaboration of the content of the right, see John Courtney Murray, "The Problem of Religious Freedom," *Theological Studies* 25 (1964), 522–27.

14. Murray, "The Problem of Religious Freedom," 529–30; see also Murray's commentary in Abbott, *The Documents of Vatican II*, 686, n. 20.

15. Universal Declaration on Human Rights, article 18 ("Everyone has the right to freedom of thought, conscience and religion; this right includes freedom to change his religion or belief and freedom, either alone or in community with others and in public or private, to manifest his religion or belief in teaching, practice, worship and observance"), in Henry J. Steiner and Phillip Alston, *International Human Rights in Context: Law, Politics, and Morals* (Oxford: Oxford University Press, 1996), 1158.

16. Murray's scholarship is a continuing point of reference for this chapter. His position on the free exercise of religion as "a freedom *sui generis*, even though it is cognate with other civil rights," is found in "The Problem of Religious Freedom," 519. Perhaps the clearest statement of how Murray conceived of the relationship of religious freedom and other political and civil rights is the following: "Along with these freedoms religious freedom constitutes an order of freedoms in society. Religious freedom cannot be discussed apart from discussion of this whole body of freedoms. All human freedoms stand or fall together—a fact that secular experience has made clear enough." Murray, "The Human Right to Religious Freedom," 240. See also "The Declaration on Religious Freedom," in John H. Miller, ed., *Vatican II: An Interfaith Appraisal* (Notre Dame, Ind.: Association Press, 1966), 565–76.

17. Murray, "The Problem of Religious Freedom," 514–16.

18. John Paul II, "World Day of Peace Message," *Origins* 17 (1987), 494; see also J. Bryan Hehir, "*Dignitatis Humanae* in the Pontificate of John Paul II," in John T. Ford, ed., *Religious Liberty: Paul VI and Dignitatis Humanae* (Brescia, Italy: Instituto Paolo VI, 1995), 169–83.

19. The most comprehensive biography of John Paul II stresses repeatedly the integral role of religious freedom in the teaching and statecraft of the Pope. See George Weigel, *Witness to Hope: The Biography of Pope John Paul II* (New York: Harper Collins, 1999), 268, 272, 274, 382–83.

~

Comment by Robert Kagan

I will begin by saying that I come at this issue as a Jewish atheist who believes that U.S. foreign policy should be concerned with the persecution of Christians and other religious persons in other countries.

We have a tendency to think that everything that comes up as a major issue in any given year is new. Religious persecution is not new. So what brought it into the spotlight at this particular time? I think that the groundswell of support for what became the International Religious Freedom Act was intimately related to overall congressional and public reaction to things that were going on in China and in U.S. policy on China. It so happens that the congressman who sponsored the legislation in the House, Frank Wolf, has also been a major figure in the battle over Most Favored Nation trade status for China. Once again in U.S. foreign policy we have a fortunate situation in which the pursuit of a moral goal coincides with at least a reasonable interpretation of national interest.

As I listen to many of those who wish to promote the issue of religious persecution as a concern of U.S. foreign policy, I feel I hear a sentence not spoken but loudly implied—that we need to support oppressed Christians overseas *because we are a Christian nation*. Certainly the original motive of the Religious Persecution bill that became the International Religious Freedom Act was to combat the persecution of Christians. This creates an interesting

Robert Kagan is a senior associate at the Carnegie Endowment for International Peace and Alexander Hamilton fellow in American diplomatic history at American University in Washington, D.C.

problem. If you are appealing to the general concern that Americans have always had for liberal values, for individual freedoms, for what is in effect an American "religion"— if you are appealing to this American religion of liberal ideals as it is outlined in the Declaration of Independence, that is one thing. If you are appealing as a member of one religious group on behalf of your co-religionists in other countries and are asking the United States to put its power behind the interests of your co-religionists overseas, then it seems to me that you are entering dangerous territory.

Now, of course ethnic groups have always sought to marshall American power or American influence on behalf of their brothers overseas. Certainly Greeks have done this, and Italians, and Irish. But that appeal in itself was never seen as a sufficiently legitimate reason to employ the power at America's disposal. If you were going to make an appeal on behalf of your brothers overseas, you needed to portray that policy goal in light of the American religion of liberal ideals, broadly construed. I think it is important to observe this line, and to identify this cause of combatting religious persecution with an overall American cause and not a purely Christian cause.

But at the same time you need to maintain a narrow focus. One of the lessons of the 1970's human rights campaigns was that by behaving "irresponsibly" the activists forced the government to incorporate human rights in a way that actually found a balance and achieved a great deal. It is not the job of human rights activists or religious persecution activists to pull together the appropriate blend of economic and strategic tools. The government will do that. If the activists begin by saying, "Well, we know there are tradeoffs between economics and strategic considerations and human rights," then the government is going to find it very easy to say, "Yes indeed, yes indeed, there certainly are, and we throw the issue of human rights out on the table every time we meet with our counterparts in this bilateral relationship to discuss the broad gamut of issues in that relationship, etc." I would urge groups that are engaged in single-issue politics to *behave* like groups engaged in single-issue politics and not like psychologists or conflict mediators or sociologists or grant administrators or anything else.

~

CHAPTER THREE

Religious Persecution and Religious Relevance in Today's World

Samuel P. Huntington

Religious liberty and religious persecution, particularly of Christians, became an item on the agenda of U.S. foreign policy in 1997 as the result of several developments. (1) Two impassioned books detailing this persecution were published—Nina Shea's In the Lion's Den and Paul Marshall's Their Blood Cries Out.[1] (2) In response to congressional prodding, the State Department produced a 50-page report on "U.S. Policies in Support of Religious Freedom: Focus on Christians," which covered the state of religious liberty in some seventy-eight countries. (3) Simultaneously, there appeared a 475-page private assessment of religious liberty, funded by the Pew Charitable Trusts—Freedom of Religion and Belief: A World Report, by Kevin Boyle and Juliet Sheen.[2] (4) The persecution of Christians received media attention, notably in column after column by A. M. Rosenthal in the New York Times. (5) On November 16, a designated Day of Prayer for the Persecuted Church, eight million Americans met in Protestant and Catholic churches across the country to protest the persecution of Christians and to commit themselves to sustained efforts to end it. And (6) Representative Frank Wolf and Senator Arlen Specter introduced the Freedom from Religious Persecution bill to create in the White House an Office of Religious Persecution Monitoring. This office would identify those governments engaging in religious persecution, giving priority to the persecution

Samuel P. Huntington is the Albert J. Weatherhead III University Professor at Harvard University, where he also is chairman of the Harvard Academy for International and Area Studies. His numerous books include The Clash of Civilizations and the Remaking of World Order, published in 1996 and translated into twenty-five languages.

of Christians, Tibetan Buddhists, and Iranian Baha'is, and the offending governments would be subject to a variety of economic sanctions. Congressional hearings were held; Trent Lott and Newt Gingrich endorsed the bill but did not bring it to a vote in 1997. The State Department, a wide range of business groups, and some mainline religious bodies opposed it.

Eventually, in 1998, the Wolf-Specter bill was passed in a somewhat altered form as the International Religious Freedom Act. The act established three new entities: a Special Adviser on Religious Persecution, in the National Security Council at the White House; an ambassador-at-large to head the Office on International Religious Freedom at the State Department; and a Commission on International Religious Freedom, an independent, bipartisan, ten-member body charged with advising the President and Congress on strengthening religious freedom and combating religious persecution worldwide. The commission first met in June 1999 and elected as its chair Rabbi David Saperstein, director of the Religious Action Center of Reform Judaism, and as vice chair, Dean Michael Young of the George Washington University Law School. In September 1999 the State Department issued its first comprehensive *Annual Report on International Religious Freedom*, as required by the Act.

How and why did all this come about? The immediate cause, it is clear, was the intense work of a relatively small group of activists determined to make religious persecution an issue. They include Shea, Marshall, Rosenthal, Michael Horowitz, and Gary Bauer, who put together a coalition encompassing some traditional human rights liberals, Jewish neoconservatives, Sinophobes, Christian evangelicals, and right-wing Republicans. Their success in bringing the issue to public attention testifies both to their commitment and to their political and public-relations skills. It is also testimony to the open and diffused character of the American political system.

But Washington is filled with small groups of activists pushing causes that fail to achieve either recognition or success. Other factors must have been at work to give this issue such visibility. Three points are relevant.

First, religious persecution *is* a reality in today's world. Recent studies document beyond doubt that it is extremely widespread and that Christians in particular are subjected to various forms of harassment and persecution in a significant number of countries, mostly Communist and Muslim—China, Vietnam, North Korea, and Cuba, on the one hand, and Saudi Arabia, Iran, Pakistan, Egypt, Iraq, and Sudan, on the other. Orthodox countries, including Russia and Greece, also impose various restraints on the practice of non-Orthodox religious groups. Employing fairly rigorous definitions and criteria, Paul Marshall estimates that in 1996, 200–250 million Christians were being persecuted for their faith while some 400 million others lived "under nontrivial restrictions on religious liberty."[3] Throughout the world, believers considered nonmainstream such as Mormons, Jehovah's Witnesses, and members of Pentecostal groups generally are the most likely to suffer persecution. Boyle and Sheen regrettably have it right when they say that "religious persecution of minority faiths, forcible conversion, desecration of religious sites, the proscribing of beliefs and pervasive discrimination, killings and torture are daily occurrences at the end of the twentieth century."[4]

Second, this widespread religious persecution has been largely ignored by liberal and secular groups in the West. It has also often been ignored or trivialized by mainstream Western churches. At least prior to 1997, violations of the rights of religious groups received far less attention than violation of the rights of political dissenters, journalists, women, ethnic minorities, and workers. The impact of the antipersecution movement has thus been enhanced by people's previous lack of familiarity with the extent and depth of violations of religious rights.

Third, while religious persecution is clearly widespread, what is not clear is whether it is increasing. Nina Shea has said that more Christians are suffering from religious persecution today than at any other time in history. That is probably true, but it is also not very meaningful, since undoubtedly more Christians also are *not* suffering from religious persecution now than at any other time in history. The 1996 State Department Country Report on Human Rights Practices more cautiously reports that "a disturbing aspect of the post–Cold War world has been the persistence, and in some cases intensification, of religious intolerance, religious persecution, and the exploitation of religious and ethnic differences for narrow and violent ends." In his introduction to Marshall's book, Michael Horowitz refers to "the mounting persecution of Christians," but in the book Marshall estimates that the number of Christians suffering persecution and harassment in 1996 was about the same as in 1980.

Democracy is not necessarily incompatible with religious persecution. Communism, however, is inseparable from religious persecution. One would assume that the collapse of Communism in the past decade and the spread of democratic regimes to so many countries during the past two decades would have enhanced religious liberty. The new Annual Report on International Religious Freedom, mentioned earlier, should make it possible to come to an informed judgment on trends in religious persecution.

The Increasing Power of Religion

If, in fact, religious persecution has not increased significantly, then we must look for another reason why the antipersecution activists were so successful in placing this issue on the public agenda. The answer, I believe, is quite simple. Religious persecution has become an issue not because persecution has increased but because the power and salience of religion have increased. We are witnessing what various observers have called "the revenge of God," "the questioning of the secular state," "secularism in retreat." The renaissance of religion throughout the world has made freedom of religion and religious persecution key issues. It may indeed have promoted increased religious persecution, if that has occurred. If religion is unimportant, it can be tolerated. If it is important, governments will insist on controlling it—regulating it, suppressing or prohibiting it, manipulating it to their own advantage. In today's world, religion has become centrally relevant to, first, the identity of states and nations, second, the legitimacy of governments, and third, the conflicts between peoples. All three of these developments provide incentives both for engaging in religious persecution and for making that persecution a political issue.

Religion and National Identity
Throughout the world secular identities are decreasing and religious identities are increasing in importance. Western secular models of the state are being challenged and replaced. Consider five very different societies. In Russia, Lenin's secular and antireligious Soviet state has given way to a Russian state that terms Orthodoxy central to "the establishment and development of Russia's spirituality and culture." In Turkey, Ataturk's concept of a Westernized, secular nation-state is under challenge from an increasingly powerful Islamist (i.e., fundamentalist Islamic) political movement. Nehru's concept of his country as a secular, socialist, parliamentary democracy is under attack by several political and religious movements that see India as a Hindu society. Ben Gurion's image of Israel as a secular Jewish social democracy has been repudiated by Orthodox Jewish groups. In the Arab world, Kiren Chaudry has shown, a "new nationalism" is emerging, fusing the formerly antagonistic old nationalism of the Nasser era and the now increasingly powerful currents of political Islam.[5] And, of course, the Shah's effort to create a modernizing, secular, Western state in Iran fell victim to the Iranian Revolution. Almost everywhere, political leaders are, in Mark Juergensmeyer's words, "striving for new forms of national order based on religious values."[6]

The part of the world where religious nationalism appears weakest is the West, but even there signs exist of a possible revival of a religion as a source of identity. Westerners think of theirs as a secular culture; non-Westerners, particularly Muslims, for good reasons identify the West with Christianity. Even with the addition of Turkey as an applicant, its admission remains problematical, and the European Union remains a Christian club. By every conceivable measure, Americans are a highly religious people, and for 87 percent of them that religion is Christianity.[7]

The major expansion of the numbers of evangelical Christians and the emergence of the Christian Coalition were in large part responsible for the several actions of Congress in pressuring the Administration to pay attention to the persecution of Christians. It is at least conceivable that Americans may be beginning a rediscovery of their Christian roots, and that Christianity may become an increasingly salient element in American identity.

The rise of religion as a source of national identity has significant consequences for freedom of religion. States that define themselves in secular terms may either prohibit or suppress all religions, as Communist states tried to do, or may indifferently tolerate all religions, as has generally been done by the United States and France. If, however, a society's identity is defined in terms of a religion, then intrusions of other religions into that society may be seen as threats to that identity. Just as Americans and the U.S. government saw Communist ideology as a threat to American society during the Cold War and took steps to counter or curtail its dissemination, so also religiously defined states discriminate against, restrict, suppress, and prohibit other religions. The Soviet state, for instance, was hostile to all religions; the Russian state identifies itself with Orthodoxy and harasses and discriminates against other religions, particularly evangelical Christianity. Patriarch Alexy II termed the efforts of Western religious groups to proselytize in Russia a threat to Russia comparable to the expansion of NATO. The overall leader of Eastern Orthodoxy, Ecumenical Patriarch Bartholomew I of Constantinople, similarly attacked Protestant missionaries as "wolves in sheep's clothing" undermining Orthodox society.

In similar fashion, the Chinese Communists view Christian missionary efforts as an increasingly dangerous threat to the unity and identify of their society. "As we open our doors wider and wider to the outside world," one internal Party document stated, "hostile foreign forces . . . use religious infiltration as their breakthrough point in their attempt to 'Westernize' and 'divide' China. . . . Forces of the various cults must be firmly banned." The movement to redefine India as a Hindu society has led to attacks on Muslims; the quite successful effort to redefine Mongolia as a Buddhist society has caused human rights problems there for Christians and others; China views Tibetan adherence to Lamaist Buddhism as an attempt to "split the country" and hence brutally attempts to suppress it. The breakup of Yugoslavia into religiously defined communities produced the terrorizing, killing, and expulsion of people belonging to religious minorities. If countries define their identity in terms of religion, deviation from or challenges to that religion become the equivalent of treason.

Religion and the Government's Legitimacy

Governments and political movements legitimize themselves through elections, effective performance, political doctrine or ideology, nationalism, and religion. Democratic governments based on *elections* are relatively stable because their legitimacy is renewed regularly through elections. Nondemocratic governments face more difficult problems. *Performance legitimacy* depends on their delivering the goods people want, and their ability to do that can be severely limited by their own incompetence and corruption as well as by external forces that they cannot control. *Ideological legitimacy* is normally a diminishing asset as fervor fades and the gap between the ideals of the ideology and the sordid realities of politics remains unbridged. Governments can bolster themselves through *nationalist appeals* against perceived hostile outside forces, but, as we have seen, peoples are increasingly defining their national identity in religious terms. As a consequence, governments are turning to *religion* to bolster their own legitimacy, suppressing religious movements that they think threaten their legitimacy, or quite often doing both.

Politics and religion cannot be disentangled. Modern democracy has its roots in Protestant Christianity, and in the twentieth century Catholicism has become equally supportive of democracy. Historically and in the contemporary world, the correlation between Christianity and democracy has been extraordinarily high. While obviously several non-Christian countries (India, Japan, Israel, among others) have sustained democracy for years, Christian countries make up well over 80 percent of the countries Freedom House classifies as "free," and outside of Africa, Cuba is almost the only nondemocratic Christian country. Christian churches, priests, and ministers (and, of course, the Pope) and Christian political leaders were decisive actors in the massive wave of democratic transitions that began in Southern Europe in the mid-1970s, swept through Latin America, engulfed Eastern Europe, and had an impact on Asia. The current president of South Korea and the immediate past president of Taiwan, who played central roles in bringing democracy to their countries, are both devout Christians.

The leaders of nondemocratic governments quite accurately see Christianity as a threat to their authority and attempt to suppress it. "The Church played an important role in the change" in Eastern Europe, a Chinese state publication observed in 1992, and in a pointed metaphor it concluded: "If China does not want such a scene to be repeated in its land, it must strangle the baby while it is still in the manger."[8] The governments of Vietnam and Singapore have similarly seen it in their interest to intimidate and repress Christian organizations, activities, publications, and believers in their countries. Until recently, so also did the government of Cuba. In 1993, however, Cuban church leaders began to assume a more active role toward their government, and government controls on religion began to loosen almost imperceptibly. In the fall of 1996, Castro invited the Pope to visit Cuba, and that visit took place in January 1998. In connection with the visit, more controls slipped away, and religious services and activities became more frequent and public.

While Americans in large part focus on the persecution of Christians, quite possibly more Muslims than Christians suffer religious persecution, and they suffer it largely at the hands of Muslim governments. Islamic fundamentalism provides a challenge to the legitimacy of nondemocratic Muslim regimes comparable to Christianity's challenge to nondemocratic non-Muslim regimes. While Chinese leaders are haunted by the image of the Pope bringing down Communist regimes in Eastern Europe, Muslim leaders are haunted by the image of the Ayatollah bringing down the Shah.

Muslim governments react to this challenge in several ways. They adopt Islamic rituals, symbols, and practices so as to give some Islamic legitimacy to their regimes. They make concessions to the Islamist movements by adopting policies those movements promote, including policies directed against Christian and other non-Muslim groups. In an attempt to divide their opposition they allow limited political participation by more moderate fundamentalists. And sometimes they ruthlessly suppress Islamist organizations, activities, and individuals. In some cases this police action is quite justified, because it is directed at terrorist groups employing violence against the regime and people. Often, however, governmental repression is also broadly applied to various groups and individuals that are acting no more violently than the Christian groups that are suppressed in China and Singapore. The rights of Muslims to support religiously based parties are surely abused when the Algerian military cancels elections that an Islamist party would win and the Turkish military force out of power an Islamist government that had been democratically constituted.

Religion and Conflicts between Peoples

Religions have dual personalities: catholic/ecumenical, and parochial/exclusionary. In their catholic and ecumenical personality, almost all of the world's great religions espouse the values of peace, justice, tolerance, and understanding and (in the words of the "Declaration of a Global

Ethic" adopted by twenty major faiths in 1993) denounce "aggression, fanaticism, hate . . . xenophobia," and violence. In their parochial and ex-
clusionary personality, religions are self-oriented, exclusive, and divisive.
Simultaneous adherence to two religions is generally impossible. Religious
leaders thus often see it as their highest duty to advance their own religion
and to counter the expansion and doctrines of other religions. When religion becomes the basis of nationalism, religious leaders became nationalists and do not hesitate to exhort their believers to march off into battle
on behalf of their nation.

As it is obvious from the news almost every day, differences in religion
mark the combatants in violent struggles over much of Eurasia, from Northern Ireland to the former Yugoslavia, the Caucasus, the Middle East, the sub-
continent, Sri Lanka, Southeast Asia, and East Africa. Most of the prolonged
and bloody conflicts going on in the world involve people of different religions. Other conflicts, such as those in Algeria and Afghanistan, are waged by
fervent devotees of one religion against their less fervent co-religionists. One
aspect of this, of course, has been the growth of what has been called "holy
terror," that is, terrorism carried out by groups that define themselves and
their goals in religious terms. By one estimate, no such groups existed in 1968,
but there were two in 1980 and twelve in 1992. Religious terrorists tend to be
more extreme and indiscriminate in their use of violence than secular terrorist groups; hence proportionally they kill more people than secular groups.

As religion has become central to the identity of nations and the legitimacy of governments, religious differences have become a source of conflict
between peoples, and religious liberty has become an issue in international
relations, particularly the relations of the West with Islamic and Chinese societies. In practical terms, campaigns against religious persecution and for religious liberty are campaigns waged by Christians and Jews on behalf of their
religions, and in particular to advance the cause of Christianity.

What Can Be Done?

Religious persecution is widely prevalent in the world today and has become a
major issue because religion has become an important force in people's lives. Religious persecution is the price of religious power. If our aim is to reduce religious
persecution and promote religious liberty, what can be done to achieve these
goals? I can see four possibilities, none of which is likely to be very successful.

First, governments and international organizations can take modest steps
to reduce religious persecution. Boyle and Sheen urge the strengthening of
the UN Special Rapporteur on Religious Intolerance.[9] In response to con-

gressional pressure the Clinton administration appointed an Advisory Committee on Religious Freedom Abroad, promised to give the issue more attention in Presidential statements, instructed our embassies to pay more attention to it, directed that foreign assistance be given to organizations concerned with religious liberties, and promised to raise the issue in the UN Human Rights Commission. And the International Religious Freedom Act of 1998 and the commission and reporting it established are certainly positive developments. Overall, some of these measures might make some difference; a few could be counterproductive; most are likely to accomplish little in promoting progress toward religious liberty.

Second, if religious persecution is in part a consequence of the power and importance of religion as a source of identity, legitimacy, and conflict, then logically religious persecution might be reduced if religion became less important in the lives of people. Although this may well happen in the future, it is hard to see what measures anyone could take now to make it happen sooner rather than later. In addition, if it did happen, the positive effects of the greater salience of religion in people's lives would also be lost.

Third, religious liberty is a Western cause, and the most egregious violations of religious liberty occur in non-Christian, particularly Islamic and Chinese societies. Hence religious liberty might be promoted by the expansion of Christianity and the conversion of non-Christians to Christianity, through a mighty missionary effort. If this occurred, however, it would also promote even more vigorous resistance from and religious persecution by other religious groups. Religious liberty would come about only if Christianity were victorious in a global war of religions.

A final course would be to attempt to encourage those tendencies and groups in non-Christian religions that support religious freedom. To expand freedom within a religious community, freedom will have to develop out of that community, the product of its ecumenical personality over its darker personality. Given the connection between religion and nationalism, a particular need here is to develop procedures for extending at least a minimum degree of toleration to non-national religions. Moving in this direction would at best be a long, slow process, but it may be the only practical one.

Religious liberty is an issue where it is difficult to be optimistic without being utopian.

Notes

1. Nina Shea, *In the Lion's Den* (Nashville, Tenn.: Broadman and Holman, 1997), and Paul Marshall, *Their Blood Cries Out* (Dallas: Word, 1997).

2. Kevin Boyle and Juliet Sheen, eds., *Freedom of Religion and Belief: A World Report* (London: Routledge, 1997).

3. Marshall, *Their Blood Cries Out*, 255.

4. Boyle and Sheen, *Freedom of Religion*, 1.

5. Kiren Aziz Chaudry, "Templates of Despair, Visions of Redemption: A New Arab Nationalism for a New International Order," in Harvard Academy for International and Area Studies, *Conflict or Convergence: Global Perspectives on War, Peace, and International Order* (Cambridge: Harvard Academy, Conference Papers, November 13–15, 1997).

6. Mark Juergensmeyer, "The New Religious State," *Comparative Politics* 27 (July 1995), 379.

7. While some commentators have made much of what they see as the increasing diversity of religions in the United States, the diversity outside Christianity is pretty minimal. Jews make up only slightly more than 2 percent of the population, Muslims about 1.5 percent, and Hindus and Buddhists each less than half a percent. *New York Times Magazine*, December 7, 1997, 60.

8. *China: Religious Freedom Denied* (Washington, D.C.: Puebla Institute, 1994); quoted in Marshall, *Their Blood Cries Out*, 10–11.

9. Boyle and Sheen, *Freedom of Religion*.

Comment by George Weigel

I want to suggest three implications of the new awareness of the role of religious conviction in world politics and the new salience of religious persecution as a foreign-policy issue. First, it means a little dose of humility for intellectuals. The world isn't turning out the way the intellectual elite of a hundred years ago and many of its heirs today thought it would. In 1900 it was widely assumed that in the twentieth century, under the impact of modernization, humanity would outgrow its need for religion. But by the end of the twentieth century, three of the four most potent culture-forming sources on the world historical stage were religious: Roman Catholicism, evangelical Protestantism, and Islam. Therefore, to repeat a point that Peter Berger has made many times, one of the great themes of contemporary Western social science, namely, that modernization necessarily involves radical secularization, has been decisively falsified by empirical evidence and by the lives of the people.

Second, we need a reassessment of realism as a foreign-policy category. We particularly need to reassess the tendency of the realist tradition to reduce the idea of power to military and economic categories alone. Realism, of the sort articulated in the Christian context by Reinhold Niebuhr, seems to me to remain an important corrective to moralism and its tendency to create a one-to-one correspondence between the ethics of interpersonal relations and the ethics of world politics. But that realism seems to me to be just that: a

George Weigel is a senior fellow of the Ethics and Public Policy Center in Washington, D.C., and the author of *Witness to Hope: The Biography of Pope John Paul II*.

corrective. It needs to be located within a more comprehensive theory of moral reasoning applied to world politics. Moral reasoning would take more seriously than the realist tradition does the truth that ideas have consequences. If one runs through the list of such prominent personalities in the history of the twentieth century as Lenin, Hitler, Mao, Churchill, Ben Gurion, Nasser, Schuman, Monnet, Adenauer, and John Paul II, one is tempted to make the case that the world is run by ideas. Those are all men who bent history to their wills through the force of ideas for good or for ill. If we take that notion seriously, then I think we have to say—against elements of the Morgenthau-ian tradition—that international politics is not an amoral realm. Moral claims and passions are important forces in the politics of nations and need to be recognized as such, rather than being treated as epiphenomena, as they often are in our domestic political rhetoric.

The nation-state may no longer be the only serious and salient unit-of-count in the world of politics. It is surely of some consequence for the future that the three culture-shaping religious forces I mentioned—Roman Catholicism, evangelical Protestantism, and Islam—all teach that the loyalty of believers to a political community is bounded by and accountable to a loyalty that transcends that political community. This raises the question whether, in a more intensely religious twenty-first century, a world we frequently call postmodern may not be in some sense postpolitical, in that the nation-state no longer remains the sole unit-of-count, and the locus of historical change is not understood to be exclusively governmental but is in nongovernmental sectors as well.

But those three religious forces that teach a transcendent loyalty that in some sense limits the loyalty to the political community then divide on how one is to live in that built-in tension. One of the three says the goal is to unite the political community and the religious community in the *Dar al-Islam*, the abode of peace, in which *shari'a*, Islamic law, prevails. But the overwhelming majority of Western Christian leaders and theologians say that the city of God and the earthly city will not be united this side of the coming again of the Messiah. "We do not seek to put the coercive power of the state behind our religious proposal," they say. "We will hold the political community accountable to transcendent moral norms. But we also recognize the legitimate autonomy of the state in the sphere of its specific and limited competencies, and we do not claim the warrant of divine revelation in resolving every conceivable issue of public policy." Now between those two visions of the relationship of the earthly city and the city of God there is a great gulf.

My third thought about what all this means is that we need to think more carefully about the definition of religious freedom. If we reduce religious freedom to just another free-standing personal-autonomy right, the result is intellectual and policy chaos. The alternative to that, I would suggest, has been spelled out by the Second Vatican Council and in the teaching of John Paul II. Both run the argument something like this: The human person has an inalienable right to seek the truth without coercion, and a fundamental moral duty to act upon the truth when it is found. The right and the duty are part of the same package. The truth is not taken to be *my* truth, nor am I taken to be the norm of truth. The truth cannot be truly apprehended unless it is apprehended freely. Any appeal to religious freedom as a means of coercing others is a false appeal. Now, we disagree about what constitutes coercion. But the principles are clear and have rather clear implications. One is that two-tier citizenship arrangements, as in the *dhimmi* system of formally constituted Islamic societies, are violations of religious freedom and need to be understood as such.

Finally, I think we Americans need to be cautious about the institutional arrangements necessary to make this concept of religious freedom viable in societies. Various ways of accomplishing this are imaginable; we should be very hesitant about proposing any one-size-fits-all institutional arrangement. But there *is* something to be said for having as the goal not a sacred public square or a naked public square but a *civil* public square.

CHAPTER FOUR

The Political Sociology of the Crusade against Religious Persecution

Allen D. Hertzke

The persecution of believers in Christ has a long history. Indeed, divine promise and earthly persecution arose conterminously, as King Herod, deeply troubled by the news of the birth of Jesus, ordered the slaughter of all male infants in Bethlehem and its environs. The Christian message from the start has relativized earthly regimes and provoked tyrants to violence.

In recent years, the persecution of Christians in many places around the globe has been well documented.[1] Thus we might have expected the free Christian churches in the West to respond with unified vigor. It has not quite happened. In what follows I will probe why this unified response has not occurred and weigh the obstacles that must be overcome to make it do so.[2] To be sure, some notable mobilization efforts have occurred, and more will surely follow. But it will take enormous energy and commitment to transform this nascent movement on behalf of persecuted Christians into a sustained and successful foreign-policy initiative. Besides the normal obstacles in our Madisonian political system, the movement will need to overcome division and passivity among Christians as well.

Many advocates for persecuted Christians see their endeavor modeled on the successful campaign for Soviet Jewry that took place in the 1970s. That earlier effort produced the Jackson-Vanik Amendment, which prohibited the

Allen D. Hertzke is the Noble Foundation Presidential Professor of Political Science at the University of Oklahoma. He is the author of *Representing God in Washington*, an analysis of religious lobbies, *Echoes of Discontent*, an account of church-rooted populist movements, and *Religion and Politics in America*, a textbook.

granting of Most Favored Nation (MFN) trade status to a country that did not allow free emigration. Can the International Religious Freedom Act of 1998 become a true successor of Jackson-Vanik? Under what conditions? Over what obstacles?

Apparent similarities between the two issues are quite striking. Just as the focus on persecuted Jews opened up other spaces in the Soviet empire, so today's advocates argue that pressuring for greater freedom for Christian minorities abroad would foster greater general freedom and openness.[3] As with Jackson-Vanik, opposition to the movement for the persecuted arises from some foreign-policy elites who see linkages to religious freedom as a transgression against *realpolitik*, and from those in the business community who chafe at any restrictions on lucrative trade. The focus on congressional legislation is another similarity, though the 1998 International Religious Freedom Act has diverse and generally milder sanctions and includes provisions related to the U.S. internal policy on asylum.[4] Finally, successful campaign tactics on behalf of persecuted Christians would have to mirror those employed by Jews nearly three decades ago—fostering public awareness through dramatic media exposure, personalizing the persecution, mobilizing congregations, and mounting sustained constituency pressure—thus making the issue one that members of Congress and executive-branch officials cannot ignore.

But there are a number of differences as well. To highlight those differences, it is helpful to note the characteristics that brought legislative success in the campaign for Soviet Jewry.

To begin with, Jews are a people, a remarkable people whose shared crucible through persecution and holocaust forged a profound solidarity on fundamental questions. Though diverse theologically and ideologically, on issues that touch on Israel or survival of their remnants Jews demonstrate unity and vigor. Indeed, among the ethnic lobbies that hope to shape U.S. foreign policy the lament often heard is, "Why can't we be like the Jews?"[5]

During the campaign for Soviet Jewry, virtually all active congregants would have heard poignant stories of oppressed brothers and sisters. Temples and synagogues sported banners demanding freedom for Jewish *refuseniks*, and Natan Sharansky became a living symbol of their plight. Popular press coverage was extensive. The message was also proclaimed in books, internal news organs, church flyers, and other publications.

In addition, Jewish lobbyists in Washington who brought their legendary skills to the issue[6] found ready allies among labor unions and anticommunists. These Washington insiders also capitalized on a vigorous grassroots response to keep the issue before Congress, which ultimately attached the

Jackson-Vanik Amendment to the Trade Act of 1974 (Section 402, "Freedom of Emigration in East-West Trade").

A final feature of the campaign was its simplicity. Advocates focused on a single goal, the freedom to emigrate, and a single system, the Soviet Union and allied regimes. The legislation promised normalized trade relations and credit if the nation met the open-emigration guidelines.

Interestingly, some of the most vigorous advocates for persecuted Christians have been Jews, such as Michael Horowitz of the Hudson Institute (who has probably done more than anyone else to get the issue on the congressional agenda), Cheryl Halpern of the National Jewish Coalition, Rabbi David Saperstein of the Union of American Hebrew Congregations, and *New York Times* columnist A. M. Rosenthal, who wrote no fewer than a dozen columns on the issue in 1997 alone.[7] Skeptics have ascribed self-interested or strategic political motives to this support, suggesting that the issue serves nicely as a weapon to contain militant Islam. Even if that is partially the case, such a strategic concern dovetails with the traditional Jewish devotion to human rights and natural sympathy for the persecuted. Perhaps just as African Americans have second sight into America's soul, Jews have especially acute eyes for persecution.

Obstacles to a United Christian Front

In contrast to Jackson–Vanik, the current campaign for the persecuted is global in reach, multifaceted in its aims (with both domestic and foreign initiatives), and more complex in implementation. Religious persecution, particularly against Christians, involves many nations with vastly diverse strategic and commercial ties to the United States. Although the initial campaign succeeded in passing legislation, continuing opposition from business interests and skepticism in elite foreign-policy circles cloud the impact and implementation of the new law. Moreover, most Washington journalists and opinion leaders have taken little or no notice of the issue; it has not received the sustained attention required to engage broad public interest. But perhaps the greatest obstacle lies within the Church itself, in the complex sociological dynamics within the community that presumably has the greatest stake in the outcome.

The Sociology of Pluralism

A central challenge for movement advocates is the lack of unity and passion for the issue among many Christian groups. With some notable exceptions, the response has been sporadic, mixed, or anemic. Nina Shea and

Paul Marshall, the foremost chroniclers of Christian persecution today, have alluded to this phenomenon.[8] What are its causes?

Unlike Judaism, which adheres to a distinct people, Christianity proclaims universal application. This represents both its strength and its potential weakness. Christianity may produce a broad civilization, as Samuel Huntington suggests, but because it spreads itself over such diverse cultures and nations, it does not produce a distinct people with natural solidarity.

Sociologists of religion have observed how the faith has been molded to fit ethnic, class, sectional, or national identities. H. Richard Niebuhr bemoaned the scandal of disunity, which he saw flowing from worldly compromises of the demanding ethical standards of Christ. But Niebuhr also offered an astute empirical analysis of how differently the message was preached and practiced in different settings. There are churches of the dispossessed, churches of the middle classes, nationalist churches, immigrant and ethnic churches, sectional churches, and so on. While this diversity was a worldwide phenomenon, nowhere was it allowed to flourish as it did in the United States, with its freedom and disestablishment. Niebuhr noted that this pluralism produced profoundly different views of the Christian message itself. Solidarity is undermined as the faith is filtered through varying ideological or cultural prisms.[9]

Moreover, the pluralism and liberalism of the American regime have often succeeded in channeling the fervor of religious sects into market competition for the faithful. As Finke and Stark suggest, the blend of disestablishment and religious freedom transformed churches into voluntary associations and created an open religious marketplace; churches that lose their evangelical zeal thus lose market share to upstart entrepreneurs.[10] In such an environment energies must be invested in evangelization, church-building, seminaries, missions, Sunday schools—in other words, in the effort to fill a market niche by meeting the spiritual hungers of people. This imperative normally funnels energies away from political engagement, creating another key obstacle to mobilization.

A review of church publications and news organs readily reveals the enormous effort that must be devoted to sustaining large, complex organizations. To take just one example, the 1997 General Assembly of the Presbyterian Church in the U.S.A. had before it some 130 resolutions, 95 of which concerned church governance, ministry issues, or internal policies.[11]

Scholars have also noted how the "denominational" society represented a kind of détente among religious groups, as well as an unconventional pact with the broader polity.[12] In return for the nation's grant of broad religious freedom, groups tacitly agreed to be domesticated, not to challenge the fundamental premises of the regime, and generally to tolerate one another.[13] This pact has tended to hold down political mobilization, especially in this century. The great examples of successful religious mobilization—the abolitionist, temperance, and civil rights movements—are more the exception than the rule; most of the visible political effort is restricted to marginal adjustments in policy.

Societal engagement by churches is impressive: they operate countless schools, hospitals, relief agencies, and other charitable endeavors. Yet such engagement can also deter churches from taking on controversial issues that might threaten their delicate relationships with the state. There is evidence that a number of church relief organizations and foreign-mission groups are concerned that making persecution a high-profile focus of American foreign policy might jeopardize their access, however tenuous, to the nations identified as persecutors. This can produce excruciating calculations. Evangelist Billy Graham, for example, though acknowledging China's record of persecution, wrote to members of Congress in the summer of 1997 urging them to support MFN status for China, because open trade would tend to facilitate keeping missionary lines open as well. Other evangelical leaders similarly argued that MFN status actually furthered the interest of ameliorating persecution.[14] But the Catholic bishops and some other evangelical groups opposed MFN. Such a babel of religious voices may provide cover when a president finds it difficult to act vigorously on the International Religious Freedom Act.

These tendencies—theological pluralism among Christians, divergent views among church leaders, preoccupation with internal church matters, and political passivity among many in the pews—pose serious obstacles to sustained mobilization. To be sure, when just a small fraction of the Christian population agitated for religious-freedom legislation in 1997–1998, Congress acted. But disunity and the apparent lack of broad salience militated against stronger legislation.

Secularization of the Elite
The secularization of major institutions and the elites who lead them presents another barrier to advocates of the persecuted. The stubborn persistence of mass religious faith and practice has led scholars rightly to doubt the simplistic modernization-secularization thesis propounded a generation ago by some of the West's great sociologists.[15] Nonetheless, an unmistakable secularization at the elite level, which had been emerging for some time, accelerated in the 1960s and has continued. From public schools to government bureaucracies, mass media to the academy and business—all these large institutions increasingly operate with purposes and logic largely detached from

transcendent faith.[16] To be sure, individual faith is generally tolerated, and religious practice is protected by First Amendment guarantees. But believers, especially the most orthodox, must cross formidable barriers to get a hearing among policy elites or secular journalists.

In his 1997 book *Their Blood Cries Out*, Paul Marshall offers a penetrating account of how the secular prism of elites has hidden or marginalized the problem of persecution. From the press to the diplomatic corps to secular human rights organizations to the academy, Marshall hears a virtual "deafening silence."[17] In a similar vein, Michael Horowitz, who has emerged as the key mover in Washington on the persecution issue, views this campaign as a test of how elite opinion will view transcendent faith in the twenty-first century.[18]

The problem of secular blinders is especially prevalent among those who fashion the news. Elite journalists largely inhabit a secular cosmos, and they often ignore what they cannot comprehend or filter it through stereotyped frames of reference.[19] Marshall contrasts extensive media attention to atrocities against Bosnians, for example, with the scant treatment given to similar treatment of Christians elsewhere. Most surprising has been the slighting of modern slavery. The topic is one that might be expected to draw extensive media exposure. Not so. Indeed, people are far more likely to know that whales are endangered than that "you can buy a black woman as a slave for as little as fifteen dollars in Khartoum."[20]

Nina Shea's survey of foreign coverage by the elite press confirms the scant attention to the persecution issue, especially from the foreign desks where one would expect the greatest sensitivity.[21] A. M. Rosenthal has also taken his fellow journalists to task for slighting both the story of persecution and mobilization against it. He contended that news media virtually ignored the "Shatter the Silence" national day of prayer on November 16, 1997, an event that organizers claimed had 50,000 participating churches.[22] Although media attention finally caught up with the day of prayer the following year, 1998, when perhaps as many as 100,000 churches participated, the press treatment was perfunctory and fleeting. It is hard to imagine a similar result four decades ago, when journalists were more anchored in the world of average citizens, less likely to enter the profession from Ivy League environments.

Secular blinders present an especially formidable obstacle when the persecuted are unfashionable evangelicals and orthodox Catholics. A number of observers have noted that when persecution is not simply ignored, its meaning is filtered through the multicultural lens of the contemporary era. In the increasingly dominant "politically correct" view, Christian missionaries were either accomplices of conquistadors in the slaughter of indigenous peoples, or cultural imperialists on the model of the minister in James Michener's

Hawaii. Richard Land of the Southern Baptist Convention argues that these images contribute to the anemic Western response to persecution: "Too often people in the West, peering through the selective prism of Christian history in the West, reflexively think of Christians as persecutors rather than the persecuted."[23] The image of Christians *qua* Christians being persecuted just cannot pass through this ideological filter. In discussions with leading journalists, Nina Shea found a similar mental barrier: many journalists view Christianity as a "white man's religion and a tool of Western imperialism." She noted that a top magazine's Middle East bureau chief, though aware of such persecuted indigenous groups as Egypt's six million Copts, saw the campaign for persecuted Christians "as mainly a strategy for repressing the culture of the Third World—an attempt to force Muslim countries to allow proselytizing by American Christian missionaries."[24]

Liberal Christian Leaders: Seeing Colonialism

The cool response of many liberal Christian leaders to the issue of persecution is in part explained by this ideological lens. Joan Brown Campbell, general secretary of the National Council of Churches, saw in the movement for persecuted Christians a dangerous "muscular Christianity," an attitude of Christian superiority that led not only to the Inquisition but eventually to the Nazi Holocaust.[25] Moreover, one finds in the documents and testimony of oldline Protestant leaders, as well as those on the Catholic left, attention to women, minorities, indigenous peoples, and peasants as objects of oppression. But the oppression of Christians as Christians is rarely noted, nor is there a recognition of the possibility that women and indigenous peoples could be persecuted because of their Christian faith.

Thus liberal Christian leaders have reacted vehemently against the special focus on the persecution of Christians, and they normally avoid the word "Christian" in their statements on religious persecution. Writing to express "concerns" about the early version of the religious-freedom legislation, one Lutheran advocate noted the special need to "defend the human rights of groups most susceptible to violations, especially all minorities, women, and children." A United Methodist leader never mentioned Christians in a long letter on China policy but did single out "ethnic and indigenous groups, especially Tibetans and others in border regions." An article on China in the liberal Catholic *Maryknoll* magazine avoided mentioning the imprisonment of Catholic bishops, and instead of uttering the word "persecution" favorably observed the lack of "tension between the underground Catholic Church group that refuses to go along with government regulations and the more open group that complies."[26] Such euphemistic language contributes to subtle equations of moral equivalence. Expressing skepticism of some aspects of the campaign on behalf of Christians, one liberal Protestant lobbyist observed that "some groups might be critical of persecution at the hands of Iraqis but not so critical at the hands of Israelis."[27]

The frame of reference that sees Christendom as colonial, of course, neglects the fact that indigenous Christian communities have existed for centuries in North Africa, the Middle East, and the Far East, and ignores the remarkable growth of Christianity in Latin America, Africa, and Asia. Conversions, demographic shifts, and lapsing faith in the West have dramatically shifted the composition of the world's Christian population. In 1950, an estimated 70 percent of all Christians lived in North America and Europe. By century's end that proportion was down to 40 percent, while over 60 percent of Christendom lived in Latin America, Asia, and Africa, and that proportion is rising. Thus while some 250 million Christians live in the United States, an estimated 258 million live in Asia, 317 million in Africa, and 448 million in Latin America.[28] Samuel Huntington suggests that inroads of Christianity in such places as Asia and Africa are spurred when "traditionally dominant religions do not meet the emotional and social needs of the uprooted people in modernizing societies."[29] Perhaps this explains the stunning fact of Christian politicians' heading the governments of Taiwan and Korea. The growth of Pentecostalism in Central America also fits Huntington's thesis,[30] suggesting that Christian faith in the Third World represents a more indigenous phenomenon than the colonial-missionary model suggests.

To be sure, pluralistic expressions of indigenous Christianity can take a variety of forms, not all of them benign. From the atrocities committed by Eastern Orthodox Serbians[31] to the participation of some Catholic priests in the genocide in Rwanda, examples of religion enmeshed with ethnic strife are striking. And even if such examples are exceptions, they provide evidence for those who see religious fervor as dangerously retrograde, in striking contrast to those movement advocates who view Christianity as a force for democracy and modernity in the developing world.[32]

The Culture Wars
A more recent sociological feature of the religious landscape presents a related challenge for advocates of the persecuted. During the past four decades American religion has been "restructured" along theological and ideological lines. Though pluralism remains, sociologists and political scientists have noted the way ecumenical alliances have congealed into two divergent, mutually hostile camps of theological liberals and conservatives. It is a division that can cut across denominational lines. As Robert Wuthnow observes, this

great cultural divide is in part a legacy of the modernist-fundamentalist clash earlier in this century but has been deepened by "the larger social unrest that emerged in the 1960s."[33] Wuthnow summarizes survey evidence of the mutual stereotyping today across this divide:

> People who identified themselves as religious liberals were prone to stereotype their conservative brethren as intolerant, morally rigid, fanatical, unsophisticated, closed-minded, and simplistic. The animosity recorded from the other side was equally blatant. Self-identified religious conservatives thought religious liberals were morally loose, were too hung up on social concerns rather than truly knowing what Christianity was all about, had only a shallow knowledge of the Bible, and were deeply compromised by secular humanism.[34]

This pattern produces deep suspicion, and makes coalitional efforts especially arduous. Moreover, it has fed into clashes over the broader culture, giving the religious divisions a harsh political edge. As James Davison Hunter and others have noted, skirmishes over abortion, homosexuality, art, the media, public education, law, family structure, welfare, and public expressions of faith together constitute a kind of *kulturkampf*. Partisans on opposite sides see each other as adversaries in a struggle for the soul of the nation. The progressive coalition sees the Christian Right as a mortal threat to gains in civil rights and liberties, women's rights, gay rights, and tolerance for religious minorities. The orthodox coalition sees secularizing culture in a moral free fall, believers ridiculed and marginalized, and liberal religious opponents in league with forces that would plunge the nation into a decadent dark age.[35]

Although the culture-war phenomenon has probably been exaggerated at the lay level, where "ideological constraint" may not operate consistently, plenty of evidence shows that among clergy and church leaders the cultural divide is real. The authors of a 1997 study found that on almost every political issue the Protestant clergy divide rather consistently into these divergent camps.[36] In Washington, one finds liberal Protestant lobbyists at odds with evangelicals and fundamentalists on almost every public issue.[37]

More than disagreements over issues, the culture wars divide partisans over fundamental visions, aims, and ways of life. All this is obviously a barrier to an effective united campaign against religious persecution. If members of Congress hear a babel of Christian voices rather than a united voice, they have reason to ignore the complaints and respond to the more comforting counsel of caution by foreign-policy elites and business traders.

To be sure, honest differences of opinion exist about the degree of the problem or the wisdom of possible remedies. But a fact of religious life is that anything that hints of Christian Right sponsorship will be seen as deeply suspect by liberal religionists. When the Christian Coalition announced persecution of Christians as a priority cause, it sent a chill through the liberal religious community. "I was afraid that it would be used politically, especially to beat up on Clinton and the State Department," said one NCC official. If a floor vote on the bill became a "line" on the Christian Coalition voter guide in the 1998 election year, he said, "we will divide up in camps."[38] Although a compromise bill ultimately passed unanimously, the divide remains.

This is one reason why Jewish and Catholic support for the cause is so helpful: it can give cover to Democrats in Congress who are wary of Christian Right causes but would not want to be seen as failing to vote against persecution.[39]

Sustaining a Focus

Successful mobilization requires a sustained focus, something that is often difficult for contemporary churches. As noted previously, the voluntary nature of American religion requires churches and religious agencies to devote considerable effort to institutional maintenance. Moreover, the complexity of religion's societal engagement and the growth of the administrative state have produced an unusually large agenda for religious advocates, as they respond to the effect of government regulations on their hospitals, relief agencies, schools, and the like. This imperative can siphon off political energies that could otherwise be used for other initiatives. Finally, the perceived threat from opposing religionists in the culture wars tends to draw partisans into an array of political battles. The issue of persecution can simply be crowded off the agenda.

For example, in the 1997 Presbyterian resolutions mentioned previously, the thirty-five dealing with outreach cover an astonishing spectrum of topics, including domestic violence, movie ratings, welfare reform, homelessness, disarmament, sexual exploitation of women and children, Middle East relationships, and international family planning. Only three of the resolutions dealt with persecution: one concerned persecution of Christians generally, another advocated prayer for the persecuted church, and a third focused on Sudan. The 1996 United Methodist General Conference similarly concerned itself with a wide array of issues, including abortion, AIDS awareness, homosexuality, health care, substance abuse, immigration, and racism, but had nothing on religious persecution. Even as the issue of religious persecution heated up in Congress, some religious groups seemed oddly silent. A month before the House bill was to come up for a committee vote, the "Legislative Update" of the Lutheran Office for Governmental Affairs contained nothing about the issue, though it had articles on campaign finance reform, food stamps, child care, health care, Haitian refugees, the land mine ban, Cuban trade, and the earned-income tax credit.

In the "ecumenical" branch of Protestantism, then, a plethora of social concerns appears to push the persecution of brethren onto the margins. But evangelicals and Catholics operate with a similarly broad agenda, encompassing issues of both religious conscience and church interests. The Catholic Church, as the operator of the largest parochial school system, has huge interests to defend and extend, and it is also heavily invested in the abortion controversy. Evangelicals, meanwhile, see themselves defending the faith against a variety of secular attacks. Maintaining a focus on a foreign-policy issue is difficult.

Context and Strategies of Religious Lobbying

The accounts of Nina Shea and Paul Marshall, along with my own interviews and my analysis of church documents, suggest a pattern in the religious response to the issue of persecution as an American foreign-policy concern. Protestant evangelicals have been the most vigorous in championing the issue, but their focus can be diverted by domestic skirmishes in the culture wars or the spiritual preoccupations of the faithful. The Catholic hierarchy is supportive, but some Catholic groups on the left are skittish. National Jewish leaders and individuals have championed the issue, though robust grassroots Jewish mobilization is doubtful. Liberal Protestant leaders in the oldline denominations, on the other hand, have been (with a few exceptions[40]) cool, suspicious, and even hostile. Their lobby opposition might thus provide cover for more economically motivated opponents of enforcing sanctions against persecuting nations.

The context of religious lobbying on persecution also suggests that various religious groups have different forms of access to the system they seek to influence. In the next section I will give some background on the different groups and then chart the nature of their engagement with the issue of persecution. The policy outcomes so far, and those in the future, will hinge in part on what these groups do, and why.

Liberal Protestant Denominations

The liberal "mainline" (or oldline) churches may have dwindling memberships, but they retain a considerable presence in American life and an even greater inherited capital of credibility, which provides access to the executive branch (especially the State Department), to some members of Congress, and to the elite press. Their world relief programs maintain contacts with the aid apparatus of the U.S. government, and their domestic agencies are often called upon to resettle refugees. Congressional committee staffs will usually listen to oldline lobbyists, who have maintained an institutional presence in Washington for decades. But members of Congress do not fear the minimal grassroots threat of liberal church leaders. Policy insiders are well aware of the gap between the liberal lobbying of the church leaders and the views of the more conservative to moderate laity, a gap that has been documented for more than three decades now.[41] Indeed, the possibility exists of a lay counter-mobilization for a more robust U.S. posture against religious persecution. The 1997 General Assembly of the Presbyterian Church U.S.A. designated the Sunday before Epiphany an annual "Day of Prayer for Those Persecuted for Their Faith,"[42] in response to a resolution from the Presbytery of Southern Kansas. That resolution cited the "Statement of Conscience" issued by the National Association of Evangelicals and also quoted the Pope's words against persecution of Christians by "Islamist and communist" regimes. This case suggests potential tension between grassroots laity and denominational leaders in Washington.[43]

When Clinton was president, liberal groups enjoyed some access after twelve years in the desert of Republican administrations. But this access was obviously vulnerable, and liberal church groups seem more comfortable working through the State Department bureaucracy rather than through the pressure system. They opposed creation of a special White House office to monitor religious persecution, for example, favoring a program anchored in the State Department. Oliver Thomas, chief counsel for the National Council of Churches, offered a series of objections to the Wolf-Specter bill, which were embraced and echoed by Assistant Secretary of State John Shattuck. The liberal churches also continue to advocate multilateral, UN-based efforts rather than sanction-oriented congressional ones.

Critics of the liberal churches see this approach as an ideal strategy to dilute the strength of the U.S. response to persecution. The State Department has come under criticism for slighting the issue and for inadequately training ambassadors to deal with it. Widely recounted in this context is the vignette of former senator James Sasser, who became U.S. ambassador to China early in 1996. After months of State Department briefings in preparation for the post, Sasser was asked about the U.S. response to Beijing's persecution of the house churches. "What's a house church?" was his reply.[44]

Although the oldline denominations pose little grassroots threat to legislation, their access to the press, coupled with the affinity of secular journalists for religious people they can understand, does pose a problem for those seeking a vigorous U.S. response to religious persecution. Since the emergence of the Christian Right, journalists and oldline denominational leaders have cooperated in producing the standard storyline: "mainline religious groups oppose the Christian Right." From school prayer to abortion, oldline denominational leaders have been available with press conferences and ecumenical letters opposing Christian Right initiatives. In this symbiotic relationship, reporters get to challenge those religionists they do not understand and liberal church leaders get to wear the now dated label "mainline."

This facet of Washington life will surely be a feature of the ongoing debate over religious persecution. From bill drafting through the legislative compromises and now in the implementation phase, most liberal church lobbyists have worked to soften the blow of the International Religious Freedom Act. In this they have become allies of big business and foreign-policy realists— an ironic outcome in light of their ideological proclivities.

A review of some events during 1996–1997 suggests that liberal Protestant leaders were caught off guard by the emergence of besieged Christian communities as a foreign-policy concern. The issue did not seem to fit their ideological lenses; on the other hand, their churches could not ignore such a manifest threat to the faithful. So they found themselves responding to initiatives of others—particularly members of Congress and the National Association of Evangelicals. Early in 1996, leaders of the National Council of Churches met with leaders of the National Association of Evangelicals and expressed general support for the NAE's "Statement of Conscience" on religious persecution. The Episcopal Church, the Presbyterian Church U.S.A., and the United Methodist Church also commended or endorsed "in principle" the statement of conscience.[45]

Other pronouncements, however, showed much greater caution. For example, Albert Pennybacker, associate general secretary of the NCC, in testifying before Congress clothed his remarks in qualifications. He expressed a concern over "genuine" persecution but noted that "the relationship between religious faith and the communities that live out such faith, and the cultural heritage of religions and nations are deep-seated, complex, and defy easy assessment from afar." Obviously such nuanced language is not meant to mobilize the troops. Pennybacker also explained why nonevangelical churches might be suspicious of claims of persecution: "The evangelistic zeal of outsiders, openly voiced or even subtly imposed, may encounter an authentic resistance as it moves on unfamiliar ground. What may appear as 'persecution' and indeed is resistance may in fact be the wish to preserve religious and cultural traditions."[46]

One thing that did emerge from the various church documents was the importance of denominational mission branches. Indeed, some leaders acknowledged that they shied away from stronger statements on persecution or sanctions because that was the counsel they were receiving from their mission boards.

Why would this be so? One explanation is rooted in a pattern of liberal witness on foreign policy. From the anti-Vietnam effort of the 1960s onward, the ecumenical churches took a left turn on foreign affairs that simultaneously embraced some Marxist "liberation" struggles in the Third World, softened criticism of the Soviet Union and China, and increasingly criticized the capitalist West, particularly the United States. This ideological posture lent itself to a relatively benign "constructive engagement" with Communist systems that, critics charged, led missions to ignore the persecution of Christians by those regimes. This pattern continues to shape the international posture of the ecumenical churches in both subtle and overt ways.[47] For example, the Reverend Jay Lintner, Washington representative for the United Church of Christ, announced opposition to the Wolf-Specter bill in September 1997. His opposition arose in part because the bill specifically mentioned the persecution of Christians in China, North Korea, Vietnam, Laos, and Cuba, and this, Lintner argued, tended to "continue a hard-line Cold War sanctions strategy." Moreover, he said, because the bill also cited Muslim countries, it would "extend the cold war to many Islamic countries."[48]

The case of China provides a vivid picture of churches potentially compromised by their ties to persecuting regimes. China requires all church groups to register with the authorities and imposes other restrictions that are spelled out in decrees 144 and 145, signed by Premier Li Peng in January 1994 and elaborated in May 1994. Evangelicals and Catholics who refuse to follow these dictates must operate underground under the threat of harsh penalties. But because the liberal churches worked through official channels in China in the past and remain largely tied to the officially sanctioned churches, they would not necessarily hear of such persecution, or they might shy away from highlighting it for fear of losing their access to the mainland. The Lutheran World Federation Assembly, meeting in Hong Kong in July 1997, shortly after the return of Hong Kong to Chinese control, rejected a resolution mildly criticizing China when Chinese delegates argued that it would endanger relations between churches in Hong Kong and churches in China.[49] The Methodist Church in Hong Kong observed that it would continue its relationship with the churches on the mainland chiefly through the officially sanctioned Council of Churches and the Three-Self Patriotic Movement (the Protestant church sponsored and approved by Communist authorities).[50]

The liberal churches did make a modest impact in the legislative process. Oliver Thomas, counsel for the NCC, drafted a memo of concerns and objections to the House bill in the fall of 1997. An experienced Washington insider with a "common sense" reputation, the former counsel for the Baptist Joint Committee was in an ideal position to make the best case for the ecumenical churches. Thomas's memo presented a series of reasonable arguments and plausible concerns about the possible unintended consequences of the legislation as written. It became the basis of a letter signed by a dozen national church leaders and distributed to all members of Congress on October 2, 1997. Bill drafters responded by making changes to accommodate NCC concerns for greater presidential flexibility,[51] but the liberal churches remained deeply suspicious of legislative remedies.

During Senate deliberations, however, one liberal church leader, Tom Hart, Washington representative of the Episcopal Church, broke ranks with his counterparts to endorse the Nickles-Lieberman bill and help assemble support. That final legislation provided even more presidential discretion, but in other ways was more far-reaching than the House bill and was certainly tougher than many in the liberal community were comfortable with. The independent commission, in particular, has staked out a forceful posture on China and Sudan that gives the lie to those in the mainline community who had previously trivialized the problem.

Evangelical Protestants

In contrast to the liberal Protestants, evangelicals tend to have grassroots strength, ideally suited to bringing pressure on members of Congress. To be sure, the National Association of Evangelicals—a longtime actor in Washington—and other established evangelical groups continue to lobby the executive branch and the White House, and the Clinton administration was relatively open to dialogue with them. But the upstart groups, such as the Family Research Council and the Christian Coalition, tend to push congressional initiatives, both because of their influence with the Republican majority and because of their formidable grassroots mobilizing capability. Evidence of this clout came when GOP congressional leaders announced support for the Wolf-Specter bill before a meeting of Christian Coalition supporters in September 1997.[52]

Thus evangelicals have infused the main energy into the campaign for the persecuted, a fact acknowledged by liberal groups. Indeed, a letter sent to Congress signed by a dozen leaders of the NCC and affiliated churches had this to say: "We very much appreciate the new energy from both evangelical Christian groups and Congress which calls attention to the pain of this issue and to the need to seek fresh solutions."[53]

Yet sustained intensity will not be automatic. Despite two decades of activism by the Christian Right, there remain strong counterweights to political engagement on this issue. Many evangelicals remain focused on the individual dimension of faith, and a number of churches are tightly focused on spiritual succor, therapeutic ministries, healing, and even promises of personal prosperity. Indeed, the most notable event in the evangelical world in the mid-1990s was not opposition to religious persecution but the emergence of Promise Keepers, devoted to rebuilding families and the culture through a reassertion of male responsibility, with a strong dose of racial healing.

My hunch is that awareness of the problem of persecution is still lacking among some evangelicals in the pews. To be sure, staffers for members of Congress noted a huge initial response when James Dobson, head of Focus on the Family, went on the air in the summer of 1997 to talk about persecution.[54] The flow dropped off by late fall, as groups moved on to other issues,[55] then picked up again in the spring and summer of 1998, when Charles Colson devoted air time to the issue. The question is whether or not sustained pressure can be maintained for vigorous implementation of the International Religious Freedom Act.[56]

One of the challenges is that the issue does not resonate with people in the way that prayer in public schools, trash on TV, or family breakdown does. Just as the mobilizing campaign for religious persecution legislation got under way in March 1998, for example, a proposed "religious freedom" amendment to the Constitution, sponsored by Republican congressman Ernest Istook, was passed out of the House Judiciary Committee on a straight party-line vote. Randy Tate, executive director of the Christian Coalition, pledged that his organization would spend up to $2 million to mobilize support for this 1990s version of the perennial effort to overturn Supreme Court decisions on school prayer and other public expressions of faith.[57] On another front, Charles Colson made reinstating the Religious Freedom Restoration Act (RFRA), overturned by the Supreme Court, a top priority of Prison Fellowship. While the Istook amendment focused on "establishment" case law, RFRA sought to reinstate broad protection for "free exercise" practice that had been narrowed by the Court. Group energies and resources can be siphoned into these issues and evangelical constituencies subjected to numerous appeals. Moreover, members of Congress often find themselves bombarded by potentially confusing and cross-cutting campaigns, and policy space may become congested.

Nonetheless, a number of key players emerged during the mobilizing campaign against religious persecution, including Charles Colson of Prison Fellowship, Richard Land of the Southern Baptist Convention, Gary Bauer of Family Research Council, James Dobson of Focus on the Family, and Donald Hodel of the Christian Coalition. Ralph Reed, before he stepped down as head of the Christian Coalition, announced campaigns in favor of Wolf-Specter and against MFN status for China, and his successors continued to speak of making persecution a priority issue for the Coalition.

Of course, this grassroots mobilization has the potential to split the Republican coalition of business interests and moral conservatives.[58] Nowhere has this come out so clearly as on the extension of normal trade status to China. In 1997, for example, when Gary Bauer of the Family Research Council showed a willingness to forge ties with unions and human rights activists on China, he received favorable press coverage and plaudits from unlikely sources.[59] And though his presidential campaign fizzled, he continues to chastise the business wing of the GOP for its willingness to "sacrifice" human rights concerns.

The other crucial backer is Charles Colson, who enjoys universal respect in the evangelical world and considerable admiration beyond. The mere mention of the fact that he will attend a committee meeting ensures the participation of a host of others. Heretofore, Colson has been able to divide his time and energy rather effectively between his domestic and international religious-freedom concerns, but maintaining his worldwide prison ministries must of course be his primary concern.

The Catholic Church

As Samuel Huntington has argued, the Catholic Church since Vatican II has put its formidable world resources behind democratization and human rights.[60] More recently, Pope John Paul II has spoken out vigorously against the persecution of the faithful in Islamic and Communist societies. As a genuinely worldwide church, the Catholic Church has a range of diplomatic and public means to advance its concerns, and thus offers tremendous benefits to a coalition fighting religious persecution. Because of its institutional strength, the Church has good elite access in Washington, and its testimony and lobbying efforts receive an attentive hearing on the Hill.

Catholic church leaders employed a two-pronged strategy. They worked through diplomatic channels, the press, and sister churches in other countries to highlight persecution and attempt to ameliorate it. They also worked as Washington insiders to offer testimony and public pronouncements on official positions taken by their bishops.

The bishops opposed extending MFN to China, citing the fact that Catholics in China face harassment and possible imprisonment for teaching Catholic doctrine and voicing fidelity to the Pope. A U.S. Catholic Conference official, John Carr, announced this opposition during a news conference conducted by Representatives Nancy Pelosi and Frank Wolf that included Gary Bauer of the Family Research Council, leaders of the AFL-CIO, and the International Campaign for Tibet.

When the U.S. Catholic Conference came out in support of Wolf-Specter, it did so in a nuanced fashion. In its characteristically Scholastic manner, the USCC offered an extended analysis of the problem and detailed the ways in which the legislation could be strengthened, particularly its asylum provisions.[61] It voiced some of the same concerns as those raised by the National Council of Churches—that the definition of religious persecution might be too narrow or might be construed as sanctioning more common violations of religious liberty, and that the automatic nature of the sanctions might not be wise—but did not see these as precluding its support.

The posture of the American bishops was supportive, if a bit phlegmatic.[62] John Carr along with Msgr. William Fay, associate general secretary of the bishops' conference, publically backed Wolf-Specter at a February 4, 1998, kickoff summit and news conference in Washington, and the final legislation probably would not have passed without the continued lobby endorsement of the U.S. Catholic Conference. Yet the church shows only limited signs of engaging in the kind of mobilization through parishes that it has done on the abortion issue, and religious persecution is probably not a salient issue yet with many Catholics in the pews. The church's major contribution is likely to remain institutional support rather than grassroots mobilization.

Jewish Groups, the Black Church, Members of Congress

As noted earlier, Jewish groups and individuals, with excellent elite access in Washington, played a crucial role in promoting the cause among opinion-makers and publicizing it through the media. Michael Horowitz of the Hudson Institute is sometimes called the intellectual father of the idea. He contributed enormously to getting it on the agenda and shepherding it, with his 1995 *Wall Street Journal* piece, his mailings to religious groups and world missions, his convening of the Wolf-Specter steering group, his continued prodding of religious groups, and his congressional lobbying. He remains active in keeping the pressure on the State Department and the Administration for vigorous implementation. Cheryl Halpern, president of the National Jewish Coalition, provided visible Jewish backing in early lobby forums, and Stacie Burdette of the Anti-Defamation League was instrumental in later ones. Rabbi David Saperstein, executive director of the Religious Action Center for Reform Judaism, endorsed the original Wolf-Specter bill and was the first chairman of the legislatively mandated Commission on International Religious Freedom. Saperstein argued that support from Christians during the campaign for Soviet Jews commanded a response from Jews now that Christians are subject to persecution. "When God's children are imprisoned for praying," he said, "then Americans must speak out."[63] Elliott Abrams, president of the Ethics and Public Policy Center, succeeded Saperstein as chair of the Commission and has written extensively about the issue.

These Jewish alliances with evangelicals have contradicted common stereotypes.[64] It remains unclear, however, how much grassroots mobilization has occurred or will occur among the Jewish constituency.

A bigger question mark attaches to the response of the black church. So far its engagement has been limited. Advocates for Sudanese Christians, in particular, have been disappointed with the response of such figures as the Reverend Jesse Jackson to the modern-day slavery of Africans in southern Sudan. Alliances with Muslims in the United States and abroad have probably influenced some responses. Probably contributing to the limited salience of the issue is the fact that black churches have such a huge task maintaining their role in the American black community and trying to rebuild the fabric of black family and community life. But there are pockets of activism on the issue that could grow.

Finally, it is important to acknowledge the important part played by some members of Congress. House members Tony Hall (D), Frank Wolf (R), and Chris Smith (R) have for years traveled extensively around the globe, issued news releases, held hearings, and testified to publicize the scope and nature of persecution. On the Senate side, passionate support of the bill by retiring Senator Dan Coats, backing by Majority Leader Trent Lott, and shepherding by Majority Whip Don Nickles proved pivotal. Even skeptics credit the genuine commitment of these members and applaud their role in highlighting the issue. The bipartisan nature of congressional support also has been a valuable asset to the advocates and a contrast to normal coalitions. Support from Democrats, such as Representative Nancy Pelosi and Senator Joseph Lieberman, conveyed to wavering colleagues that the issue is not just a Christian Right cause. Indeed, Nancy Pelosi spoke at the 1998 Religious Persecution Summit, and lauded the efforts of Republican Frank Wolf, whom she referred to as her "leader" on the issue.[65]

Taking Stock

The issue of persecution has come a long way in the past decade. Barely a blip on the screen at the beginning of the 1990s, the issue was taken up by previously obscure religious groups such as Voice of the Martyrs and Open Doors, pressed by some members of Congress and a cadre of key staff members, documented by scholars such as Paul Marshall, publicized by journalists such as Abe Rosenthal, advanced by the fervent advocacy of Nina Shea and Michael Horowitz, and backed by evangelical groups and the Catholic Church. By 1996 Clinton was moved to create a White House Advisory Committee to the

Secretary of State, and Congress voted to mandate a State Department report providing a country-by-country summary of treatment of Christians around the world. The China MFN debate propelled the issue further, and the Wolf-Specter bill was put on the fast track by Republican leaders. By early 1998 the coalition of evangelicals, Jews, and Catholics pushing for legislation expanded to include Buddhists represented by the International Campaign for Tibet. House legislation passed in the spring of 1998, and intense Senate deliberations followed. After being written off as dead by late summer, a compromise Senate bill was pushed through in the waning days of the 105th Congress, passing unanimously in both houses before the October adjournment.

Given the opposition, the barriers, and the challenges we have noted, such an impressive achievement deserves fuller treatment, and I hope to give it this in the future. But the impact of the legislation remains uncertain, and the battle is far from over. Activists hope that the annual State Department report on persecution, along with recommendations to the president by the new U.S. Commission on International Religious Freedom, will turn the issue of persecuting nations into an ongoing aspect of U.S. foreign policy. But a single piece of legislation will surely not be enough to achieve this aim, and other initiatives are under way. For instance, a Freedom House–sponsored campaign, modeled after the South African protests, mobilized some Christian college students and churches to bring pressure on the Islamic government of Sudan, which has waged a brutal war—bordering on genocide—against its largely Christian and animist African populations.

Potential opposition to making religious persecution an ongoing concern of U.S. foreign policy remains formidable, of course. Some in the State Department remain wary of the implications of the legislation, which they claim will create a "hierarchy of human rights," privilege religious persecution over other forms of oppression, and reduce diplomatic flexibility. Trade-oriented big business will continue to provide the most muscular lobby opposition, not only in the obvious cases, such as China, but even in places like Sudan, which happens to be the main provider of an essential ingredient in soft drinks and other foods, gum arabic. Congresswoman Nancy Pelosi noted that even though trade was not involved in the Wolf-Specter version of the legislation, business lobbyists opposed it for fear of offending trading partners. "The real opposition is business," she remarked.[66] Battles will continue over implementation of the International Religious Freedom Act and also over other efforts to link U.S. policy to the persecution record of other nations.

As this narrative suggests, I am sympathetic with the aims of the act and with the broader cause—though as a political scientist I acknowledge that there are legitimate concerns about the potential for unintended consequences. But I remain sobered by divisions within the Christian community and by the difficulty of reaching into the pews and sustaining lay involvement on an issue so far from home. Are we American Christians just too comfortable to relate to the persecution of our sisters and brothers around the world?

Notes

1. Paul Marshall estimates that some 200 million Christians in the world live under severe threat of persecution. See *Their Blood Cries Out* (Dallas: Word, 1997).

2. I wish to acknowledge research support from the Carl Albert Center and the Pew Charitable Trusts, which funded interview trips to Washington, D.C., and the diligent research assistance of University of Oklahoma undergraduate students Hans Seidenstucker and Northon Arbelaez.

3. Nina Shea, *In the Lion's Den* (Nashville, Tenn.: Broadman and Holman, 1997), and interview with congressional staff member involved in drafting the legislation.

4. A result of numerous compromises, the final 1998 legislation provides more flexibility than Jackson-Vanik, particularly in allowing the president to choose from a menu of sanctions against countries found to be practicing religious persecution. Most of the sanctions are far milder than those set forth in the 1970s legislation aimed at the Communist world.

5. Kenneth Cosgrove, "The Tangled Web: Ethnic Groups, Interest Groups, and Congressional Foreign Policy Making," Ph.D. dissertation, University of Oklahoma, 1993.

6. See Allen Hertzke, *Representing God in Washington* (Knoxville: University of Tennessee Press, 1988).

7. The A. M. Rosenthal columns appeared in the op-ed section of the *New York Times* on the following dates in 1997: February 11 and 14; April 4, 25, and 29; May 13; June 10 and 17; July 25; September 16; October 10; and December 2.

8. Shea, *In the Lion's Den*, and Marshall, *Their Blood Cries Out.*

9. H. Richard Niebuhr, *Christ and Culture* (New York: Harper and Row, 1951).

10. Roger Finke and Rodney Stark, *The Churching of America* (New Brunswick, N.J.: Rutgers University Press, 1992).

11. "Issues Before the 209th General Assembly (1997)," Presbyterian Church (U.S.A.), June 14–21, 1997, Syracuse, N.Y.

12. See Andrew Greeley, *The Denominational Society* (Glenview, Ill.: Scott Foresman, 1972); and Will Herberg, *Protestant, Catholic, Jew* (New York: Doubleday, 1955).

13. See Robert Booth Fowler, *Unconventional Partners: Religion and Liberal Culture in the United States* (Grand Rapids, Mich.: Eerdmans, 1989).

14. Sam Ericsson, a highly respected former counsel for the Christian Legal Society, is now with Advocates International. As one fellow lobbyist noted, he "caught the devil" when he supported extension of MFN to China. Interview with Oliver Thomas, December 1997.

15. See *The Desecularization of the World: Resurgent Religion and World Politics*, edited by Peter L. Berger (Grand Rapids, Mich.: Ethics and Public Policy Center/Eerdmans, 1998).

16. This theme is developed in Robert Booth Fowler and Allen D. Hertzke, *Religion and Politics in America* (Boulder, Colo.: Westview, 1995), chap. 12.

17. Marshall, *Their Blood Cries Out*, chap. 8.

18. Horowitz has spoken and written about this view and reiterated it in several conversations with me.

19. S. Robert Lichter, Stanley Rothman, and Linda S. Lichter, *The Media Elite* (Bethesda, Md.: Adler, 1986).

20. Charles Jacobs, director of American Anti-Slavery Group, as quoted in Marshall, *Their Blood Cries Out*, 201.

21. Nina Shea, in "Atrocities Not Fit to Print," *First Things*, November 1997, 33, said that over the past year "not a single story on Sudanese religious persecution has appeared from the foreign desks of the *New York Times*, the *Washington Post*, the *Wall Street Journal*, or *USA Today*."

22. A. M. Rosenthal, "Is This a Story?" *New York Times*, December 2, 1997.

23. Richard Land, as quoted in Shea, *In the Lion's Den*, 5.

24. Shea, "Atrocities Not Fit to Print," 34–35.

25. Joan Brown Campbell, as quoted by Jeffrey Goldberg, "Washington Discovers Christian Persecution," *New York Times Magazine*, December 21, 1997.

26. Mark Brown, "Religious Persecution Act Introduced," Legislative Update, Lutheran Office for Governmental Affairs, July 1996; Letter to Members of Congress from Rev. Dr. Thom White Wolf Fassett, general secretary, General Board of Church and Society, United Methodist Church, June 23, 1997; Jack Connell, "Getting to Know China—Again," *Maryknoll*, January 1998, 33–35.

27. Interview, December 1997.

28. Because categories employed by demographers have changed over time, precise comparisons cannot be made. For example, the categories in 1950 were North America versus South America, with Central America attached to the North; by 1995 the more descriptive categories of Northern America and Latin America were used. Problems dealing with the former Soviet Union also muddy the analysis. Nonetheless, the basic pattern remains unmistakable, and the figures noted in the text may underestimate the scope of the transformation, because Russia, with its large Orthodox population, had been added to the European figures. Thus even when Northern America, Europe (including Russia), and Oceania (including Australia and New Zealand) are combined, their proportion of the globe's Christian population is only 43 percent. 1995 figures are from *The World Almanac and Book of Facts 1997*; 1950 figures are from *Britannica Book of the Year 1950*.

29. Samuel Huntington, *The Clash of Civilizations and the Remaking of the World Order* (New York: Simon and Schuster, 1997), 98.

30. Ann Hallum, *Beyond Missionaries: Toward an Understanding of the Protestant Movement in Central America* (Lanham, Md.: Rowman & Littlefield, 1996).

31. It is important to note that the Eastern Orthodox autocephalous churches developed without the kind of structures and traditions that Huntington, in *The Third Wave: Democratization in the Late Twentieth Century* (Norman: University of Oklahoma Press, 1991), identified as conducive to democracy. When movement activists or scholars speak of the democratizing force of Christianity, what they really mean (though not always self-consciously) is Western Christianity.

32. This is especially the position of Michael Horowitz.

33. Robert Wuthnow, *The Restructuring of American Religion* (Princeton: Princeton University Press, 1988), 145.

34. Wuthnow, *Restructuring of American Religion*, 132.

35. James Davison Hunter, *Culture Wars: The Struggle to Define America* (New York: Basic Books, 1991).

36. James L. Guth et al., *The Bully Pulpit: The Politics of Protestant Clergy* (Lawrence: University Press of Kansas, 1997). This book analyzes a large set of original surveys by the authors and is the definitive account of the subject.

37. Hertzke, *Representing God in Washington*.

38. Oliver Thomas, interview, December 1997.

39. It mattered which Jews supported Wolf-Specter. The fact that Michael Horowitz, a former Reagan administration official, was championing the issue did not allay suspicion that the issue was a Trojan horse for another agenda.

40. The Washington Office of the Episcopal Church did take a visible stand in favor of the Senate version of the legislation in the summer of 1998.

41. See James Adams, *The Growing Church Lobby in Washington* (Grand Rapids, Mich.: Eerdmans, 1970); Jeffrey Hadden, *The Gathering Storm in the Churches* (Garden City, N.Y.: Doubleday, 1969); Harold Quinley, *The Prophetic Clergy* (New York: Wiley, 1974); and Hertzke, *Representing God in Washington*.

42. 209th General Assembly, Presbyterian Church (U.S.A.), June 14–21, Syracuse, N.Y., news release.

43. Overture 97-43 to the 209th General Assembly Presbyterian Church (U.S.A.), from the Presbytery of Southern Kansas.

44. Marshall, *Their Blood Cries Out*, 75.

45. The NAE statement and church endorsements are contained in the appendix of Nina Shea's *In the Lion's Den*. The National Council of Churches statement is from a news release dated February 16, 1996. In joining with NAE, it stressed the unique vulnerability of minorities and women.

46. Testimony by Albert M. Pennybacker, associate general secretary, National Council of the Churches of Christ in the U.S.A., before the House Subcommittee on International Operations and Human Rights, February 15, 1996.

47. For a summary of this story see Allen D. Hertzke, "An Assessment of Mainline Churches since 1945," in James J. Wood Jr. and Derek Davis, eds., *The Role of Religion in the Making of Public Policy* (Waco, Tex.: Dawson Institute, 1991).

48. News Release, "Activist Speaks Out on Proposed Legislation," September 15, 1997, United Church of Christ.

49. "Lutherans Back Away from Rebuking China," Special Reports from the Lutheran World Federation Assembly, Hong Kong, July 8–16, 1997.

50. News Release, "Methodist Finds Christians in Hong Kong Have Hopeful But Cautious Attitude," *United Methodist Daily News*, July 17, 1997.

51. Interview with Ann Huiskes, staff member for Frank Wolf on religious persecution, December 1997.

52. Steven A. Holmes, "GOP Leaders Back Bill on Religious Persecution," *New York Times*, September 11, 1997, A3.

53. The letter was signed by the Rev. Dr. Joan Brown Campbell, general secretary of the National Council of Churches, and the following church leaders: Curtis Ramsey-Lucas, American Baptist Churches, U.S.A.; the Rev. Dr. James M. Dunn, Baptist Joint Committee; David Radcliff, Church of the Brethren; Fr. Robert Brooks, Episcopal Church; the Rev. Russell Siler, Lutheran Office for Governmental Affairs; Florence Kimball, Friends Committee on National Legislation; Dr. Ronald Mathies and Lynette, Mennonite Central Committee; the Rev. Elenora Giddings Ivory, Presbyterian Church (U.S.A.); Jay Lintner, United Church of Christ; and the Rev. Dr. Thom White Wolf Fassett, United Methodist Church.

54. Discussions with a number of congressional staff members.

55. Interview with committee staff member, December 1997.

56. Three crucial elements of the 1998 Act involve (a) nominations to the nine-member Commission on International Religious Freedom, (b) Commission annual findings and recommendations to the president for action, and (c) presidential action on Commission recommendations. All three involve opportunities for backsliding from the spirit of the legislation. Partisans know that continued pressure will be necessary to keep that from happening.

57. Chris Casteel, "House Panel Gives Blessing to School Prayer Amendment," *The Daily Oklahoman*, March 5, 1998. The vote to report the proposed amendment out of committee was 16 Republicans for and 11 Democrats against.

58. Goldberg, "Washington Discovers Christian Persecution."

59. See Jacob Heilbrunn, "Christian Rights," *The New Republic*, July 7, 1997, for an unusually sympathetic account of persecution of Christians as a new conservative issue; and Fred Barnes, "Bauer Power," *The Weekly Standard*, December 22, 1997.

60. Samuel Huntington, *The Third Wave: Democratization in the Late Twentieth Century* (Norman: University of Oklahoma Press, 1991).

61. Written testimony by the Rev. Drew Christiansen, U.S. Catholic Conference, September 10, 1997.

62. Some critics have charged that the bishops are cautious so as not to upset dialogue with the American Muslim Council, which fears the focus of the campaign against persecution.

63. "Bill Proposed to Combat Christian Persecution," in Baptist Joint Committee, "Report from the Capital," vol. 52, no. 11 (July 3, 1997).

64. The author of the *New York Times* story on Republican congressional support for Wolf-Specter seemed to struggle to define the politics of the issue, downplaying Jewish support and noting that "traditional liberal human rights groups and mainstream religious organizations" have "normally been involved in foreign policy matters." Ironically, while the article highlighted "Christian Right" muscle as the reason Republicans embraced the issue, the accompanying photograph showed Trent Lott and Newt Gingrich with Cheryl Halpern of the National Jewish Coalition and Fr. Richard John Neuhaus, a Catholic who is editor-in-chief of *First Things*. See Holmes, "GOP Leaders Back Bill."

65. Religious Persecution Summit, Washington Court Hotel, Washington, D.C., February 4, 1998.

66. Nancy Pelosi, interview, February 4, 1998, Washington, D.C. Pelosi also attributed President Clinton's opposition to his business ties.

~

Comment by Norman J. Ornstein

Although I have heard quite a lot about religious persecution of late, much more of it was about the persecution of Scientologists in Germany and Buddhists in Tibet than the persecution of Christians anywhere else. No doubt having John Travolta or Richard Gere as a spokesman helps a lot with visibility of an issue. But why isn't more being written about the persecution of Christians in China and elsewhere?

I agree with Allen Hertzke that journalists are probably the most secular group within what is an extraordinarily religious society. I have been involved with various polls looking at religious values in American society, and it is striking to see how religious Americans are compared to almost anybody else. But this issue of persecution of Christians is simply not on the radar screen with most people. Journalists would, I think, be writing a lot more about it if they had that sense of a buzz from below.

It was different at the time of the Jackson-Vanik Amendment. There we had a tremendous convergence of interests that struck a spark. The issue brought the cause of Jews and Israel together with anticommunism; activists with very different political viewpoints came together to accomplish common goals. At the time you could not go into a synagogue without having a sermon or a leaflet or a poster suggest to you that the way to promote the interests of Israel, to promote the interests of Jews, was Jackson-Vanik. The amendment itself was the product of a convergence: Henry Jackson and Charles Vanik

Norman J. Ornstein is a resident scholar at the American Enterprise Institute in Washington, D.C., a widely published writer, and a frequent TV commentator.

93

represented different wings of the Democratic party that were at the time struggling for control but nevertheless could work together in this cause.

The other part of this was, of course, the very effective lobbying by dissidents within the Soviet Union. We don't have that same kind of inside-outside phenomenon with the opposition to religious persecution today. There aren't highly visible figures like Sharansky opposing the persecutors within their own country.

Another factor is the political division that exists now in the American Christian community. Conservatives and liberals are unlikely to join in a common effort if they see the cause as something likely to give an advantage in a broader range of issues to one side over the other side. What was striking about Jackson-Vanik was that everyone could see a conjunction of interests that would not give political advantage to one side.

Some interesting surveys have shown recently that the American people are more interested in a broad and significant international role for the United States than policy makers think they are, or indeed than many policy makers themselves are. I fear that most of the people who have come into Congress in the last ten years have not spent ten minutes thinking about America's role in the world. They are not geared up to think about these issues—people who come to lobby them find that the larger world is simply not on their minds.

I think it's clear that our foreign-policy decisions are going to be more and more event-driven and television-driven. And until we see examples of the persecution of Christians right on our television screens, until we see Christians shot in a city square, the issue is not likely to capture public attention or press attention in a way that would unite these struggling forces as Jackson-Vanik did.

~

CHAPTER FIVE

China's Christian Connections

Charles Horner

Common in the worlds of both faith and politics is the word *peace*—a word particularly relevant to modern China and modern Asia. Peace is the proper benchmark for beginning any discussion of contemporary Chinese affairs, for the scale of violence in that country for the past hundred and fifty years has been truly extraordinary. During the nineteenth century, China was, at one time or another and to some degree or another, at war with Britain, France, Japan, and Russia singly and sometimes with all the Western powers collectively. These foreign wars, not especially devastating in themselves, were outward manifestations of a far greater domestic upheaval that claimed tens of millions of lives and caused incalculable collateral damage.

The collapse of the imperial system in 1912 gave rise to a shadowy era now known as the period of the "warlords." Though the Western notion of warlord connotes more the racketeer than the soldier, these Chinese warlords did practice war, sometimes on a large scale and with damaging results that compounded the country's ongoing misery. There followed eight years of war between China and Japan from 1937 to August 1945. Only the German-Soviet front in Europe rivaled in ferocity this underappreciated theater of World War II. Its representative event, the notorious "Rape of Nanking," accounted for only about 300,000 of the many millions lost.

Charles Horner is a senior fellow at the Hudson Institute, with a special interest in Asia. He previously was president of the Madison Center, a public-policy organization. His posts in the Reagan and Bush administrations included deputy assistant secretary of state for science and technology and associate director of the United States Information Agency.

When that war ended, the Chinese civil war resumed. Millions fought on both sides, with northern China feeling most of the effects. In 1950, the new People's Republic of China sent its forces into Tibet, meeting armed resistance that was not suppressed until 1959. Turkic peoples in the northwest of the country who offered sporadic resistance to Chinese rule were also bloodily put down. The new government then turned against the Chinese people themselves. During the so-called Great Leap Forward in the late 1950s, it produced horrific destruction comparable to Stalin's in the Soviet Union. In the 1960s the Great Proletariat Cultural Revolution claimed still more lives and caused still more destruction.

The Communist regime also fomented and abetted violence in neighboring countries. It plotted the Korean War in 1950, losing perhaps a million of its own soldiers during its subsequent intervention to save the North Korean regime from defeat and collapse. It supported the rural insurgency of the "Huks" in the Philippines in the 1940s and 1950s, and the insurgency in Malaya in the 1950s. It was involved in various ways in all the warfare, external and internal, in Indochina after 1945—in Vietnam, Laos, Cambodia, Thailand, and Burma.

We still do not fully appreciate the combined horror of these events, mostly because violence in Asia has become so routine. And we are not prepared for the situation in the region today, which—to put it cautiously—is beginning to resemble peace. It is a peace not officially proclaimed, of course. Yet even more striking than the appearance of peace *near* China is the appearance of peace *within* China. Given the close historic ties between China and the region, two questions come to mind: Is there some relation between internal peace in China and general peace in Asia? And what has happened in China to produce the semblance of peace inside and outside the country?

This peace must continue if the situation of China's people is to improve further. Progress cannot be made without it. How, then, can peace be sustained and expanded? Certainly the United States must continue to maintain military forces and security relationships sufficient to deter the use of military force by China outside the country. But as Alexander Solzhenitsyn reminded us back in the 1970s, "peace and war" is too limited a polarity; it is more accurate to speak of "peace and violence." Whenever the Chinese government resorts to major violence against its own people, it threatens peace not only within China but also within the rest of Asia.

The Limited Powers of Prediction
During the many upheavals in China's modern history, both domestic and foreign observers have tried to relate events to China's immense and varied

tradition. At the beginning of the twentieth century, reformers looked to precedents of consultation, renewal, and deliberation to support their efforts to transform the decrepit reigning dynasty into a modern constitutional monarchy. But this period of internal disorder heightened in others an interest in the careers of the country's great autocrats and unifiers, including some of the nastier ones, like China's first emperor in the third century B.C. or the no-nonsense, fourteenth-century founder of the Ming dynasty.

More recently, when the struggle between the Nationalists of Chiang Kaishek (1887–1975) and the Communists of Mao Zedong (1893–1976) resumed in earnest at the end of World War II, there were arguments about how the Chinese tradition might prefigure the outcome. Some saw in the complexity and diversity of Chinese society—its family orientation, localism, penchant for voluntary associations, suspicion of intellectual absolutism—the ingredients for political democracy. Others saw its long history of imperial autocracy and intolerance of social order the roots of a violently reimposed dictatorial authority.

In any event, it was the appearance of Chinese totalitarianism in 1950 that demanded an explanation. Here, Westerners could readily cite a concept of their own invention—Oriental despotism, enriched by many unpleasant episodes in China's history. And because totalitarianism was imposed on China by a self-proclaimed Marxist-Leninist-Communist party, observers could also connect it to what had happened in the Soviet Union. But the phenomenon that might have been called "totalitarianism with Chinese characteristics" soon appeared more complicated. The Great Leap Forward of the 1950s and the Great Proletariat Cultural Revolution of the 1960s were marked by a passionate intensity and a seeming reliance on mass upheaval and barely managed chaos not in keeping with proper Stalinist methodology. What was this about?

Yet even as we search for the origins of these startling episodes in the past, we find ourselves in the middle of yet another unanticipated transformation of China and Chinese society. The current change seems to have some staying power, as well as consequences that expand exponentially over time. Twenty years ago the Chinese Communist Party, which had once been determined to be the farthest "left" in the world, put the country on a new course. While obviously stimulated by the economic prowess of kindred societies in Japan and South Korea, this course was inspired—pridefully inspired, we should assume—by the successes of Chinese societies in Taiwan, Singapore, and Hong Kong, and the successes of individual Chinese throughout the world.

China is now two decades into this project, initiated by the late Deng Xiao ping (1904–1997), and China watchers of a generation ago would have

been stunned by the results. The essence of Deng's program was a commitment to the release of individual energy and the willingness of the state to
live with the consequences, though certainly not all the consequences. The
regime has periodically struck back against the results of its own program,
and has done so in cruel, arbitrary, brutal, and bloody ways. But the program
has continued, even accelerated, and the stresses and strains it has caused do
not seem to have yet produced genuinely serious divisions in the upper
reaches of the political system. The society continues to be thoroughly re-
made. In the program put forward in October 1997, moreover, the state proposed "restructuring" the 30 to 40 percent of the economy still in state hands.
In addition to dislocating tens of millions of workers, this requires a thorough
revamping of previously government-run social programs, the creation of a
financial system capable of tapping into and allocating domestic savings, and
increasing reliance on the international trade and financial system. Inevitably this will mean an expanded openness to outside economic, intellectual, and cultural forces.

Of course, like their predecessors who launched the Great Leap Forward
and the Great Proletariat Cultural Revolution, leaders of the present regime
think they can manage the consequences of the forces they have unleashed.
The "imports," they assume, can be dominated by "objects," like capital and
technology, while the consequences of intangibles—like ideas—can somehow be contained.

Buddhism and Chinese Consciousness

The events of the last twenty years in China, and what its rulers contemplate
for the next twenty, constitute a development of historic dimension, bound
to have important consequences for ourselves and for the world. The role of
religion in this emerging China, and more specifically the condition of
Christianity, must be examined within the context of both China's religious
history and the social upheaval now under way. Of first importance is understanding how the acceptance or rejection of various creeds fits into a larger
Chinese sense of the way things ought to be. Especially for its government
but also for its people, a religious teaching can have both an "orthodox" and
a "heterodox" character in China. It can simultaneously *support* and *subvert*
a larger moral, ethical, and philosophical consensus about how the country
ought to conduct its public and private business.

Buddhism, of course, presents the best-known case. Though it originated
outside China, it came to be thoroughly embedded in Chinese consciousness.
Yet since its gradual introduction into the country it has experienced both
official favor and rejection, both occasional patronage and periodic suppres-

sion. Over the centuries, there developed a large Buddhist infrastructure of temples and monasteries, donors, foundations, and trusts that from time to time figured in the calculation of China's internal balance of power.

At the same time, some Chinese thinkers worried that the metaphysical aspects of Buddhist doctrine could erode the this-worldly aspects of practical Confucianism. Likewise, they were frequently concerned that indifference to the here-and-now might undermine the larger Confucian system of familial and public ethics. Nevertheless, stimulated by the cosmic expanse of some Buddhist thought, Chinese thinkers became more adept at addressing philosophical issues in an abstract fashion, often trying to reconcile the practical with the metaphysical.

Some parts of the Buddhist outlook were thought of as slow-motion subversion, then, but over the centuries Buddhism presented quite another kind of challenge, sometimes to the entire secular order. Despite its reputation in the West for passivity and nonviolence, Buddhism has another side to it—messianic, totalistic, apocalyptic, and prone to trigger violent social upheavals. Dynastic histories frequently record the brutal suppression of this sort of ultimate heterodoxy. In addition to impressing whatever rulers held sway at the time, such violent peasant uprisings became part of Chinese lore, defining one mode of resistance to oppressive government. This insured that future governments would indeed worry about what they viewed as exotic and dangerous ideas loose among an unsophisticated, all too easily misled populace. And in fact, these older episodes came to prefigure many events in China during the past century and a half.

In sum, Buddhism represents the thorough assimilation of a foreign teaching, its complex "sinification" leading to both harmony and conflict. This religion is a basis for both acquiescence in and resistance to the power of the state, and a contributor to every kind of cultural expression—art, literature, philosophy, music. But things never stand still. In the more open Chinese society of today, a revitalized Buddhist infrastructure, supported financially by Chinese in China and around the world, is starting to press up against the limits of state control. Seeking autonomy and self-government, Buddhism offers another kind of political rallying point. In Tibet, for example, which China wishes to retain as part of its imperium, organized Buddhism is at the core of local resistance and the focus of outside interest.

Islam's Power in China

While Buddhism is a foreign-born creed that has deeply influenced every aspect of Chinese life, Islam is one of the great foreign teachings that have had a more modest impact on "Chinese-ness." Islam has indeed been important in the history of China, but in a much narrower way. Muslims in China fall into two groups: Chinese-speaking Han Chinese, and non-Chinese-speaking people ethnically related to the peoples of Central Asia and beyond. The presence of this latter group inside the Chinese imperium is arbitrary. Inhabiting some strategically important and oil-rich real estate in the far northwest of the country, they are today restive at best, and their objections to China's rule have become more frequent and more violent.

In earlier eras, the emperor's non-Han Muslim subjects would periodically revolt against his authority, drift out from under his control, or find themselves involved by happenstance in some larger imperial rivalry. They were involved, for example, in tensions between the Romanovs and the Manchus, and later, between the Soviet Union and the People's Republic of China.

Islam's power inside China derives from the relation of China's Muslims to centers of Islamic power outside China. Indeed, non-Han Chinese Muslims, long subjected to the heavy-handed rule of an overwhelming Han majority, find their room for maneuver and self-assertion in the ever-changing balance of power between the Islamic and Sinic worlds. The emergence of independent, predominantly Muslim states in what once was Soviet Central Asia, for example, makes the continued nonindependence of an Islamic Chinese Turkistan—Xinjiang, as the Chinese call the region—seem quite arbitrary. China must maintain important relations with several Islamic countries on its border—Kazakhstan, Tajikistan, Kyrgyzstan, Pakistan, Afghanistan—and nearby Bangladesh, while cultivating Persians, Turks, and Arabs in the Islamic Near East. The trick for Beijing is to expand Sinic influence in the Islamic world without somehow enlarging the maneuvering room of Muslims who happen to live inside China. The Chinese must give Iran and Saudi Arabia, those bases of activist Islam, some persuasive reason of their own for not stirring up their co-religionists in China.

To add to the complexity of these relations with Central Asian, Near Eastern, and South Asian Muslims, there is yet another Sinic-Islamic frontier, with Malayan Islam in Malaysia and Indonesia. The prosperous Chinese minorities in these countries are crucially involved in the ongoing renovation of China proper. They provide China with capital, expertise, and commercial connections. Indeed, these Chinese communities have become a major strategic asset for the motherland, but they are also very vulnerable to the vagaries of anti-Chinese resentment among majority Muslim populations. China has thus developed a substantial practical interest in "tolerance," "open-mindedness," "multiculturalism," and "cosmopolitanism." Like some other great powers, it has come to think of itself as a protector of minorities in potentially hostile foreign situations, except that its motives are entirely practical and straightforward.

The Case of Christianity

If Buddhism and Islam represent opposite poles of the experience of foreign-originated religions in China—that is, assimilation versus marginalization—Christianity in China rests somewhere in between. Christianity, unlike Islam, has had a substantial influence in modern Chinese history; yet, unlike Buddhism, it remains quite conspicuously "foreign" and therefore vulnerable.

There have been Christians in China for centuries. Catholic communities that exist today can trace their founding back to the time of the pioneer Jesuit missionaries of the sixteenth and seventeenth centuries. The Jesuits also brought with them the first systematic intellectual challenge to Chinese since the arrival of Buddhism centuries before. The Jesuits had an influential presence at the imperial court until the early eighteenth century, when the promising contacts with China's rulers, mandarins, philosophers, and scientists, so painstakingly cultivated over decades, were severed.

The next great wave of missionary effort, primarily Protestant, began in the mid-nineteenth century and held the attention of millions of Americans for decades. Drawing on the enthusiastic support of Christians in Europe and especially in the United States, these missionaries built up a substantial infrastructure, most of it near the coast but some deep in China's heartland. Over time, moreover, treaties between China and the Western powers came to include protection for both Western Christian missionaries and their Chinese converts. This relationship to the West made the position of Christianity in China both powerful and precarious.

The contemporary state of Christianity is marked by a mixture of problems, such as intolerance and oppression, and opportunities, such as growing affiliation and influence. This mixture has a long and complex history. First, the experience of the nineteenth century, when the propagation of a Western religious faith was clearly related to the presence of Western power inside the country, still resonates in China today. Christianity continues to be dogged by deep tension between being a good Chinese Christian and being a good Chinese patriot. The two are certainly reconcilable, but they are always harder to reconcile when China's relations with the West are under stress.

Second, Christianity has been deeply subversive of the existing order in a variety of ways. In the mid-nineteenth century, one Chinese man's heterodox reading of Christian teaching led him to conclude that he was the younger brother of Jesus Christ with a mission to replace the entire social order. The Taiping Rebellion he started led to fifteen years of civil war that claimed tens of millions of lives, further weakened the reigning dynasty, and expanded Western influence. At the end of the century, some inside the imperial court thought they could tap into anti-Christian sentiment by backing the efforts of a xenophobic sect, the so-called Boxers, to drive out foreigners and murder their Christian converts. The result was a united Western-plus-Japanese military response—and a huge financial indemnity that further limited China's independence.

Christian Prominence: Sun Yat-sen, Chiang Kai-shek

During the same turn-of-the-century period, however, Chinese Christians were involved in efforts of Western-style reform and revolution. Sun Yat-sen (1866–1925) is the representative figure here, and his enduring symbolic role as the father of the Chinese republic, both on the Chinese mainland and on Taiwan, suggests the powerful appeal of his political and philosophical eclecticism.

Sun was born in southeast China (close to British-owned Hong Kong). He left at an early age to join an older brother in Honolulu, where he was educated in Christian schools and later baptized. He then studied Western-style medicine in Hong Kong. Dr. Sun became an inveterate campaigner against the Manchu dynasty, traveling in North America, Europe, and Asia to enlist overseas Chinese (especially the disproportionate number of Christian converts among them) in his many plots. He also maintained close ties with Western missionaries and Chinese Christians in and around his home region. In these respects, Dr. Sun was a worldly man who was somehow able to balance his trust in Christianity, science, and republicanism with ties to such mysterious and obscurantist elements in Chinese society as the Triads, all the while riding herd on a coalition that included constitutional monarchists and radical republicans. Toward the end of his life he added his own idiosyncratic understanding of Russian Bolshevism to the mix.

Sun's present place in both the Communist and the Nationalist pantheon results, of course, from his having died at the right time—that is, before either side prevailed. Nevertheless, his life and legacy still have a practical relevance. When President Jiang Zemin visited the United States in October 1997, he stopped in Honolulu en route to Washington. In addition to wanting to remind Americans that China and the United States were once allies against Japan, Jiang (who reportedly began his study of English in a Christian mission school near Shanghai) wanted to send a message to the Chinese. He invoked Sun Yat-sen's time in Hawaii to highlight both China's proven capacity to be open to the world and the long role of overseas Chinese in the growth and development of the motherland.

After Dr. Sun's death, as the quarter-century struggle between the Communists and the Nationalists intensified, Christianity—especially American Protestant Christianity—became deeply involved in Chinese politics. Beginning about 1915, the Christian establishment in the United States had become increasingly pro-Chinese and anti-Japanese in its outlook. Major American denominations had made substantial investments in the China missions, and an Americanized Chinese elite emerged from the experience of higher education in the United States. The Christianization of prominent members of the Nationalist government—particularly General and Madame Chiang Kaishek—seemed even more providential. Madame Chiang came from a prominent Chinese Methodist family and brought her husband to baptism in the same faith. The United States' great efforts on behalf of the Nationalist regime, the religious underpinnings of those efforts, and the bitter political consequences of their failure are all well known. They are particularly important to the inner history of the Republican Party since 1950 and have hovered over the larger debate about American Asian policy ever since.

Christians' work of a century seemed to collapse suddenly with the decisive victory of the Communists in the Chinese civil war. The churches, schools, and universities constructed throughout the country by the 1940s, a new Chinese professional class educated in Christian institutions and insinuated into the highest reaches of government, the well-schooled intellectuals carefully trained for philosophical combat—all this seemed to count for nothing. The optimists of the 1930s and 1940s were insufficiently alert to other, more predictive countertrends. After World War I, for instance, many Chinese intellectuals followed the lead of their Western colleagues, turning away from "Christianity" and embracing "socialism" as the defining doctrine of Western modernity. Anti-Christian movements led by Chinese politicians were aided by Chinese intellectuals who issued manifestos informing the Chinese people that the West itself seemed to be turning on its own core tradition.

At the end of World War II, only the United States remained as a "Western" power in Asia, the position of Britain and France having collapsed with Japan's conquest of their East Asian domains. China's long, immensely destructive struggle with Japan had enormous and underappreciated effects. In destroying the European position in China, the Japanese achieved more than they knew. In particular, to the extent that Chinese Christianity was a Western multinational enterprise—supported not only by American Presbyterians but also by French Catholics, English Methodists, and German Lutherans—the toppling of the European pillar of support was a devastating

blow. American Christians were the only ones still interested in and capable of lending their Chinese brethren a hand, but their position was not to
be wholly restored either.

Chinese Christians on Their Own

The war against Japan, the ensuing civil war, and the Communist consolida-
tion of power all presented enormous difficulties for Chinese Christians. Despite Americans' keen interest in China's fate between 1937 and 1945, the
churches in China had to learn how to fend for themselves. Their connections to the outer world, which had established and sustained the congregations, began to dissolve. Japan's occupations of large parts of China had, by
itself, created "underground" churches that refused to cooperate with the
regnant political authority—in this case, an occupying power and its pup-
pets. But this severing of relations with the world was insignificant compared
to the subsequent pressures of Communist rule.

It is valuable to view the contemporary problem of so-called patriotic (i.e.,
government-managed) Christian organizations as against so-called underground (i.e., government-repressed) ones in this historical context. That the
churches had any capacity at all for independent action during Japanese occupation and Communist repression can be attributed, in some measure, to
the prescience of the earliest missionaries who recognized that Chinese
Christians had somehow to create their own church. They should not become Canadian Presbyterians or American Baptists who happened to "look"
Chinese. They needed not only self-government but also financial independence, for a Chinese church perpetually reliant on overseas largesse could
never escape suspicion about its "true" motives. This conscious effort to promote an independent Chinese Christian establishment—observed more in
the breech than in actual practice, to be sure—spoke to the problematic relationship between Christianity and the Chinese government and between
that government and foreign countries.

How could such political tensions be overcome? As Chinese felt forced to
reconcile Christianity with Chinese patriotism, many Americans made an effort to separate their missionary impulses from American patriotism. In response to those missionaries for whom American Protestantism and American Manifest Destiny were one and the same thing, others began to argue that
spreading the Gospel was not a nationalistic or patriotic enterprise of any sort.
Rather, it should be seen as a withdrawal from participation in the United
States' self-aggrandizement or even as a rejection of politics altogether.

While surely high-minded, this idea lost much of its sublimity as it traveled through American religious organizations over the decades. In particu-

lar, the original notion—that American missionaries ought not to be agents of anything other than their creed—was seriously warped during the period of China's self-enforced isolation from the rest of the world between 1950 and the late 1970s.

There were many consequences. By not effectively challenging the political Left's anti-American interpretation of modern Asian history, U.S. churches did nothing to educate the American public about what was actually happening in Asia. Worse still, "enlightened" religious opinion came to take up the larger anti-Christian feelings among Western intellectuals, even to the point of condoning criticism of Asians who had embraced Christianity in the first place. Somehow, Asia's Christians became major villains, prominent especially in the Indochina melodrama between 1945 and 1975. The government of South Vietnam was portrayed as a collection of quislings, for instance, because practicing Catholics helped run it. This period must have been doubly discouraging for China's Christians, whose Communist oppressors were afforded a standing in the Western world never enjoyed by any prior modern Chinese regime.

How Chinese Christianity came to survive not only the Great Leap Forward and the Great Proletariat Revolution but also the relative indifference of the non-Chinese world during these dangerous periods is not well understood. To assess Christianity's future prospects in China, we need to comprehend this unanticipated persistence both as a testament to the strength of personal convictions and as a reminder that there are limits to the reach of even the most brutal of police states.

Christianity in a Transforming Society

It is important to remember that China is no longer either the ever-repressive, murderously crazed, totalitarian state of 1950 to 1976, which drove Christianity deep into the underground, or the disintegrating country of 1850 to 1950, which provided opportunities for Chinese Christians and their foreign patrons to exercise influence all out of proportion to their tiny numbers. Nor does China have a secretly enlightened regime whose hidden agenda is to transform the country into a liberal democracy, or a regime that will go quietly away if liberal democracy is somehow the outcome of years of economic reform. Caution should be the rule in thinking through the implications of the post-1976 era in Chinese affairs and in evaluating how the transformation of Chinese society—especially its system of political economy—is likely to affect China's relations with the rest of the world, especially with Asian neighbors traditionally under its cultural influence.

In this age of greater openness, China's international Christian connections are being rebuilt, alternately aided by increased tolerance and hampered by brutal repression. The repression is constrained because the regime does, in fact, respect the power of outside opinion on this subject, and knows that the condition of Chinese Christians can be a powerful element in shaping attitudes in Western countries. The tolerance comes from a recognition of the value of China's Christian connections; the regime has long since given up the simple-minded idea that Christianity was a wedge for "imperialism" and nothing else. It now sees Christianity as a force for modernization and education.

Christianity is also understood, still, as a gateway to the world for many young Chinese. It has, moreover, become a means of re-linking many older overseas Chinese with the motherland. After all, well before missionaries gained entry into China itself, they were active in such places as Singapore, Indonesia, and the Philippines. Later, the system of Christian schools and colleges built up in China and in these way stations became important in educating Chinese elites in China and in the diaspora. Today, alumni networking attracts both sentiment and money back to Christian institutions—support that is welcomed and encouraged by the Chinese regime for its own purposes.

Small developments of this kind call attention to something very important in contemporary Asia, namely, the growing role of Christianity in the region as a whole. Properly appreciated and supported, Asian Christianity and Asian Christians can spur the development of civil society inside China, thereby improving the prospects for religious freedom there. It is significant that the Philippines, a Catholic country for centuries, has produced something recognizable as a democracy in an Asian setting. South Korea, also a functioning electoral democracy, is now about 30 percent Christian; its former president, Kim Yung-sam, is a Presbyterian, and its current president, Kim Dae-jung, is a Roman Catholic. Catholics in Vietnam are among the natural mediators between that country and the larger world, which the still-too-Communist regime haltingly wants to re-enter. Indeed, should Vietnam ever become serious about internal reform, its cosmopolitan Catholics would be likely to play a disproportionately large role.

In the Chinese world, there are more than a few heirs to Dr. Sun Yat-sen's belief that Christianity has a place in China's ongoing revolution. Li Teng-hui, head of the Kuomintang on Taiwan and president of the republic of China from 1988 to 2000, is a Presbyterian. Christians are well represented in the upper reaches of the government of Singapore. In Hong Kong the best-known advocate of democratization, Martin Lee, is a Roman Catholic, as is Mrs. Anson Chan, the city's highest-ranking civil servant. Harry Wu, a prominent proponent of political reform in China, who has become an American citizen, is a Catholic, and a graduate of St. John's University in Shanghai. Asia's Christians, still relatively tiny in number, now play a striking role in introducing new ways into their old world, whether in commerce, culture, or politics. That influence is bound to increase. Christians will be to twenty-first-century Asia what Jews were to nineteenth- and twentieth-century Europe.

The American Role
Just as China's opening to the rest of Asia provides an unexpected opportunity for various Christian communities in the region to help improve the condition of Christians inside China, China's growing connection to the world beyond Asia gives Americans new opportunities. But on what basis should Americans assert their interest? What is the objective? How much support should be provided to Chinese Christianity as a religious movement? How much as a political movement? How much should Christians inside China determine the nature of American involvement? How should their wishes be weighed against Americans' own interest in developing a strategy for dealing with the growing power of China over the long run? Are these interests in conflict?

If democratic Asia's growing acceptance of the Western religious outlook seems clearly beneficial, the advantages of the "New World Order" should be even more apparent. This seemingly secular web of international agreements, covenants, and declarations about human rights—products of the United Nations and other public and private transnational organizations—is, in fact, closely related to Christianity. Though this particular way of thinking about the organization of the world is associated with Woodrow Wilson, Wilson himself got it from an already well-established strain of thought about politics and human rights within Christianity. In his mind, the secular trappings of "Wilsonianism" were actually the servants of high Christian purpose. A great friend of the Christian mission in China, Wilson was even once prepared to appoint one of its leading figures to serve as ambassador to China.

China is now deeply involved in this New World Order, and seeks further entanglement. Although it may not *like* this new order, it sees no alternative to it for the foreseeable future. In particular, Beijing's signature on a host of international agreements that spell out individual rights of every description makes China's treatment of its own citizens, including its Christian citizens, a matter of interest to many nations, not just to the United States. Americans who attack the legitimacy and the authority of these international agreements are needlessly weakening powerful weapons in this important struggle. The New World Order helps develop and solidify contacts between Christians inside China and those throughout Asia and beyond. It also establishes a high order of accountability for China, diminishing the credibility of Beijing's claim that Americans' interest in the religious freedoms and political rights of Chinese Christians is merely one more in a list of pesky problems in U.S.-China relations. For, properly speaking, it is a problem for China's relations with the entire world.

The Confucian Angle

Those interested in religious freedom in China and its political liberalization generally have—in addition to the progress of Christianity within Asia and the benefits of old-fangled American internationalism—yet another ally, the Chinese tradition itself. Because Westerners know so little about this tradition and often assume that it stands in opposition to Western beliefs about political and social life, they have yet to tap into its resources.

Chinese people around the world, however, are now discussing the meaning of their modern history and contemporary existence in the context of the vast thing called "Confucianism." This term obviously encompasses a range of thought, parts of which are in opposition to other parts, and opinions about it have changed as circumstances have changed. At one time, most Chinese intellectuals saw Confucianism as an obstacle to national survival, something that needed to be discarded if China were to continue as an independent and powerful nation in the modern world. Later, Confucianism was used to explain the success rather than the failure of Chinese in the modern world; upon reflection, it was discovered that Confuciansim was a functional equivalent to Protestantism as a catalyst for capitalist-type achievement. Today, Confucianism is often proffered, not so much as a way for the Chinese to succeed in the modern world, but rather as a way for Chinese to resist the corrosive social effects of the modern world.

Of special interest is the way that Confucianism has been invoked in defense of authoritarian government and in opposition to things like the rule of law and human rights. This is, at best, a shaky assertion. Over the centuries "Confucians" have argued among themselves about the same issues that have engaged Western political philosophers—the dividing line between public and private, the boundary between the state and civil society, the relation between virtue in individuals and good order in the nation, private economic activity and governmental regulation thereof, and limits on the power of the state, especially its arbitrary power. Moreover, over those same centuries, some "Confucians" had an open and expansive view toward the outer world; they were industriously curious about the natural world and heartily embraced the human world.

Who, then, ought to have custody of this tradition today? Which side in contemporary China will succeed in co-opting the venerable Chinese tradition? Who, outside of China, is allowed to participate in this interesting battle? Just as the Western tradition has become the world's common property, to be both defended and attacked outside the West, so too is the Chinese tradition common property. The study of it has long involved non-Chinese of many nationalities and of widely varying political and religious opinions. *Their* view of the meaning of the Chinese tradition in the modern world can have influence, for Chinese and non-Chinese can educate each other.

The example of the Russian Jewish Sinologist Vitaly Rubin (1923–1981) is instructive. Rubin focused on ancient Chinese thought and came to appreciate Confucianism as the deep enemy of totalitarianism. This view, which he expressed in *Individual and State in Ancient China* (1970) and other writings, got him into trouble with the Soviet authorities because of the obvious critique of the Soviet Union. Rubin compounded his difficulties when, in 1972, he applied to emigrate to Israel. There was, however, an unusual international effort among Sinologists on his behalf, and four years later he was allowed to leave. He became a professor at Hebrew University in Jerusalem.

But though it was Rubin's personal situation that first directed the attention of his colleagues to the relationship between free expression and arbitrary power, it was his scholarship that sustained their interest. The relation of the Chinese tradition to questions of the human rights and moral obligations of individuals and citizens, the legitimacy of the state and the requirement for personal protest when the state behaves illegitimately, absorbed Rubin. And there is some evidence that his point of view may now be growing inside the Chinese world as Chinese thinkers apply their intellectual heritage to contemporary conditions.

Chinese now seek to compress into decades a process that took centuries in the West. This undertaking is very disorienting, and the rapid refashioning of Chinese society has set off a large and busy discussion about the meaning of the country's modern history and recent experience. Philosophers and religious thinkers of every sort are engaged, and Christianity is once again an important presence in the discussion. While this intellectual effort has lagged behind China's technical and economic advances—and also behind comparable efforts in such countries as Germany—the Chinese are starting to realize that an analysis of their hideous modern era is the starting point for thinking about their country and its relations with the rest of the world.

There is, then, some basis for optimistic speculation, though it relies on a leap of faith. The hope is that a great tradition of tolerance and compromise built up in the West can be joined to, and strengthened by, a great tradition of personal cultivation and civic responsibility built up in the East. This is hardly a new ambition; a search for the commensurability of these great traditions has gone on intermittently since the Jesuit missionaries began it centuries ago. And it is not a project that will be completed any time soon. But it has long had a special fascination for Christians, and to the degree that Christians in the Western world can sustain their interest and faith in it, their brethren in the Sinic world can only benefit.

Comment by Arthur Waldron

Charles Horner made a number of important and subtle points in his paper. One that I'd like to comment on is his stress on the bloodiness of China's recent history. Where is it coming from, all that suffering and killing, all that destruction? There is scarcely anybody in China who has not been touched by it emotionally if not physically. My wife is from China, and two members of her immediate family died directly or indirectly as a result of the Communists. This is really what the revival of Christianity is about in China. Many non-Christians in the West tend to think of a kind of social-gospel, American Friends Service Committee model of Christianity. That's not what it is in China. It is very much about understanding the meaning of the devastation, the meaning of all that suffering and death, how it can be redeemed. I remember once being with my wife in the Catholic cathedral in Beijing. She looked at the people praying and said to me, "Look at these faces. Every one of them tells an extraordinary story." Those faces are documents of a process of historical destruction, the only parallels to which are found in the other great Communist country. They're not seeking to promote a social or economic agenda; they're simply asking to be left alone with their faith.

The Three-Self Autonomous Church, which Charles Horner calls a government-managed church, is even more than that—it's a government-run church. It's not simply a question of getting licensed. You don't say, "We started a new congregation and we need an occupancy certificate" and

Arthur Waldron is Lauder Professor of International Relations at the University of Pennsylvania and director of Asian studies at the American Enterprise Institute.

wait for the fire marshal to come around and approve your facility. Basically the police run the registered churches in China. Now, within those churches, of course, many people are trying to operate in ways that are not in keeping with what the government wants.

A lot of Christian churches in China are entirely indigenous. The big one today is the so-called True Jesus Church, which began in China and now has spread all over the world. When I was in Leicester, England, recently, I noticed what was obviously a formerly Anglican church with a big sign in Chinese: True Jesus Church. They have missionaries and foreign congregations. This is a very vital group, and it is an unanticipated consequence of liberalization.

The collapse of liberal Protestantism in the West has had a big effect on Chinese Protestantism. In the days when liberal Protestantism was still a force to be reckoned with, there would have been strong pressure in the United States for a close embrace of the official church and a tendency to view believers in the unregistered churches as troublemakers who were just being unreasonable in refusing to join the police-run churches. That's not the case today. Likewise, there is a great awareness within the Roman Catholic Church of both the aboveground and the underground Chinese churches. From time to time there's pressure within the Catholic Church to embrace the official church—and essentially hang a lot of the underground out to dry. I think that the present pope has clearly shown he is unwilling to do that.

We in America tend to be extravagant in what we promise. We should only promise what we really intend to do and are able to do. Remember, the Chinese invented bluff. We are never going to beat them at that game, and we shouldn't even play it. I think the most important thing we can do is simply to tell the truth, to call things by their true names. When South Africa broke relations with Taiwan and recognized the PRC as the sole legitimate government of China, I found it appalling that no less a person than Nelson Mandela, when he was asked about the repression of democracy in China, said something like "it is not appropriate for me to comment on the internal affairs of China."

We must not allow ourselves to be co-opted into silence. We have to be steady, persistent, and reliable, and we have to tell the truth about human rights violations.

CHAPTER SIX

Political Islam and the Roots of Violence

Habib C. Malik

Certain phrases conceal worlds of meaning. "Islam's Bloody Borders," lifted from Samuel Huntington's seminal work on the clash of civilizations, is one such phrase. Indeed, it seemed that wherever the Islamic world came in contact with a different "other," there was blood to be found. What is more arresting is that in today's world this appears to be true *only* with respect to Islam—no "other" is encased in a circumference of red the way Islam is, from Egypt to Kashmir and Mindanao, from Bosnia and Kosovo to Chechnya, from southern Sudan to East Timor and the Moluccan islands. The phenomenon cries out for explanation, but the accounts one comes across—whether in Huntington or elsewhere[1]—while useful, tend at best to be truncated and not to dwell on the primary reason: the inherent, even organic connection that has always existed between *Political Islam* and violence.

What follows is in no way premised on a presumed (and therefore tendentious) association between Islam and violence. Certainly a stroll through the writings of the great philosophers of Islamic civilization, from Averroes in the twelfth century to Mohammad Iqbal in the early twentieth century, would support no such association. Nor would a similar excursion through the writings of Islam's early Sufi mystics, from Rabiah al-Adawiyah (d. 801) to al-Hallaj (tenth century) and Ibn Arabi (thirteenth century). And the vast majority

Habib Charles Malik teaches history and cultural studies at the Lebanese American University (Byblos branch). He is the author of *Between Damascus and Jerusalem: Lebanon and Middle East Peace* and of *Receiving Soren Kierkegaard: The Early Impact and Transmission of His Thought*. He has a Ph.D. in modern European intellectual history from Harvard University.

of these thinkers and mystics regarded themselves as devout Muslims. The violent fate many of them suffered at the hands of Muslim authorities underscores the culpability of Political Islam, while leaving no room for doubt that such a culture of violence is not pervasive in every Islamic context, and that it preys as easily upon the sons and daughters of the faith as upon the outsider. (Witness the case of intra-Islamic violence in present-day Algeria.)

The standard portrait presented of Political Islam as it has functioned through the centuries does not always depict reality, a reality steeped in antagonism and violence. The "anecdotes of tolerance" typical of so much of the specialized literature on Political Islam cannot mask the sordid conditions that native non-Muslim communities living in a predominantly Islamic environment have had—and continue to have—to endure.[2] In the contemporary world, Islamic moderation finds itself in a generally sorry state, besieged on all sides by a virulent militancy. Where and when such moderation existed in the past, it usually derived from the fortuitous benevolence of a particular ruler and had little staying power.

Since Islam does not separate the realms of religion and politics, peculiar ingredients in the religion bear directly on the behavior of Muslims in positions of power, and have an adverse effect upon the daily life of non-Muslims under Islamic rule. Taken together, these ingredients create a perception of the alien "other" that becomes a handy excuse for violence and persecution. It is certainly true that to speak of "Islam" or "Muslims" in monolithic terms can be misleading; there are many variations of Islam and a correspondingly diverse community of Muslims. However, a remarkable degree of uniformity is apparent among Islamic portraits of "the other"—especially of the Christian, and even more so of the Jew. In this context it is not much of an oversimplification to refer to an "Islamic view" or "Muslim outlook."

The Two Realms

Islam divides the world into two sharply segregated realms: the Abode or House of Islam (*Dar al-Islam*), where Muslims live in a majority as an *umma* (Islamic community) and exercise political power, and the Abode of War (*Dar al-Harb*), which includes everywhere outside the first realm. This division serves to anchor an a priori attitude of hostility toward the non-Muslim. It was spawned and nurtured during the early period of conquests, when Islam confronted and overcame its surroundings through the sword, and it gradually became ingrained in the official as well as the popular Muslim mindset. The Abode of War was looked upon as the realm where confusion and falsehood reign. Infidelity, or *kufr*, was its prevailing feature. The Abode of War was the dwelling place of the *aghyar* (the different others) or the *munafiqin* (the hypocrites), who displayed *istikbar* (the arrogance of the oppressor) and who needed to be fought and killed.

The *shari'a*, or Islamic Law, makes *jihad* (holy war) a duty for all Muslims. In several places the Koran exhorts believers to fight or kill "in God's way"; for instance, "Prescribed for you is fighting though it be hateful to you. Yet it may happen that you will hate a thing which is better for you; and it may happen that you will love a thing which is worse for you; God knows, and you know not."[3] "So fight in God's way, and know that God is All-hearing, All-knowing."[4] "Count not those who were slain in God's way as dead, but rather living with their Lord, by Him provided."[5] "God loves those who fight in His way in ranks, as though they were a building well-compacted."[6] The recurring phrase "in God's way" means, according to one authoritative source, that whoever fights so that the Islamic *shari'a* prevails does so "in God's way."

Islam's founder, Mohammad, was himself an exceptional military leader and strategist who fought many battles and slew enemies with his own hands. So did all the early Islamic rulers or caliphs, many of whom also died by the sword. Killing for the faith—which is the same as *jihad*—was from the start a natural activity sanctioned and required of all the faithful.[7] A harsh fate awaited the opponents of Islam, both in this life and in the next: "This is the recompense of those who fight against God and His Messenger, and hasten about the earth, to do corruption there: they shall be slaughtered, or crucified, or their hands and feet shall alternately be struck off, or they shall be banished from the land. That is a degradation for them in this world; and in the world to come awaits them a mighty chastisement."[8]

Despite Islam's claim to be the final fulfillment of both Judaism and Christianity, with Mohammad being proclaimed as the Seal (the last) of the Prophets, the standard Islamic designation of everything that preceded Islam as *jahiliyya* (the age of ignorance) represents a radical *break* with history and an abrupt discontinuity in its progression. Such a view automatically cancels the intrinsic value of the predecessor, who is then never studied on his own terms nor assessed through the prism of his frame of reference.[9] This disruption of history in effect predisposes to violence: smashing idols, battling the vestiges of ignorance, and rectifying religious waywardness by force become compelling obsessions for the Muslim believer. Hence there is no permanent peace with the forces of infidelity, only temporary truces; such truces are to be broken by the Muslim, and *jihad* resumed, whenever more favorable conditions prevail.[10]

The *Dhimmi* System

Islam distinguishes between two categories of unbelievers: those whom the Koran calls "People of the Book" (namely Jews and Christians) and all the rest (members of other religions, and pagans). Being grounded in a reworking of certain Old Testament stories as well as in Christian heterodoxy (Arianism and Docetism), Islam from the start was very conscious of its Jewish and Christian roots. The last two lines of the opening passage of the Koran, for instance, refer to two groups not "in the straight path": "those against whom Thou art wrathful" (meaning the Jews), and "those who are astray" (meaning the Christians).[11] With a pervasive fixation on Christianity, the Koran repeatedly speaks of the absolute unity of God (Allah); of God's not having been begotten and not having himself begotten; and of *shirk*—introducing external associates into the One Godhead—as the most odious form of idolatry.[12] Koranic verses vary in their severity toward Christians. Side by side with verses that call for confronting the unbelievers in battle and that consign them to the fires of hell in the next life are verses of a more tolerant sort: "no compulsion is there in religion," and, in a characteristic expression of Islamic fatalism, "if thy Lord had willed, whoever is in the earth would have believed."[13]

From the earliest Islamic period, means had to be devised to accommodate the presence of non-Muslim minority communities within the Abode of Islam. Members of these communities were called *dhimmis* (i.e., those under the protection of Muslims) and included Jews, Christians, and later—when the authorities needed additional revenue from taxation—Zoroastrians. Specific rules attributed originally to the Caliph Omar were instituted to govern the daily life of *dhimmis* and their relations with Muslims.[14] Although it became customary both in Islamic sources and among Western apologists for Islam to view the *dhimmi* system as compassionate and humane simply because it eschewed direct physical violence against *dhimmis* who strictly observed the rules, the system was in fact discriminatory and demeaning.[15] It legally instituted a second-class status for these conquered non-Muslims (a kind of religious apartheid), and *dhimmi* prescriptions taken collectively constituted a subtle form of religious persecution.

To be a *dhimmi* meant one had first to pay a special poll tax (the *jizya*, literally "penalty tax") for being allowed to remain an infidel. In addition, the *dhimmi* had to exist in a state of perpetual humiliation in the eyes of the Muslim. He could not build new churches nor renovate dilapidated old ones. His house had to be built lower than those of Muslims, and the entrance also had to be low, forcing the occupants to stoop when passing through it. Most of the time *dhimmis* had to remain on the side streets and alleys. This too was where they held their funeral processions, in silence. The ringing of church bells (sounds of infidelity), the displaying of crosses and other religious symbols (symbols of idolatry), loud singing during church services, and religious processions during particular festivals such as Palm Sunday—all these outward manifestations of *kufr* (infidelity) were strictly forbidden. *Dhimmis* were prohibited from selling alcohol; had to wear distinctive dress (usually gray-colored for Christians); were required to shave the front of the head; were not to be greeted first by Muslims; were not allowed to ride horses but only donkeys and mules in a sideways posture; and were barred from carrying any arms and exempted from military service. They enjoyed no political rights whatsoever but served in bureaucratic posts and held low-level administrative jobs that often required technical expertise. They were not accepted as witnesses in court in cases involving a Muslim. They had their own special courts for settling matters of personal status such as disputes, divorce, and inheritance. A *dhimmi* man could not marry a Muslim woman, though a *dhimmi* woman could marry a Muslim man.

All this should make it evident that the *dhimmi* concept is in great need of demythologizing; it should cease to connote tolerance. The best that can be said in its favor is that it entails violence "with a human face." The gradual dehumanization of non-Muslim minority communities—which is what the *dhimmi* system achieves—represents a form of cumulative abuse. And this slow erosion of the *dhimmi*'s humanity could be abruptly transformed into physical violence as punishment for any violation of *dhimmi* precepts, such as preaching to Muslims, or having sex with a Muslim woman, or cursing the Prophet. Offenses of this sort result in the automatic revocation of the "protections" of *dhimmi* status and a relegation of the offender—including sometimes his entire household—to the Abode of War.

Over time, the *dhimmi* system has functioned as a means not of tolerance but of liquidation, with the expectation that it would eventually lead to *hidaya* (bringing the lost to the right path). Communities toiling under the *dhimmi* burden were greatly reduced in numbers, either through wholesale conversions to Islam to escape the stifling restrictions of the system, or through emigration out of *Dar al-Islam*. When places of worship cannot be maintained nor can new ones be built, and when men of the dominant community can marry women from the other community while the reverse is forbidden, the ultimate result is material and physical eradication of the minority community.

The reputed economic prosperity of some non-Muslim minorities living in predominantly Islamic urban areas, in the sporadic instances when it occurred, was due to two main factors unrelated to any supposed good will on the part of the authorities: the state needed the expertise of these unbelievers, and they did not constitute a political threat since they could have no aspirations to the caliphate. "Dhimmitude," as Bat Ye'or aptly calls it, becomes with time a state of mind embodied as much in ideology and legal texts as in collective perceptions. Ye'or writes:

> Dhimmitude can be defined as the totality of the characteristics developed in the long term by collectivities subjected, on their own homeland, to the laws and ideology imported through *jihad*. Dhimmitude represents a collective situation and is expressed by a specific mentality. It affects the political, economic, cultural, sociological, and psychological domains—all these aspects being interdependent and interactive.[16]

Most striking about dhimmitude are the lasting psychological scars it inflicts on the victim communities, scars that long outlast any political and/or legal liberalization in Islamic lands. Thus the *dhimmi* syndrome, according to Ye'or, is one of "psychological conditioning": "The basic components of the . . . syndrome lie in the combined psychological effects of vulnerability and humiliation."[17] Neither the heterodox Christian sects surviving as outcasts on the fringes of the Byzantine Empire, who were the first to be overrun at the dawn of Islam, nor, centuries later in 1453, the besieged inhabitants of Constantinople could have imagined at the time what it would be like to live under Political Islam.

The *Dhimmi* Christian Communities

Two distinct historical experiences shape native non-Muslim communities scattered throughout the Islamic world. Specifically among indigenous Christians, these two experiences can be classified as *dhimmi* and free. Each of these conditions bred over time a set of perceptions and metaphors, a reading of events and an evaluation of outcomes, unique to the circumstances of communal subjugation or communal liberty. The perspective of each group of communities, *dhimmi* or free, retains its own validity for interpreting the causes of the periodic violence visited upon its members by Political Islam. Taken in isolation, neither the *dhimmi* experience nor that of the native Christians who remained free can provide a comprehensive explanation for the phenomenon—ancient and modern—of religious persecution. The two perspectives contain complementary elements of legitimacy and truth and need to be interrogated in tandem.

The vast majority of Christian Arabs in the Middle East, who today number somewhere between 10 and 15 million, live in *dhimmi* communities. Having been subjugated in the early period of Islamic conquests, these communities long ago gave up a free existence and succumbed to the insidious inferiorization of dhimmitude. Over time they tended to adopt and internalize many of the ingredients that inform the worldview of antagonistic dualism embraced by their Muslim masters. Although they shared the Muslim majority's general distaste for the West, and although as *dhimmis* they were technically entitled to protection, these communities often became the local scapegoats for frustrated Muslim mobs (and rulers). They found themselves associated with the excesses and hostilities of their co-religionists in the West whenever the latter made incursions into Muslim lands; such incursions included the Crusades, the concessions to European powers (Capitulations) allowing foreign protection for Christians (France for Catholics, Russia for Orthodox, Great Britain for Protestants and Jews), and the colonial and imperial experiences in modern times.

In fact, the Middle Eastern penchant to spin, and then act on, conspiracy theories very often places native Christian communities directly in harm's way by branding them as fifth-column accomplices in the devious Western plots (real or imagined) directed at local Muslims.[18] Alternatively, whenever local Christians have tended to prosper economically, as individuals or as communities, they have run the risk of becoming objects of envy by other *dhimmis* and resentment by the Muslims. This happened during the 1950s to the Syrian and Lebanese Christians living in Egypt after Nasser came to power, and it happened again in December 1997 when Muslims attacked ethnic Christian Chinese in Jakarta, Indonesia. The latter of these attacks has since mushroomed, particularly after the bloody independence in 1999 of East Timor, to encompass other segments of the Indonesian archipelago.

Christians in the Ottoman Empire

Induced by the success of the Greek War of Independence (1821–1829) and accompanying pressures from European states, the Ottomans pledged to institute legal and administrative reforms throughout their sprawling empire, which spanned most of the Middle East, North Africa, and the Balkans. The two edicts proclaiming the new reforms, the Rose Pavilion Decree of 1839 and the Imperial Rescript of 1856, both spoke explicitly about granting equality to all citizens of the empire, Muslims and non-Muslims alike.[19] This novel and liberalizing measure, officially undertaken by the sultan himself, in effect terminated the legal component of *dhimmi* status—though not the psychological damage inflicted by dhimmitude. With the new reforms, known as the *Tanzimat*, liberal influences followed closely by nationalism crept in from the West and steadily became entrenched in many corners of the empire, eventually including Istanbul itself.

One would have reasonably expected such a development to ease the burden of discrimination and persecution suffered by the non-Muslim subjects of the Ottoman Empire. Paradoxically, the opposite occurred. The roster of massacres perpetrated against various Christian populations of the empire from the mid-nineteenth century to the eve of the Second World War speaks for itself.

Barely four years after the appearance of the Imperial Rescript proclaiming equality for all Ottoman citizens, the city of Damascus was the scene of a vicious massacre of Christians. Responding to events in neighboring Mount Lebanon that saw the outbreak of hostilities between Christians and Druze, Muslim mobs in Damascus began to harass the Christians of the city, verbally at first and then physically. The result, according to contemporary documents, was that in July 1860 alone between 6,000 and 7,000 Christians were slaughtered in Damascus, and an untold number of women and children were abducted east into the desert, where a gruesome fate of rape, sale into slavery, and death befell them.[20]

Centuries of oppression of Christians included the deliberate settlement of Turkish populations in southeastern Europe and eastern Anatolia, as well as the regular snatching of Christian children from the Balkans for forced conversion to Islam and incorporation into the Ottoman army (the *devshirme* system). These coercive measures reached a height with the atrocities committed against the Bulgarians in 1876 and repeatedly against the Armenians in 1895, 1909, and 1915. Nor were the Syriac-speaking inhabitants of southern Anatolia and northern Syria spared, for in 1895 in Diyarbakr, Merdin, and Tur Abidin, and again between 1915 and 1918 in conjunction with the wholesale genocide against the Armenians, scores of Syriac villages were attacked and hundreds of people were slaughtered. Often on these occasions Kurds, who were themselves victimized by the Turks, would take part in the attacks on Christians. Assyrian and Chaldaean communities in southeastern Turkey and today's region of northern Iraq were also targeted in 1915 and again in 1933.[21]

Such was the sad record of the so-called era of emancipation, the much-hailed period when *dhimmi* status was abrogated from the books by imperial order, but hardly eradicated from the hearts and psyches of both victim and oppressor. In a curious way, in the eyes of strict believers the official proclamation of equality in citizenship for non-Muslims moved them from the camp of *dhimmis* to that of *harbis* (citizens of the Abode of War), thereby releasing the devout Muslim from the obligation to protect them and rendering them vulnerable to persecution. Add to this the mounting intrusiveness of Western ideas, economic and colonial influence, and military assertiveness, and the stage is set for the atrocities cited, where the Christian victims within the empire were suddenly perceived as subversive extensions of the predatory West. Much of the slaughter took place under the ultranationalist Committee of Union and Progress in Turkey, for example, and the massacres, enforced famines, and demographic dislocations continued well after Turkey had been proclaimed a secular republic. The first to be killed was usually the *millibashi*, or religious leader of the *millet* (religious community), such as the Patriarch in the case of the Christians. The low-intensity violence of the *dhimmi* and *devshirme* systems, where some constraints on arbitrariness operated, gave way to swift physical elimination, facilitated by the imported improvements in weaponry.

Similarly, the movement of pan-Arabism inspired by the example of nationalism in Europe and egged on by an assortment of Arab Christian *dhimmi* intellectuals was, as Bat Ye'or insightfully explains, "inevitably destined to revive and renew the values created by the Arabs, those same values that had borne them to the height of their power at the time of the conquests and which had presided over the formulation and application of the *shari'a*." A lethal yearning for a more righteous past was born, and, Ye'or again, "[n]ostalgia for the period was a factor in the recall, revival, and satanization of the *dar-al-harb*."[22] Thus the *dhimmi* populations of Arab lands did not get the chance to taste the fruits of liberal policies envisaged, and in a few cases actually implemented, during the early part of this century, or shortly after decolonization and independence.

At mid-century a host of military coups swept the Arab world, erasing any hope for liberalizing trends to take root. And as if this were not enough, the 1979 Islamic revolution in Iran unleashed a militant fundamentalist tidal wave that shook the entire Islamic world and eclipsed the ailing authoritarian regimes and dynasties ruling over the bulk of Muslim populations.

Christians in Iran

All non-Muslim minority communities in Iran experienced a setback in 1979 following the establishment of Ayatollah Khomeini's Islamic Republic. *Dhimmi* existence returned in full force after the relaxed liberal period under the shah. Some of these minority communities, such as the Baha'is, suffered exceedingly after the fall of the shah because the mullahs (the religious leaders) regarded them as foreign agents needing to be purged, which they did mercilessly. Among Iran's Christians, who make up about 1 percent of the total population, the traditional Eastern churches native to the country did not undergo as radical a deterioration in their position as the Anglican and Protestant churches of more recent vintage. Also adversely affected were Catholic monastic orders such as the Dominicans, who were active in Isfahan and other cities.

Since the Protestant churches have historic and ongoing links with missions coming from England and the United States, and since their congregations often include some first-generation converts from Islam, their situation under the new regime became dire. Legal recognition of their status was revoked, and their schools, hospitals, and other institutions were confiscated and shut down. The Anglican bishop Hassan Deqani-Tafti, himself a convert from Islam, now resides in exile in London. *Ridda*, or apostasy, the term given to the free choice by a Muslim to convert to another faith, is punishable by death in Iran.[23] Other features of *dhimmi* segregation in the country include the requirement that shops owned by Christians display a sign saying "Religious Minority" so as to warn a Muslim not to purchase goods polluted by the infidel. Similarly, Christian school children have their own drinking fountains to prevent the "contamination" of the Muslim pupils.[24]

A booklet distributed in the early 1990s by the Iranian embassy in Beirut purported to show how well Iran's Christians were being treated. In fact, all the photographs of churches included in its pages reveal run-down buildings that have not been maintained for decades. The booklet also contains, as a way of emphasizing their patriotism, lists of Iranian Christians who fought and died for Iran in the Iran-Iraq war of the 1980s. Noteworthy is the fact that none of these listed Christians has a military rank even of corporal, which is indicative of the discrimination to which such groups continue to be subjected.

The Copts in Egypt

By far the largest Christian community in the Middle East is the Egyptian Copts. Historically the Copts have been the quintessential *dhimmis*, both because of the way they have consistently been mistreated and because of their way of responding to this abuse. Their actual numbers are a matter of wide dispute. One reliable source, writing in the mid-1960s, gave an estimate of around 4 million. Most Copts today insist that their numbers are more than twice this, while the Egyptian government's official census figures for 1986 put them at no more than 2.8 million. An estimate given by an independent source in 1989 was 5.2 million.[25] This unresolved controversy involving disparities in the millions points to the marginalization to which the Coptic community has been subjected over the centuries.

As with any *dhimmi* condition, there have been both bad times and worse times for Egypt's Copts, and never a free existence. In the tenth and eleventh centuries they underwent periods of severe persecution under a series of cruel rulers. They had already been suffering from the added burden of a property tax, the *kharaj*, over and above the compulsory *jizya*. Matters eased a bit during the Crusades, when the Monophysite Copts were barred by the Latins occupying Jerusalem from making pilgrimages to the holy city; this convinced the Muslims that the Copts were truly different from the invading European Christians. In the early nineteenth century, under Mohammad Ali's rule, conditions improved further, and by the second half of the century Copts could even be found in high positions in government. A shared feeling of nationalism propelled the Copts to support the 1882 rebellion of Urabi Pasha, an officer and an Egyptian nationalist.

This Coptic nationalistic fervor, however, eventually received a jolt when the struggle for independence began increasingly to take on Islamic and anti-Christian undertones. A rekindled Coptic embrace of European protection ensued. Boutros Pasha Ghali, grandfather of the recent UN secretary general Boutros Boutros Ghali, became prime minister under British rule, only to be assassinated in 1920 by a zealous Muslim.[26] By 1952, when a group of army officers led by Gamal Abdel Nasser staged a successful coup, the Copts were feeling very insecure. The officers harbored sympathies for—and in the case of the young Anwar Sadat, ties to—the Muslim Brotherhood movement. Coptic fears after 1952 were reflected in, among other things, a plummeting birth rate.[27]

Egypt soon went the way of other "secular republics" sprung from military coups in the Arab world. The cancellation of religious tribunals meant that the Copts became subject to a law that could not escape being influenced by Islamic *shari'a*. This development spelled a reinforcement—instead of an easing—of second-class status for the Copts. One paradoxical consequence of the secularizing, egalitarian trend was that the study of the Koran became compulsory for everyone attending the state schools. To make matters worse, Nasser's brand of socialism expropriated lands, nationalized businesses and industries, and introduced land reforms that destroyed landowners and prosperous businessmen who were mostly Christian.[28] Meanwhile, the Muslim Brotherhood (precursor to today's *Gama'a Al-Islamiyya*) was busy in the 1950s and 1960s dynamiting cinemas, restaurants, night clubs, and other "monuments of Western decadence," and killing innocent civilians in the process. According to the hard-line Sayyed Qutb, who took over the leadership of the Brotherhood, "Islam could not accept any compromise with other religions or political doctrines concerning the way of life in a Muslim community."[29] Being a total system of life, Islam had to be applied in full, and this was a religious duty for the believer. Qutb was put to death by Nasser in 1965.

Today's confrontation between the Mubarak regime and the *Gama'a* is an extension of the earlier falling out between the Brotherhood and the revolutionary officers who seized power in the 1950s. In this ongoing tug of war between an authoritarian Arab regime and local militant fanatics, non-Muslim communities like the Copts often become caught in the crossfire and are abused by both sides. This phenomenon of being caught in the middle is not restricted to Egypt; it has occurred with varying degrees of severity in nearly every Muslim country where minority non-Muslim communities live, such as Syria, Iraq, Iran, Pakistan, and the Palestinian territories.

After Nasser came to power there was a steady exodus of Christians, mostly Syrians and Lebanese who had made Egypt their residence for decades if not generations. The Copts as a community retreated south to Upper Egypt, where their ancestral villages lie. They were soon followed by Islamic fundamentalists, who set up shop in those same towns, and periodic attacks on the Copts and the burning of their churches have continued unabated to this day. Pressures have mounted to a point that each year several hundred Copts are estimated to pass over to Islam in order to escape persecution.[30] The same people who torch Coptic churches in Upper Egypt also spray bullets at busloads of Western tourists in Cairo and around the archaeological sites, as happened in Luxor in November 1997. To these extremists of the *Gama'a* there is a clear association between the "crusading infidels" from abroad (tourists) and the local infidels (Copts).[31]

In light of the recurring incidents of persecution against Christians in Egypt, perpetrated not only by the *Gama'a* but by government authorities as well, it is somewhat odd to read in one otherwise respectable source that recent restrictions placed on Coptic Pope Shenooda III by the Egyptian government ought to be understood as "a balancing act to avoid increasing outbursts from Muslim extremists who had made vilifying charges against him."[32] Some truth may reside in this interpretation, but in no way does it absolve the authorities from responsibility for a number of reported incidents of extreme harassment directed against Christians, in particular those who are new converts from Islam.[33] Traditional Coptic reticence and ambivalence regarding Western attention to their plight can only be explained as a typical, and predictable, *dhimmi* reaction of caution and circumlocution. When mounting concern in Washington for the condition of the Copts was brought to the attention of Pope Shenooda by expatriate Copts residing in the United States, his reply was blunt and simple: "This is purely an internal matter to be resolved in Egypt, not in America."[34]

Christians in Sudan and Saudi Arabia

Things get nastier for Christians in two neighboring fundamentalist Islamic states, Sudan and Saudi Arabia. Since the mid-1950s, and then again since the early 1980s, the ethnically African and largely Christian and animist region of southern Sudan has been locked in a bitter civil war with the predominantly Arab and Islamic north, mainly over Khartoum's bid to impose *shari'a* law on the non-Muslims of the south. In 1983 the Khartoum authorities—a radical Sunni Muslim regime—transformed the country's penal code into a carbon copy of the *shari'a* and began a campaign to implement it by force in the south. Whippings for various offenses, amputation of limbs for theft, beheading for capital crimes or *ridda* (apostasy), and the denial of testimonial competence in law courts for non-Muslims and women—these are but the highlights of this *shari'a* justice. Torture, forced conversions of children to Islam, sale of women and children into slavery, deliberate starvation, and occasional crucifixions were, and still are, the standard practices of the Sudanese government and its security forces. Details of these brutal policies aimed at the country's Christians, who make up between 3 and 4 percent of the population, have been steadily surfacing in the West.[35]

Behind the strategy of forced Islamization looms the figure of Hassan Al-Turabi, the Western-trained leader of Sudan's Islamic National Front, a fundamentalist organization bent on imposing a militant Islam throughout the country and beyond. Turabi studied law in Britain and France and, in a typical application of the classical Islamic dualism, took all that is useful from the Abode of War in order to use it to fight that same realm. When writing about *shari'a*, Turabi employs a deliberate "style of generalization and evasion" intended to obfuscate the precise impact of strict Islamic legal precepts on women and non-Muslims.[36] Matters remain vague regarding the precise rights and obligations of non-Muslim citizens of the state. Can these citizens, for example, express their disapproval of specific provisions of *shari'a*, and will they be exempted from adhering to them in that case? If *shari'a* is the ultimate legal yardstick, as Turabi wishes it to be, then clearly the answer would be no.[37] As one informed analyst puts it, "although observers may differ in their assessment of the various social, economic, and political causes of the north-south conflict in the Sudan, all would agree that the imposition of Shari'a is a major, if not the primary, cause of the current phase of the civil war."[38]

One place where *shari'a* is indisputably—and brutally—imposed is Saudi Arabia. Never has there been a case of such flagrant human rights abuses and systematic religious persecution coupled with a stony silence on the part of Washington and other Western democracies. The reason is painfully glaring: extensive oil interests. The Saudi dynasty is classified as "moderate" in

Washington because it acquiesces to the demands of U.S. foreign policy in the Middle East. At home, however, the same dynasty is anything but moderate on every level that counts in the daily lives of its citizens. Reluctance to shine the spotlight on the appalling record of Saudi religious persecution turned into active compliance on the part of the U.S. government with official Saudi demands that Christian religious services in embassy and consular compounds and at American military installations in the kingdom be discontinued.[39] The Saudi dynasty, whose Bedouin origins lie embedded in the strict puritanical Islam of Wahhabism, has to contend with the added responsibility of being custodian over Islam's holiest shrines. Both these reasons breed a sustained momentum toward extremism. The victims, in addition to the Saudi people, are the thousands of expatriate Christians (mostly Indians, Filipinos, Koreans, and Westerners) temporarily residing and working in the kingdom.

If the Sudanese government has been trying to apply *shari'a* by force on its non-Muslim population in the south of the country, the Saudi state already imposes it with an iron fist on everyone within its borders, whether native or foreign, Muslim or non-Muslim. Documented cases of detention, beatings, torture, forced confessions, amputations, indefinite imprisonment, and beheading are plentiful, and many of them involve Christian expatriates and foreign migrant workers. Notorious among these cases are the imprisonment, torture, and execution in the early and mid-1990s of a number of Filipino Christians for organizing or attending secret prayer services. Information about these persecutions came to light when a Filipino named Donato Lama, imprisoned on similar charges, was released.[40]

Similar abuse, though usually to a much lesser degree, occurs in the Gulf States, especially Kuwait. There some of the educational and medical establishments owe their origins to abortive Christian missions. One statistic from 1989 placed the indigenous Christians living along the entire Gulf coast from Kuwait to Oman at 150, with another 400 in Yemen.[41] This is minuscule compared to the tens of thousands of foreign Christians strewn throughout the Emirates and Saudi Arabia. Undoubtedly, rapid development of these traditional societies accompanied by Westernization precipitated inevitable backlashes among the rulers and populace at large, which led to severe instances of repression and persecution directed at Christians.

However, with Saudi Arabia a homegrown culture of intolerance and exclusion plays the leading role in fueling persecutions. Even the *shari'a* category of *aman*, meaning the temporary license defining the terms and conditions of the stay of nonbelievers in the Abode of Islam,[42] is flouted by the Riyadh authorities in favor of going after Christians merely for expressing their basic beliefs in private. The *Mutawa'a*, or religious police, make it their job to go around sniffing for the slightest evidence of Christian worship in order to squash it and punish those responsible.

And the Saudi kingdom does not confine its obsessive vigilance for a purer Islam to its portion of the Arabian peninsula. Like Iran and Sudan, Saudi Arabia is in the business of exporting Islamic fanaticism and all the trouble that comes with it to other parts of the Middle East and anywhere else that offers fertile soil. Unlike Sudan and to a lesser extent Iran, however, the Saudis operate with a version of Islamization that is guided by a geopolitical subtext. The aim is to make of the kingdom a regional power broker. This could entail using financial clout to meddle in regional disputes, support one side against another, destabilize certain regimes, compete with other Islamic states like Shiite Iran for influence, and so on.

But invariably with the Saudis there exists an anti-Christian agenda beneath all this. In Lebanon the Saudis have their man, former prime minister Rafiq Hariri, who dips at will into their coffers in order to promote a Sunni Muslim preponderance at the expense of both Christians and Shiites. In Uganda the Saudis supported the repugnant regime of Idi Amin, among whose atrocities was persecution of the country's Christians. The same holds true of Saudi support for the Sudanese government. In the Horn of Africa the Saudis backed the despotic Muslim regime of Siad Barre in Somalia against Christian Ethiopia. Muslim rebels in the southern Philippines were financed by the Saudis out of pure fanaticism because the rest of the Philippines is Christian. And we must not forget the role Saudi money played in the late 1960s to starve the Biafrans (mostly Christians) out of existence.

Palestinian Christians

According to reliable sources, the number of Christians today in Israel (including Jerusalem), the West Bank, and Gaza is somewhere in the neighborhood of 150,000,[43] about 7,000 of whom are in Jerusalem.[44] Back in 1947, there were more than 45,000 Christians of all denominations in the Old City and its environs, but by 1967 they had declined to 28,000.[45] The trend is clearly toward an emptying out of the city's Christian population: "emigration has for some time threatened to reduce Jerusalem to a museum of Christian history rather than the center of a living Christian community."[46]

Informed Palestinians often speak about an identity crisis that afflicts Christians. Being neither Muslim nor Jewish, they feel they are not accepted by either of the two larger communities. Being Palestinian, they can never be a part of Israel even if some of them carry the Israeli passport. And being Christian Arabs, they are not easily integrated into the wider Christian world. Many of them face economic difficulties, in particular land seizures and arbitrary practices of hiring and firing, and experience obstacles in trying to get a higher education (only 5 percent of the students at Israeli universities are Arab). Add to these factors the rising tide of an assortment of fundamentalisms—Muslim, Jewish, and evangelical Christian—and the pressures to emigrate become very palpable.[47] And of course it does not help for the upper hierarchy of the largest Christian denomination, the Eastern Orthodox, to consist of ethnic Greeks, thereby creating a linguistic and cultural rift between the church authorities and their Arab congregations.

By and large, Palestinian Christians have tended to find in Palestinian nationalism a meeting ground with their Palestinian Muslim counterparts. This point of intersection between the two communities, however, has all too often been mythologized by intellectuals and clergymen, who never tire of insisting that harmony has always prevailed between Muslims and Christians in Palestine.[48] Obviously, this sort of emphasis is motivated primarily by a desire to maintain a unified political stand vis-à-vis Israel. But it also stems from a deeper *dhimmi* psychological state: the urge to find—or to imagine and fabricate if need be—a common cause with the ruling majority in order to dilute the existing religious differences and perhaps ease the weight of Political Islam's inevitable discrimination.

The history of Palestinian Christianity has, for the most part, been no different from that of *dhimmi* Christianity throughout the Levant—the Christians of Lebanon being a notable exception. Without Israel in the picture, the problem of *dhimmi* subservience would still exist for Palestinian Christians. And even with Israel as the perceived and proclaimed enemy of all Palestinians, reducing Muslims and Christians alike to second-class status, according to them, the specter of *dhimmi* inferiorization continues to lurk just below the surface. Palestinians, particularly Christians, get very defensive when they are confronted with reports of persecution of Christians by Muslim Palestinians.[49] Their reflexive attitude is to dismiss such reports as lies inspired by Israeli disinformation.

Although Palestinian Christianity, like most other Middle Eastern Christianity, is of the *dhimmi* variety, it differs from the rest in that it is marked by a singular obsession: the Arab-Israeli conflict and the Palestinian problem. This fixation relates to the improbable thesis that *all* regional instances of persecution of Christians would be alleviated, if not halted altogether, if the Palestinian problem were solved. The mythical idea behind this view is that everything was fine between Christians and Muslims in the region until Israel came along. The very presence of Israel and the often unconditional support it receives from the West constitute such an affront to Muslims—

according to this interpretation—that in the absence of a just solution of the Palestinian problem, Christians will always be at risk of reprisals from Muslims, who continue whether willfully or unconsciously to perceive the West as Christian.

Two flaws plague this Christian Palestinian interpretation. First, as a blanket reductionism it does not account for the convoluted nuances of a region like the Middle East. Removing Israel from the equation and satisfying the Palestinians beyond their wildest dreams would not eliminate the tendency toward violence against non-Muslims inherent in Political Islam. And second, the priorities implied in this interpretation are not shared by the vast majority of the region's Christians, whether *dhimmi* or free. The largest and most significant Christian communities of the Arab world are those of Egypt and Lebanon, and they simply do not espouse the same set of anxieties as the relatively small and uni-directionally traumatized Palestinian Christians. In other words, the Christians of the wider region know better than to entertain fantasies that all will be well with them once the Palestinian problem is laid to rest and Israel is put in its place, or wished out of existence. Moreover, these other Middle Eastern Christian communities do not exhibit the same discomfort with the Old Testament as the Palestinian Christians, who suffer from a misguided confusion of history, theology, and current politics. They cannot recite certain Psalms or read the Old Testament stories without making immediate associations with today's state of Israel and the Arab-Israeli conflict. Palestinian Christians are free to think like this, but they should be aware that other Christians in the region do not share their outlook.

The Free Native Christian Communities

Free native Christians, that is, Christians who have managed to live free of the shackles of dhimmitude, are the second distinct group of Christians indigenous to Islamic regions. They are fewer in numbers than the *dhimmi* Christians. In the Middle East—indeed, anywhere between Morocco and Indonesia—these free native Christians are to be found only in Lebanon and Cyprus. The importance of freedom as the principal indicator of both identity and historical conduct becomes apparent when these free Christian communities are compared to the *dhimmi* Christians of the rest of the Levant (Syria, Iraq, Jordan, and the Palestinian areas).

Levantine *dhimmis* are generally better off than their counterparts in Egypt and further afield. Even this relatively modest improvement in their situation sets them markedly apart from the other *dhimmi* communities. In Jordan, for example, it is due in part to conscious efforts of the Hashemite dynasty to provide the country's Christians with better economic opportunities, make available to them certain political and military appointments, and accept their upward social mobility. In Syria and Iraq, the minority and nominally secular Ba'thist regimes assume an opportunistic attitude with respect to Islam and therefore often find it in their interests to ease the tight grip on Christians by relying on them in sensitive political and military posts. Consequently, the little and precarious freedom these otherwise *dhimmi* Levantine Christians are allowed now and then (though it is never backed by legal or democratic institutions) is greatly appreciated by them and regarded as a forward leap.[50] By contrast, if the hard-won free existence of Lebanon's Christians is curtailed at all—as has been steadily happening since 1975—the community views it as tantamount to a historical catastrophe.

Maronites and Other Christians in Lebanon

Despite the setbacks in recent years, today's beleaguered Christians of Lebanon continue to be freer than any of the other Christian communities native to the Middle East. Much about Lebanon is unique. The country's Christian minority is reliably estimated to make up between 40 and 45 percent of the population.[51] The largest subgroup of Lebanon's Christians, the Maronites, constitute the backbone and also the spearhead of free, native Christianity in the Middle East, and indeed in Asia and Africa. The Maronites are to Lebanon what Catholicism is to Poland and Ireland, Orthodoxy to Russia, and Shiism to Iran: there is an existential symbiosis on the deepest level between the land, especially the mountains, and the Maronite community. The Maronite reading of their history as contrasted with that of the wider Christian communities of the East—a reading shared in varying degrees by members of the other Christian communities in Lebanon—is the story of 1,400 years of resistance to the threat of dhimmitude. One by one, the other Christian communities of the region succumbed to Islamic rule and forfeited their freedom; only the Christians of Lebanon, namely the Maronites and those who threw in their lot with them, managed, with great difficulties and suffering, to retain their freedom.

These free Christians of Lebanon see the roots of the violence perpetrated upon them entrenched firmly in the creeds of Political Islam. Prominent stations of violence throughout Political Islam's history include: the assassinations of the early caliphs, culminating in the murder of Ali and the Sunni-Shiite split; the strange cult of the Assassins in Persia, going back to Hassan Sabbah of Qom in the eleventh century; the Fedayeen, or direct descendants of the Assassins, who also employed narcotics, brainwashing, poisoned daggers, and physical elimination to unleash mayhem on the unsuspecting camps of the Crusaders; the esoteric Ismailites of Persia and their frequent use of violence; and, in modern times, Hassan al-Banna of the Muslim Brotherhood in Egypt, Ayatollah Khomeini's Islamic revolution in Iran, the Taliban and Osama bin Laden in Afghanistan, Khattab and Basayev in Chechnya, Hezbollah in Lebanon, Hassan al-Turabi and the government of al-Bashir in Sudan, Abu Sayyaf in Mindanao, and the GIA (Armed Islamic Group) in Algeria. An inherent dialectic of violence emerges that seems to sustain both the established order of Political Islam and the various extremist offshoots periodically spawned as a reaction to particular manifestations of this established order. In such an environment, free Christianity, where it exists, must of necessity experience rough sailing. Political Islam's propensity to violence is not simply a reaction to external threats, although such incursions do aggravate the latent tendency and whip it into a frenzy.

Yet Lebanon's free Christians, particularly the Maronites, were always openly proud of their associations with the West, never slinking away for fear of the consequences. And these carefully cultivated ties were not confined to the political and economic domains; they extended to encompass matters of the intellect and the spirit. During the Crusades, the Maronites entered doctrinal communion with the Roman Catholic Church and were officially recognized by the Pope. They fought alongside the Crusaders against the Mamluk occupiers. As a result, the persecution they had been enduring under Islamic occupation was intensified; churches and monasteries were burned with greater frequency. But the Maronites held on and, in the process, developed a unique blend of monastic and mercantile prowess that left its special imprint on Lebanon.[52]

At the time of Sultan Selim I's conquest of Syria and Lebanon in the early sixteenth century, the local Christians—Maronites and others—constituted a good 30 percent of the total population of those two countries. (Muslims had become a majority in the Levant around 1400 as a result of the steady erosion of Christian communities throughout the east.[53]) Later, in the nineteenth century, and on the eve of being attacked in 1840, the Maronites numbered 140,000 and were well armed.[54] They had reached half a million at the outbreak of the First World War, but owing to a devastating famine and Ottoman persecution their numbers declined, with close to 100,000 dying during the war years and tens of thousands emigrating.[55]

Dhimmitude could not secure a foothold in Lebanon until the opportunity provided by the turmoil of the Lebanon war, which stretched from 1975 to 1990. In terms of religious persecution, the war involved classic manifestations of attacks on unarmed groups and the burning down of places of worship for no reason other than that they belonged to another religion. All sides were involved in this, but a more careful examination of events and patterns reveals a far greater portion of incidents in which Christians were victimized and compelled to go on the defensive to ward off recurring assaults. One authoritative Western source documents eight out of ten massacre victims during the war in Lebanon as having been Christian.[56] Scores of Christian churches were burned and destroyed; dozens of villages with exclusively or predominantly Christian inhabitants met the same fate.

The years 1975–1976 and 1983–1985 witnessed the worst atrocities of a sectarian nature, and in both instances Christians, particularly Maronites, bore the brunt of the attacks. Monks and civilians alike were killed by an assortment of Palestinian, Syrian, local Muslim, and imported mercenary attackers. In mixed areas like Tripoli and West Beirut, those Christians who were unable to leave were subjected to a campaign of terror that parallels anything to be found elsewhere in the sordid annals of religious persecution. Forced teaching of the Koran in some places, repeated assaults on the persons and property of individuals and families, widespread pillage and plunder, bombing of religious institutions and places of worship, and verbal insults often terminating in physical violence—these are some of the more common forms of abuse directed at Christians in isolated neighborhoods.

Surprisingly, in light of Lebanon's recent dark years and their aftermath, in 1997 a seventy-seven-page U.S. Department of State special report on Christian religious freedom around the world devoted just half a page to Lebanon and said nothing about the daily pressures to which Christians continue to be subjected.[57] Now it is probably true that if you assemble in a single room in Lebanon any six clergymen representing the six main religious communities in the country, they will differ on many things, but one item they will agree upon is the absence in Lebanon of religious persecution, in the sense of the violation of every person or group's right to religious liberty and worship. Leaving matters at that, however, can be highly misleading. While no one interferes with a Lebanese Christian's right, alone or in community, to pray and worship as he or she pleases, subtle and cumulative measures of intimidation and discrimination are deliberately being brought to bear upon the Christian community. Over time, these will bring about the same results as crude and outright persecution.

In short, a relentless campaign of Islamization, orchestrated by prominent figures within the Beirut authorities with the blessings of outside powers, has been under way for some time in Lebanon. If left unchecked, this campaign will usher in the hitherto avoided state of dhimmitude so detested by the country's Christians. Signs of this creeping Islamization-leading-to-dhimmitude are already in evidence: demographic tampering, as in the case of the 1994 Naturalization Decree, which brought on board nearly 300,000 Muslims, roughly 10 percent of Lebanon's population; endless obstacles placed in the way of a return of displaced Christians to their ravaged villages; the minutest of financial trickles allocated by the government for rebuilding or renovating destroyed churches and homes; an unhampered rise in Saudi influence via former prime minister Rafiq Hariri, paralleled by an increase in Iranian influence through the unfettered activities of Hezbollah; wide-ranging real estate purchases in traditionally Christian areas by wealthy Muslims with foreign connections; and a persistent policy of diminishing Christian representation and effectiveness in the country's sensitive political posts.

Indicative of the atmosphere of belligerence with which Christians increasingly have to contend is the coordinated outcry that met a speech delivered in March 1997 at the St. Joseph University in Beirut by the rector of that institution, Father Selim Abou, S.J. In his talk, Abou spoke candidly of the abstraction of "the Arab nation" and the amalgamation in the collective unconscious of the words "Arab" and "Muslim" that much of the ideological discourse of the day tends to bring about. He went on to make clear that such concepts "misrepresent" both Muslims and Christians by tending to dissolve into the Muslim Arab legacy the distinct contribution of the Christians of the Orient. Such Christians, he said, cannot appropriate the Arab historic legacy on the same terms as their fellow Muslim citizens. He then mentioned "communitarian pluralism" entailing "cultural diversity" and lamented that "it is forbidden to speak about this pluralism lest one be accused of sectarianism."[58] A bold yet innocuous speech of this sort was sufficient to elicit the harshest retorts (coupled with thinly veiled threats) from an assortment of politicians, journalists, commentators, Arabists, Islamists, and loyalists to the Syrian master across the border.

Does Islamic Moderation Exist?

The efforts of Western leaders to deal with Islam as a foreign-policy issue are impaired by an ongoing crisis: the crisis (or the mirage) of Islamic moderation. To state it simply, Islamic moderation when it exists usually has a short life span. On the whole, liberal-minded individual Muslims are a pathetic and lonely lot. Sooner or later, if they survive physically, these liberal Muslims discover that it is almost impossible to remain outspokenly critical in an environment governed by the writ of Political Islam. Either they have to stop speaking out or at least tone down their rhetoric appreciably, or they have to pack up and head for freer pastures—meaning the West. Often so-called moderate Islamic regimes find they are compelled to restrain, or even clamp down on, critical liberal voices in their midst in order to placate a more dangerous and determined extremist faction or fringe. The pull toward repression is very strong in an Islamic setting, and the ideological rationalizations for this behavior are all there to be resorted to when needed. Lone liberal Muslims here and there, especially at "dialogue conferences" or among exile émigré communities in the West, will speak of the need to reinterpret doctrines like the "Two Abodes" dualism, the *dhimmi* designation, the fusing of religion and politics, and so on. The Islamic establishment by and large remains conservative and unyielding, however, refusing to entertain seriously such reformist outlooks.

The liberal voices eventually discover how unrepresentative of Islamic realities they really are. *They* may discover it, but their Western audience, out of either ignorance or wishful thinking or both, more often than not doesn't—to the detriment of a sound foreign policy. "Actually Existing Islam," as Salman Rushdie calls it (and he of all people ought to know), exhibits "granite, heartless certainties" (again, Rushdie's words). It can be defined as "the political and priestly power structure that presently dominates and stifles Muslim societies."[59] It is what I have chosen to refer to in this essay as Political Islam.

Western excitement about the emergence of presumed moderates within this power structure ought to be tempered, for three reasons. First, such moderates are likely to have little staying power. Second, what one is seeing might be a studied façade, a kind of elaborate Islamic disinformation; Shiite or Alawite Islam, for example, can be very esoteric and often exhibit *taqiyya*, or "precautionary dissimulation." Third, misleading analogies with the historical development of Christianity are ever present, usually advanced by academics with a positivist bent of mind who apply a determinism of progress to everything, including Political Islam. The idea they advance is that Islam today is where Christianity was in the Middle Ages; it is slowly heading for a more benign presentation of itself. Such an analogy is flawed on two counts: because it compares apples with oranges, so to speak, and because, even if it were valid, the time scale would be prohibitive, thus rendering the point irrelevant for current foreign-policy debates.[60]

Dialogue with Islam

The travails of Islamic moderation also create problems for those in the West seeking to engage in meaningful dialogue with Islam. In the abstract, almost any form of dialogue is preferable to the complete severing of contacts. However, dialogue with Islam requires clearly defined goals and a clear sense of the built-in, and therefore inescapable, limitations of such a dialogue. Both the clarity of goals and the awareness of limits are woefully lacking in the kinds of contacts that pass for dialogue between Christians and Muslims nowadays. When the churches of the West, in particular the mainline churches, engage in dialogue with representatives of the Islamic faith, the outcome, at best, is usually a form of least-common-denominator ecumenism expressed in a string of platitudes: we are both Abrahamic–monotheistic religions; we worship the same God; the Christ of Christian faith and the Jesus (Issa) of the Koran are really one and the same; and so on. Aside from being essentially dishonest, such platitudes serve nothing but the *political* agendas of those exchanging them. This is dialogue for the sake of dialogue. It is politicized dialogue. By serving to legitimate a repressive status quo, this form of dialogue is providing Muslim authorities, whether religious or political, with tangible political gains and an image facelift. To add insult to injury, the dialogue process is often predicated, on the Christian side, on an assumption that the only valid form of Christian existence in Islamic settings is the *dhimmi* one. This is tantamount not only to condoning persecution but to canceling out a rich and entirely other experience in history: that of free and dignified Christian existence in a Muslim environment.

Dialogue between two world views riddled with glaring incompatibilities has clear limitations. It must have as its modest objective the honest and open presentation of each position *as it is in itself*, with little regard paid to points of intersection (real or imaginary), and with the aim of increasing understanding of the other. This would also open the way for "witness through dialogue," which is what the Christian churches ought to be doing anyway in a situation like this. And caution needs to be exercised lest contacts at conferences with Muslim liberal intellectuals living and writing in the West be interpreted as contacts with Rushdie's "Actually Existing Islam." As an occasion for witness, dialogue above all must entail compassion that does not degenerate into patronizing, comprehension that does not stop at admonition, and an honest exchange that is not satisfied with platitudes. Some environments are just unsuitable for constructive Christian-Muslim dialogue. Lebanon, for instance, is notoriously bad for two reasons. First, Lebanese Muslims, in particular the Sunnis, are generally poor representatives of their faith. Far more knowledgeable and authoritative Muslims are to be found in places like Egypt's Al-Azhar, or in Tunisia and Morocco. Also, everything in Lebanon tends to become politicized, and this includes attempts at dialogue. Very often, under the guise of Christian-Muslim dialogue in a place like Lebanon, political points are being scored to promote narrow local objectives by one side or the other.

If mere platitudes for their own sake are to be avoided, the benefits of discovering real points of intersection and common ground must not be lost. In the realm of interreligious dialogue, the Roman Catholic Church as a worldwide institution ought to be considering how to apply its highly successful approach of enculturation, that is, of adapting the presentation of the same universal message to the particular historical, cultural, and temperamental givens of the target audience while assimilating in the process whatever is salvageable. Perhaps creative thinking in this context should go toward establishing a "Church of Islam" as the ultimate mediator in any meaningful dialogue with that faith. A great deal that is of substance in Islam is fully compatible with Christianity, and so an open-minded Muslim willing to explore seriously the spiritual territory beyond his or her traditional faith might find it more congenial to interact with, and maybe enter, a church that already incorporates many familiar ingredients from the native tradition and faith.[61]

Yet any dialogue, no matter how rewarding, will not eliminate the virulence of Political Islam. Both Christianity and Islam have had bloody histories. It hardly makes sense to try to determine which of the two is less bloody. The central difference between the two religions, however, becomes apparent when one looks at their founders. Taking into account the last 150 years of textual criticism, from Renan's quest for the historical Jesus to today's postmodern theologies, it is still possible to distill a sentence or two on each of the two founding figures that would describe accurately their very different attitudes toward violence. The glaring difference that emerges explains why in one system there are recurring and sincere attempts at self-accountability and acknowledgment of guilt, whereas in the other system there is a near total absence of this whole dimension, which, in fact, many Muslims regard as a sign of weakness.[62] To use Ruth Benedict's classifications in her book *Patterns of Culture*: Islam comes out of a shame culture, whereas the West is a guilt culture. Guilt cultures have shown they have a better chance of engaging in critical self-examination leading to self-rejuvenation and reform from within. Built into Christianity and retaining a strong imprint on post-Christian secular culture is a mechanism that, because of the very nature of the founder of this religion, causes people who have misbehaved to pause, feel ashamed, take stock, and rectify bad behavior. But a religious system utterly lacking in the ability to examine behavior and acknowledge guilt represents a daunting anomaly in international relations.

Toward a Conceptual Framework for Policy

An attempt to distill a conceptual profile of Political Islam would yield the following:

- The total outlook on life exhibits a number of rigid givens, including inalterability of the sacred text and a jurisprudential infrastructure that sanctions violence (for example, *jihad* against the infidel, and death to the *murtadd* or apostate).
- Religion and politics are fused on all levels.
- The "us and them" dualism of the Two Abodes leads to a more or less streamlined (and negative) view of "the other" that transcends whatever intra-Islamic variations and manifestations do exist. In other words, there is as it were an Islamic foreign policy.
- Islamic moderation tends to be weak and short-lived. If the system shows evidence of leniency and flexibility, it invariably comes under threat from the inside and is compelled to harden.
- The historical record of the treatment of non-Muslim minorities is abysmal, notwithstanding romanticized presentations of Political Islam as tolerant. This points to the crisis of pluralism in an Islamic context.
- Ideological underpinnings, and the appeal to the founder, seem to preclude the possibility of acknowledging guilt.
- Serious and responsible dialogue is virtually unobtainable. The only purpose Political Islam sees for engaging in contacts is tactical, entailing political gain or a temporary respite or advantage.
- No real, lasting peace but only temporary truces are contemplated.
- The system is reluctant or unable to reciprocate positive gestures with the West; for example, the treatment of Christians in Islamic countries is generally quite inferior to the treatment of Muslims in the West.
- Evidence of regressive radicalization is mounting: the rising tide of Islamic fundamentalism and militancy; Ayatollah Khomeini's *wilayat al-faqih* (guardianship of the juris-consult), a recipe for absolute power in the hands of one man; the lurking internal threat to Turkey's Kemalist experiment in secularism; the fundamentalist mayhem in Algeria; and the seeming inability of the Wahhabi Saudis to contemplate introducing greater freedom and openness.
- A paranoid disposition (bred by the Two Abodes dualism) convinced that there is a perpetual conspiracy by "the different other" to attack, undermine, and subjugate. Even if it were only half-true, this profile would present a bleak picture. Painfully apparent is the great disservice done by the flawed and romanticized dialogue that has encouraged many to project subconsciously onto Political Islam their own Judeo-Christian or secular humanist values. Since Political Islam has a unified view of the outer non-Muslim world irrespective of whether individual Islamic states adhere to it consistently at any given point in time, this

necessitates a corresponding conceptual framework on the part of the
United States, and the West generally, to serve as the basis for a coordinated policy response. Following are six suggested items for such a
policy response.

1. Cultivate a political culture in Washington and elsewhere in the
   West that is sensitive to matters of religious persecution, specifically
   to the fortunes of non-Muslim minority communities scattered
   throughout the Islamic world. This would be similar to the heightened awareness that now exists regarding human rights issues.[63]
2. Try to move away from an obsession with the primacy of socioeconomic factors to a deeper appreciation of personal, communal, existential, metaphysical, and ideological issues. A funny thing happened on the way to victory in the Cold War: the West defeated
   Communism all right, but not before embracing and eventually
   swallowing whole the Marxist scale of values that gives precedence
   in any analysis to socioeconomic and political causes.
3. Pursue a long-range policy of reducing dependence on anything
   the Islamic world has to offer—mainly natural resources and oil.
   Not only is there a compelling environmental imperative to do
   this, but there is also a political imperative, one of national security. Reducing dependence is not the same as disengagement, nor
   is the latter realistic or desirable in today's complex and integrated world. Diversification, viable alternatives, not putting all
   the eggs in one basket—this is forward thinking for the twenty-
   first century.
4. Since a stark "us and them" dualism pervades the thinking of Political Islam about the rest of the world, responding with a taste of the
   same medicine from time to time could be healthful. As regards specific points of crisis and confrontation, a case-by-case approach favoring separation (instead of integration) whenever feasible seems
   advisable. For example, the United States ought to push for an independent southern Sudan, promote a federal solution for both
   Lebanon and Cyprus, and assist in peaceful population transfers out
   of areas where native Christians or minority Muslims are experiencing mounting persecution—for instance, the Christians fleeing religious and ethnic violence in Timor, the Christians of Syria and Iraq
   after Saddam Hussein passes from the scene if matters should turn
   ugly, or isolated pockets of Muslims, say in parts of the Balkans. It
   should not be overlooked that *all* minorities, even Muslim ones (for

example, the Shiites of Saudi Arabia), are unprotected under Islamic regimes. Whenever the principle of reciprocity can be advanced, it should be.

By and large, Muslims in the West enjoy far greater freedom than Christians do in Islamic countries. It is not advisable, then, to favor the evolution of Bosnia or Kosovo into independent states with Islamic majorities inside Europe (one Albania is enough), or the eventual unconditional inclusion of Turkey in the European Union. This is not to suggest a recipe for Europe as a "Christian Club"; it is only to say that too much intermingling, especially when Political Islam is or may be involved, could be a source of future headaches. The case of Turkey is delicate: we do not want, by excluding it, to precipitate an Islamic backlash, but then including it might bring that about as well.

5. Everyone in the West is all too aware of the dangers of proliferation of weapons of mass destruction. Currently, radical Islamic states and shadowy substate actors hostile to the West have nuisance value. But they would quickly turn into an awesome threat once they became armed with nuclear, chemical, and biological capabilities, coupled with ballistic delivery systems for states and a willingness to martyrdom for fanatic individuals and groups. It goes without saying that a heightened state of vigilance ought to be maintained at all times, and preemptive surgical operations undertaken whenever and wherever the need arises. The free and open nature of Western societies makes them especially vulnerable to acts of chemical and biological terrorism. Great emphasis needs to be put on advance warning through improved intelligence capabilities.

6. Despite the absence in Political Islam of the concept of permanent peace, the Middle East peace process needs to be vigorously revived and sustained to fruition. Objections of extremist groups like Hezbollah and Hamas notwithstanding, a successfully concluded Middle East peace would serve to reduce overall tensions in the region and beyond. It would also have a good effect on Muslim-Western relations, especially if followed by tangible economic benefits for the states and peoples of the area.

Islam is a major world religion with close to one billion followers. It is sheer illusion to think the West could devise an airtight foreign policy that would eliminate religious persecution from the world of Islam. Holding the line, exercising damage control, massaging certain crises and points of tension, responding firmly and decisively in others, salvaging what can realistically be reclaimed for freedom—these are more practical options.

In the West, and in Washington specifically, the momentous significance of the ongoing eclipse—leading over time and with the requisite level of neglect to the extinction—of free Christianity in a place like Lebanon has not been appreciated. Free Christianity fought for centuries to survive in Lebanon. Its fluctuating fortunes have acted alternately as a beacon of hope and a barometer of danger for the wider arena of *dhimmi* Christian Arabs scattered throughout the region. To ascertain this one has only to tour the various denominational and apostolic seats located throughout the greater Beirut metropolitan area and talk to the local representatives of the many Christian minorities in Arab lands. In this sense, Beirut continues to act as a listening post and a sounding board for the conditions, grievances, and aspirations of indigenous Middle Eastern Christians. In short, the freer Lebanon's Christians are, the better it is for the rest of the region's Christians. Lebanon may be peripheral in geopolitical or economic or strategic terms; it is absolutely central when the issue is freedom and religious persecution.

Future historians will record that the abandonment of Lebanon by the West in 1975, and then again after 1982, was the single most damaging blow to the fortunes of Middle Eastern, African, and Asian Christianity combined. If the West does nothing to change the situation, then from their vantage point in the distant future, these historians will also confirm that what is slowly transpiring in Lebanon today was in time comparable to the fall of Constantinople in 1453 in its impact on eastern Christianity. Perhaps one reason why the persecution of Christians is currently on the increase in Islamic settings has to do with the perceived "victory" Political Islam has scored against Lebanon's free Christianity, and the related perception of the West's impotence or indifference.

Something can still be done to keep these future historians from having to write such a devastating tale.

Notes

1. Samuel P. Huntington, *The Clash of Civilizations and the Remaking of World Order* (New York: Simon and Schuster, 1996), 254–65. For examples of a Western apologist's socioeconomic and political explanations, see John L. Esposito, *Islam and Politics*, 3rd ed. (Syracuse, N.Y.: Syracuse University Press, 1991), and *The Islamic Threat: Myth or Reality?* (Oxford: Oxford University Press, 1991).

2. Invariably, one comes across descriptions of the moderation, gentleness, and humanity of Islamic rule, and its tolerance of non-Muslims. Albert Hourani, for example, barely touches on persecutions and tends to emphasize the harmony of Christians and Jews under Islam in urban areas; see his *A History of the Arab Peoples* (Cambridge: Harvard University Press, 1991), 117–19. See also the rosy accounts by Sir Adolphus Slade (1802–1877) of the life of Christian subjects under Ottoman rule, taken from his *Records of Travel in Turkey, Greece, etc.*, published in 1832 and quoted in Bernard Lewis, *Islam in History: Ideas, People, and Events in the Middle East* (Chicago: Open Court, 1993), 69–71. This type of account, despite its defects, remains far superior to more recent ones that blame the victim for persecution; see, for example, Kenneth Cragg, *The Arab Christian: A History in the Middle East* (Louisville, Ky.: Westminster/John Knox Press, 1991). See also my review of Kragg's book in *The Beirut Review: A Journal on Lebanon and the Middle East*, no. 3 (spring 1992), 109–22.

3. Koran, sura of The Cow, 215. All English translations of Koranic verses are taken from *The Koran Interpreted*, trans. Arthur J. Arberry (Oxford: Oxford University Press, 1985).

4. Koran, sura of The Cow, 243.

5. Koran, sura of The House of Imran, 168.

6. Koran, sura of The Ranks, 3.

7. The Islamic concept of *jihad* is very different from the Christian concept of "just war." Whereas *jihad* meant spreading Islam through the sword, just war for Christians would take place only under strict conditions; for instance, it may be undertaken only as a last resort, after all peaceful means have been exhausted. For an analysis of the Christian position, see the classic work by Roland Bainton, *Christian Attitudes toward War and Peace: A Historical Survey and Critical Reevaluation* (Nashville, Tenn.: Abingdon, 1960), 91–100, on St. Augustine, for example. On *jihad*, see Bat Ye'or, *The Decline of Eastern Christianity under Islam: From 'Jihad' to Dhimmitude, 7th–20th Centuries*, trans. (from French) by Miriam Kochan and David Littman (Madison, N.J.; Fairleigh Dickinson University Press, 1996), 43–68 and 271–302. On *jihad* and just war see John Kelsay and James Turner Johnson, eds., *Just War and Jihad: Historical and Theoretical Perspectives on War and Peace in Western and Islamic Traditions* (New York: Greenwood, 1991).

8. Koran, sura of The Table, 32. See also Koran, sura of Mohammad, 3: "When you meet the unbelievers, smite their necks, then, when you have made wide slaughter among them, tie fast the bonds; then set them free, either by grace or ransom, till the war lays down its loads."

9. It is amazing how much ignorance there is of both Old and New Testaments in learned Islamic circles. One scholar called it "Islamic self-sufficiency." See William Montgomery Watt, *Muslim-Christian Encounters: Perceptions and Misperceptions* (London: Routledge, 1991), 41–44.

10. "So do not faint and call for peace; you shall be the upper ones, and God is with you, and will not deprive you of your works" (Koran, sura of Mohammad, 34). Historically, at the frontiers of the Abode of Islam there existed temporary "abodes of truce" (hybrid zones) that once again became points of violent confrontation when conditions favored

the Muslims. All the treaties with the Jewish communities of Arabia were broken by Mohammad and the early caliphs: in the year 657 the Egyptian wali concluded a truce with the Nubian Christian kingdom; the Umayyad Caliph Mu'awiyah made a temporary agreement with some Armenian princes; later, the Ottomans had to accept "coexistence" with European powers when faced with their formidable might; in 1535 Suleiman the Magnificent signed the first document recognizing peaceful relations between the Ottoman Empire and a Christian state (France); in modern times, territorial sovereignty of other states was reluctantly accepted by Muslims, which led eventually to United Nations membership; under the influence of modern liberal trends even the concept of *jihad* itself was modified for mainstream Muslims to mean an exertion of energies directed internally at the excesses of one's own passions and whims.

11. Koran, sura of The Opening, 7. For the authoritative source that offers this interpretation, see the Koranic exegesis of Tabari (c. 838–923) in Abi J'far Mohammad Bin-Jarir Al-Tabari, *Jami' Al-Bayan 'an Ta 'wil Aay Al-Qur'an*, vol. 1, 2nd ed. (Cairo: Mustafa Al-Baba Al-Halabi, 1954), 79 ff. (on the Jews) and 83 ff. (on the Christians).

12. See, as examples, Koran, sura of The Cow, 162; sura of The Table, 109 ff., and sura of Sincere Religion, 1; sura of The Bee, 85ff., respectively. On the issue of *shirk* (introducing associates in the One Godhead) the Islamic objection stems from a misunderstanding of the Christian Doctrine of the Trinity as signifying three gods. Hence Christians were often identified with *mushrikin* (those who introduce associates).

13. Koran, sura of The Cow, 255, and sura of Jonah, 98. See also sura of The Table, 81, where "Jews and idolaters" are designated the most hostile of men, while Nasareans (Christians) are labeled "the nearest to the believers": their monks and priests, when they hear the words of the Messenger, become teary-eyed and believe in God. More rigid, fundamentalist interpretations tend to identify Christians with idolaters every time. According to one authoritative interpretation, however, the absence of compulsion in religion applies only to the "People of the Book" and not to pagans and other unbelievers, where other sayings about battling infidelity take precedence.

14. These rules, known as the Pact of Omar, eventually received wide approval by doctors of Islamic jurisprudence and were initially collected and published by Ibn Qayyim Al-Jawziyya (d. 1350) in his book *Ahkam Ahl Al-Dhimma*. The best discussion to date in English translation of *dhimmi* regulations is found in Ye'or, *Decline of Eastern Christianity*, esp. 69–99.

15. For an example of a Western apologist's misleading view see John Esposito, *Islam: The Straight Path*, exp. ed. (Oxford: Oxford University Press, 1991), 36, where he says *dhimmis* paid lower taxes and enjoyed greater local autonomy and religious freedom!

16. Ye'or, *Decline of Eastern Christianity*, chap. 9.

17. Ye'or, *Decline of Eastern Christianity*, 235.

18. See Daniel Pipes, *The Hidden Hand: Middle Eastern Fears of Conspiracy* (New York: St. Martins, 1996), 128–31. Pipes documents broad-ranging instances of the recurring accusations of treason and complicity with foreign powers that Muslims periodically level at Christian Arabs. Statements by Muslim clerics often betray conspiratorial reasoning. One example comes from a speech given in 1950 in Qom, Iran, by the founder of the Feday-

een of Islam, Sayyed Mohammad Nawab-Safavi, in which he declares: "Islam is encircled by its enemies. The Cross-worshippers of the West and the Jews who really guide them have only one objective: to eliminate Islam, which is the last true religion revealed to Muhammad." This is quoted in Amir Taheri, *Holy Terror: The Inside Story of Islamic Terrorism* (London: Hutchinson, 1987), 59.

19. On the two edicts see Bernard Lewis, *The Emergence of Modern Turkey*, 2nd ed. (London: Oxford University Press, 1968), 106–8 on the Rose Pavilion/Chamber decree and 115–18 on the Imperial Rescript.

20. The figures are taken from reports dated 20 July 1860 by Western consuls stationed in Damascus and consolidated in a set of documents translated into Arabic as *Al-Muharrarat Al-Siyasiyya wa Al-Mufawadat Al-Dawliyya an Suriyya wa Lubnan* [Political documents and international negotiations on Syria and Lebanon], trans. by Philippe and Farid El-Khazen, vol. 2, 2nd ed. (Beirut: Dar Al-Ra'ed Al-Lubnani, 1983), 179–84. Other reports in this collection of documents speak of dogs being adorned with crosses by the mob and given names of famous European leaders like Napoleon and Victoria, and of Christians being forced to kneel and worship the dogs in the streets of Damascus before being slaughtered (206–10). For related accounts see also Jean-Pierre Valognes, *Vie et Mort des Chretiens D'Orient: Des origines a nos jours* (Paris: Fayard, 1995), 85, 95, 378, 646–47, 707. See also the collection of documents on these massacres included in Ye'or, *Decline of Eastern Christianity*, 401–8, and in her earlier work *The Dhimmi: Jews and Christians under Islam*, trans. (from French) by David Maisel, Paul Fenton, and David Littman (Madison, N.J.: Fairleigh Dickinson University Press, 1985), 259–78.

21. On the Bulgarian atrocities see Lewis, *Emergence of Modern Turkey*, 159, 214. On the Armenians the literature is considerable; regarding Armenians, Syriacs, and Assyro-Chaldaeans see Valognes, *Vie et Mort*, 90, 96–98, 100, 344, 359, 417–19, 435, 461–62, 742, 745, 775, 808, and 810. For related documents on the Armenians see Ye'or, *The Dhimmi*, 281–88, and *Decline of Eastern Christianity*, 192–98 and 437–46. See also Youssef Courbage and Philippe Fargues, *Christians and Jews under Islam*, trans. (from French) by Judy Mabro (London: I. B. Tauris, 1997), 109–15. According to one firsthand source, by 1965 there remained fifty-eight Syriac villages in Turkey. Massive emigration of the community first to Germany in the 1960s and then, beginning in 1967, to Sweden, where currently there are 60,000–100,000 Syriacs, reduced the Syriac Christians in Turkey today to around 2,000. (Interview with Syriac Bishop George Saliba, November 1997, Beirut.)

22. Ye'or, *Decline of Eastern Christianity*, 219–20.

23. The severe punishment for *ridda* under Islamic *shari'a* is incompatible with Article 18 of the Universal Declaration of Human Rights, which guarantees the right of every person to change his or her religion. On Middle Eastern Christians including those of Iran, see Norman A. Horner, *A Guide to Christian Churches in the Middle East: Present-Day Christianity in the Middle East and North Africa* (Elkhart, Ind.: Mission Focus, 1989), 57–58, 67, 76–77, 94–95, and 105–6 (on Iran).

24. The Beirut newspaper *Al-Nahar*'s weekly supplement of January 10, 1998, was entirely devoted to the topic of the Christians of the Middle East and displayed the provoca-

tive title: "Stop the Emigration of Oriental Christians!" It featured several articles deal-ing with the situation of the Christians in various Middle Eastern countries.

25. For conflicting statistics on the Copts of Egypt, see first Robert Brenton Betts, *Christians in the Arab East: A Political Study*, rev. ed. (Atlanta: John Knox, 1978), 60, where the 4 million figure is quoted; see also Courbage and Fargues, *Christians and Jews under Islam*, tables 197 and 203, for the government's 2.8 million figure for 1986; see also Horner, *Guide to Christian Churches*, 104–5, for the 5.2 million figure. Most specialists estimate that the Copts over the years have roughly remained close to 10 percent of the overall Egyptian population, which means today around 6 million; however, the trend is toward a reduced proportion owing to a rising Muslim birth rate and an increase in Coptic emigration. See Valognes, *Vie et Mort*, 545, where the author also says that if Coptic baptism registers are to be relied upon, the faithful in the Coptic Orthodox Church number 11 million.

26. For a brief historical survey and profile of the Coptic Christians, see Antonie Wessels, *Arab and Christian? Christians in the Middle East* (Kampen, Netherlands: Kok Pharos, 1995), 124–50 (esp. 130–39). See also Valognes, *Vie et Mort*, 216–18, 235–76, 545–50.

27. Courbage and Fargues, *Christians and Jews under Islam*, 178–79.

28. Courbage and Fargues, *Christians and Jews under Islam*, 178–79.

29. Quoted in Taheri, *Holy Terror*, 48.

30. Courbage and Fargues, *Christians and Jews under Islam*, 232 (n. 30). A much higher figure of between 15,000 and 40,000 Copts turning annually to Islam is given by Ralph Ghadban in the *Al-Nahar* weekly supplement for January 10, 1998, 5.

31. In a radio interview broadcast on the BBC World Service ("Focus on Faith," Nov. 21, 1997) an Egyptian fundamentalist named Abu-Hamzah stated ambiguously that vio-lence is justified in Egypt against tourism, but not against tourists: "They just happened to be in the line of fire, in the target area," he declared. When asked about "Moubarak," Abu-Hamzah replied that the Egyptian president only has a Muslim name and that in re-ality Mubarak is worse than the British colonialists.

32. See Horner, *Guide to Christian Churches*, 84; see also 30–31.

33. See Nina Shea, *In the Lion's Den* (Nashville, Tenn.: Broadman and Holman, 1997), 43–47, for brief accounts of actual incidents, involving the authorities, of persecution of Christians in Egypt.

34. See the article by Salaheddine Hafez whose title translates into "American 'divine providence,' and the persecution of the Copts" in Egypt's leading government-controlled newspaper *Al-Ahram* November 12, 1997; the writer makes light of the problem and ac-cuses the U.S. Congress of giving in to pressure from the combined alliance of "fanatic Christians and the Zionist-Likud Jewish lobby."

35. See, for example, Shea, *In the Lion's Den*, 31–35. On the percentage of Christians see Horner, *Guide to Christian Churches*, 114. Other sources have placed the number of Su-danese Christians as high as 10 percent of the country's population.

36. Abdullahi Ahmed An-Na'im, *Toward an Islamic Reformation: Civil Liberties, Human Rights, and International Law* (Syracuse, N.Y.: Syracuse University Press, 1990), 39; on Turabi and the *shari'a* see 39–42, and 127–33. The author is a liberal Sudanese Muslim living in exile in the United States.

37. An-Na'im, *Toward an Islamic Reformation*, 41.

38. An-Na'im, *Toward an Islamic Reformation*, 133.

39. See the revealing article by Tom Bethell entitled "Saving Faith at State: Why Won't the State Department Stand Up for Christians?" in *The American Spectator* (April 1997), 20–21. See also Shea, *In the Lion's Den*, 40–42. For firsthand examples of persecution of Christians by the Saudi authorities including the breaking up of Christian fellowships and the destruction of Christmas ornaments, see Sandra Mackey, *The Saudis: Inside the Desert Kingdom* (Boston: Houghton Mifflin, 1987), 14–15, 92–97, 254.

40. Barbara G. Baker of Compass Direct, a California-based news service that specializes in disseminating information on the persecution of Christians around the world, broke the story on July 16, 1997, of two Filipino Christians beheaded in Saudi Arabia; she relied in her account on eyewitness details from released prisoner Donato Lama. On Lama and other persecuted Christians in Saudi Arabia see also the Amnesty International report "Behind Closed Doors: Unfair Trials in Saudi Arabia" (Nov. 25, 1997), 5, 11–12. For shocking revelations of torture and executions, see Amnesty's briefing, "Saudi Arabia: End Secrecy, End Suffering" (March 2000). For background see the Amnesty report on Saudi Arabia, "Religious Intolerance: The Arrest, Detention, and Torture of Christian Worshippers and Shia Muslims" (Sept. 14, 1993).

41. Horner, *Guide to Christian Churches*, 89.

42. An-Na'im, *Toward an Islamic Reformation*, 88.

43. Anglican Bishop Riyah Abu-'Assal, Diocese of Jerusalem, Episcopal Church of the Middle East, gave me this figure during an interview in Beirut in December 1997. It is less than the overall figure of around 164,000 supplied in 1989 by Norman Horner in his *Guide to Christian Churches*, appendix B, 107 and 112–13. The discrepancy can be explained by the effect of Christian emigration during the intervening eight years.

44. This is an average of the figure of 8,000 (most of them elderly) given by Bishop Abu-'Assal and 6,000 published in late 1997 by Beirut journalist Rajeh El-Khoury in *Al-Nahar*, November 12, 1997.

45. Horner, *Guide to Christian Churches*, 84–85, gives the 45,000 figure for 1947. Bishop Abu-'Assal provided the 28,000 figure for 1967. Ghadban, in his article in *Al-Nahar*'s weekly supplement for January 10, 1998, gives the figures of 31,000 in 1948 and 10,000 in 1967. Other figures for Christians provided by Abu-'Assal include Nazareth (30,000), Haifa (20,000), Bethlehem (20 percent of the town's population), Ramallah (15–20 percent of the town's population), and Nablus (700). The majority are Eastern Orthodox.

46. Horner, *Guide to Christian Churches*, 84.

47. Interview with Bishop Abu-'Assal.

48. "The entire history of Palestine never witnessed any religious conflict between Christians and Muslims," Bishop Abu-'Assal emphatically declared. See also Hanan Ashrawi, *This Side of Peace: A Personal Account* (New York: Simon and Schuster, 1995), 24, where the author poetically declares that as she was growing up she felt no difference between Palestinian Christians and Muslims: "[W]e did not know who was what, and it was not an issue." For his part, Edward W. Said in *The Question of Palestine* (New York:

Vintage Books, 1992), 147, contrasts the religious factionalism in Lebanon with its alleged absence among the Palestinians, thereby reinforcing a blind spot that is proving to be costly for Palestinian Christians.

49. See as an example the revealing article by Steve Rodman, "Report: Christians Persecuted by PA," *Jerusalem Post*, October 24, 1997, in which details, statistics, and places of persecution are mentioned, based on reliable eyewitness reports.

50. In both Iraq and Syria in recent decades the Christian communities have seen some relief in their situation, but it has been erratic. While the Chaldaeans of Iraq (about one-third of the country's Christians) opted for integration and largely adopted an Arab identity, the Assyrians did not and suffered the consequences of clinging to ethnic apartness. They had already endured persecution from Turks and Kurds in the north and had migrated to the cities in the center of the country as a prelude to emigrating abroad, mainly to Scandinavia and North America. In Syria between 1958 and 1990 some 250,000 Christians left the country. Prior to 1975, many of these went to Lebanon, but difficulties with the Beirut authorities hampered speedy naturalization, and following the outbreak of fighting in Lebanon large numbers of Syrian Christians left for the West. In both Iraq and Syria, foreign monastic orders and foreign-run schools were nationalized or closed in the late 1960s. The Jesuits, who had established Baghdad College in the 1930s and Al-Hikma University in 1958, were expelled from Iraq in 1968, and foreign Protestant personnel followed in 1969. Emigration of Christians out of Iraq accelerated after the Gulf War of 1991 and has not abated since the economic sanctions have been imposed on the country. As a recurring expression of a region-wide phenomenon, Christian birthrates in both these countries have been generally lower than Muslim rates.

On Syria and Iraq, see Horner, *Guide to Christian Churches*, 35, 48–50, 63–64, 86–87, 115 (Syria); and 36, 40–42, 58, 88, 106 (Iraq). Horner gives the number of Syrian Christians as 850,000, that is, around 10 percent of the overall population; and about half that number for Iraq's Christians, that is, some 2.5 percent of the country's population. See also Courbage and Fargues, *Christians and Jews under Islam*, 190–92; and Ghadban's piece in *Al-Nahar*'s weekly supplement for January 10, 1998, 5.

51. No accurate demographic data exist for Lebanon's Christians, but there are reasonably reliable estimates. Horner, writing in 1989, places them at just under 45 percent of the country's population (*Guide to Christian Churches*, 89 and 109–10). Another source estimates them at around 1,514,000 in a total population of around 3,114,000, that is, just under 50 percent; see Gerard Figuie, *Le point sur le Liban 1994* (Beirut: Anthologie, 1994), 36–54. Citing a 1992 study, Courbage and Fargues write that "the Christians today still form about 40–45 percent of the Lebanese population" (*Christians and Jews under Islam*, 185).

During the war years in Lebanon, many tried to deflate the numbers of the Christians in order to serve specific political agendas. Syrian officials and some of their Beirut mouthpieces are still in the habit of repeating that the Lebanese Christians do not exceed 25 percent of the population. As a reaction to this, certain local Christian sources have erred in the opposite direction by inflating the figures.

The spring 1997 visit by Pope John Paul II was an eye-opener on the number of Christians in Lebanon. A close analysis of those attending the Pope's open-air Mass at the

Beirut port, along with some logical extrapolations, would yield a percentage of around 45; see Habib C. Malik, *Between Damascus and Jerusalem: Lebanon and Middle East Peace* (Washington, D.C: Washington Institute for Near East Policy, 1997), 78. However, owing to the combined effects of high Christian emigration and low Christian birth rates, the Naturalization Decree of 1994, which with the stroke of a pen added some 300,000 Muslims to the Lebanese population (two-thirds of them from neighboring Syria), and the impending prospect that the Palestinian refugees now in the country, who are almost all Sunni Muslims, will remain, future demographic trends appear heavily weighted against the Christians.

52. On the Maronites, see Matti Moosa, *The Maronites in History* (Syracuse, N.Y.: Syracuse University Press, 1986), especially chap. 26, "The Maronites in Modern Times"; and Wadih Peter Tayah, *The Maronites: Roots and Identity* (Beirut: Bet Maroon, 1987).

53. Charles A. Frazee, *Catholics and Sultans: The Church and the Ottoman Empire, 1453–1923* (London: Cambridge University Press, 1983), 49.

54. Frazee, *Catholics and Sultans,* 277.

55. Frazee, *Catholics and Sultans,* 283.

56. See Theodor Hanf, *Coexistence in Wartime Lebanon: Decline of a State and Rise of a Nation* (London: Centre for Lebanese Studies in association with I. B. Tauris, 1993), 342.

57. The report, released July 22, 1997, is entitled "United States Policies in Support of Religious Freedom: Focus on Christians."

58. See Selim Abou, S.J., *Les defis de l'Université* (Beirut: Université Saint-Joseph Press, 1997). An English translation entitled "The Challenges of the University" was made by Chibli Mallat. On the automatic identification of the words "Arab" and "Muslim" in the minds of many and the problems this generates, see Habib C. Malik, "The Future of Christian Arabs," in *Mediterranean Quarterly: A Journal of Global Issues,* vol. 2, no. 2 (spring 1991), 74–75.

59. Quoted from a speech given by Salman Rushdie in December 1991 in New York City entitled "What Is My Single Life Worth?" and later printed in Brian MacArthur, ed., *The Penguin Book of Twentieth-Century Speeches* (New York: Penguin, 1992), 485. Rushdie goes on to declare: "Actually Existing Islam has failed to create a free society anywhere on earth."

60. Furthermore, there are instances in Islamic history of movement in both directions. The Khawarij, who were extremist in the past, are more moderate today and can be found in Oman and the North African oases. The Ishmailis (Fatimids in Egypt) were originally the Assassins but today are represented by the moderate Agha Khan. On the other hand, Sufis in the nineteenth and twentieth centuries became very fanatic and participated in many massacres. The ultraconservative Wahhabis of Arabia are a relatively late arrival on the Islamic scene. And the liberal experiments of the Mu'tazila and Ikhwan Safa were long ago brutally suppressed.

61. Actually a project for a Church of Islam already exists. See the book by the Dominican Father Ramzi Habib Malik entitled *La Bonne Nouvelle de l'Eglise de l'Islam* (Beirut: Dar Al-Ba'th, 1987).

62. Examples of *mea culpa* are plentiful on the Christian side, especially in recent years. In September 1997 the Roman Catholic bishops of France apologized and asked for

forgiveness from the Jews for what happened during World War II. In October of that year the Ecumenical Patriarch of the Eastern Orthodox Church, Patriarch Bartholomew, made a similar apology while visiting the Holocaust Museum in Washington, D.C. On November 2, 1997, Pope John Paul II denounced anti-Semitism and repeated the apology to the Jews. In fact, back in 1965 at the Second Vatican Council the Catholic Church officially addressed this issue in an encyclical (*Nostra Aetate*). And these are only a few of the prominent instances of *mea culpa* exercised by responsible Christians. Of course, the most significant and dramatic instance of apology came in March 2000 before and during the Pope's Jubilee visit to the Holy Land, when on behalf of the Roman Catholic Church he apologized for all past wrongs and transgressions committed against anyone—Jews, Muslims, other Christians, and others—over the past two millennia.

63. Opinions that in the name of political realism play down the importance of the "values component" in foreign policy ought to be given less of a hearing for a change. See as an example the op-ed piece by Anthony Lewis entitled "An Unnecessary Focus on Religious Persecution," *International Herald Tribune*, September 13–14, 1997. In their well-argued book, Graham E. Fuller and Ian O. Lesser—two sophisticated Western apologists for Islam—conclude that Political Islam, in its dealings with the West, is the "functional equivalent of nationalism." Maybe so (and only in a narrow geopolitical sense). But in its dealings with its own non-Muslim minorities, Political Islam has shown it can be a repressive force backed by an intolerant creed. It is time such a fact mattered to the West. See Fuller and Lesser, *A Sense of Siege: The Geopolitics of Islam and the West* (Boulder, Colo.: Westview, 1995), 165 ff.

Comment by Daniel Pipes

Habib Malik's paper is quite an extraordinary polemic written by a free Christian. In my thirty years of studying the Middle East I have never heard anything quite like it, and I applaud its excellence and its bravery. My remarks will touch lightly on a few of his points, highlighting differences, of course, for who needs to hear me repeat what he said?

First I want to comment on Samuel Huntington's suggestion that Islamists in Algeria and Turkey are like Christians in China. I would revise this formulation and compare Islamists in those two countries to *Communists* in China. They are, in other words, the persecutors, not the persecuted. Islamists are the third and most recent harbingers of the century's utopian radicalism, following on the heels of the fascists and Marxist-Leninists. All three of them have a clarion vision of how to structure society and are ruthless in attaining it. They all happily break eggs to make their particular flavor of omelet. That said, some radical utopians break more eggs than do others. Not every Communist is a Stalin, not every Islamist is like the Taliban in Afghanistan.

On the question of moderate Islam: from 1880 to 1940, Islam became more modern. Muslims in those years were influenced by Western liberal thought. The subsequent sixty years have seen regression. It has reached the point that Muslims find it hard to be at all critical of Islam in public—I'm not talking about blaspheming the Prophet Muhammad but, for example,

---

Daniel Pipes is director of the *Middle East Forum*, editor of the *Middle East Quarterly*, and a columnist for the *Jerusalem Post*.

opposing the application of Islamic law. Liberal voices find it difficult to speak out.

I disagree with the notion that liberal Islam must be based on the Koran, that one has to find the right verses and then have a tolerant spirit grow out of the verses. Rather, it's possible for a liberal spirit to grow out of the right circumstances, out of trends that are taking place in the world. However tenuously based in Islam, the last two centuries have shown that Islamic liberals are people influenced by the West. Should favorable conditions prevail, moderate Islam can once more find strength, and I predict this will happen, though I have no idea when. Sixty years in our direction, sixty away; things will again turn around some day.

What can Americans do to encourage moderate Muslims? The global influence of the U.S. government specifically, and of Americans more generally—of churches, businesses, nonprofit organizations, filmmakers, you name it—is extraordinary. Washington and Hollywood have an outsized presence around the world, to the point that things that are quite minor here—some prize given, some grant bestowed, some resolution passed—can have considerable importance in the outside world. Recognition by Americans of beleaguered moderates can help them feel that they belong to something larger, that they're not quite so isolated as it may seem, and that powerful forces support them.

I differ slightly with Habib Malik on the question of the *dhimmi* status. Yes, by today's reckoning it is uncontestably an inferior position, even a form of religious persecution. I certainly would hate to live as a *dhimmi*. But in historical terms, the *dhimmi* status was not that bad. Compare the position of Jews in the Christian world with those in the Muslim world through the long middle era, from, say, A.D. 700 to 1700. In both civilizations Jews were a small, somewhat despised minority, but the Jews in Muslim countries were unquestionably better off, in good part because they had a legal status. Inferior though it was, this offered them a security that was far more assured than anything in Christendom. It also bears note that when the European colonial powers conquered Muslim lands and eliminated the *dhimmi* status, finding it anathema, the Jews and Christians in Muslim lands suddenly lost their legal standing. The persecution of Jews and Christians notably increased after the *dhimmi* status disappeared. Do not misunderstand, however: I abominate its continuance today and especially oppose efforts to impose it in the West.

Finally, I'd like to note how the Middle East stands out as a place where religion has central importance for politics. From an American point of view, our interests in the area basically boil down to two: those connected to religion and those connected to petroleum. As an example of the former, note Jerusalem, which is lacking in either strategic or economic importance. It is the purest of religious issues in U.S. foreign policy. Note too how American policy there is determined by a religious ambition: for fifty years, the U.S. government has supported a plan to internationalize Jerusalem, which effectively means withholding it from either an Israeli or a Palestinian state and placing it under Christian control. That remains on the books as the official U.S. goal, but in practical terms it is defunct. At this point and forward, Jerusalem will be under some combination of Jewish and Muslim control, not Christian.

Still, this is perhaps a unique issue where Christendom still exists politically and has much to say about the disposition of Jerusalem. The issue today is: Will Jerusalem be wholly under Israeli control or will it be divided between the Israelis and the Palestinians? Jewish Israelis and Muslim Palestinians realize that which side the Christians come down on will be critical—I sometimes draw the analogy of two siblings fighting for the favor of the third. This explains why both Jews and Muslims are actively making their case to Christians, for example in recent dueling full-page advertisements in the *New York Times*. Some Christians—generally those on the left—favor the Palestinian viewpoint, while others—generally on the right—adopt the Israeli viewpoint. The side that prevails in this contest to win Christendom's favor will probably prevail in Jerusalem.

CHAPTER SEVEN

~

The Rise of Christian Mission and Relief Agencies

Paul E. Pierson

Mission, defined in terms of both reaching those outside the Church with the Christian message and doing works of compassion for those in need, is inherent to the Christian faith, though many in the Church fail to exemplify this. Like every other institution in any society, the Christian Church is inextricably entangled with the values and presuppositions of its society; it must constantly try to distinguish the essentials of its faith and action from values and assumptions that are simply a part of its culture. One way to view the history of mission and of relief and development organizations in the United States is to see it in terms of this effort. For the nearly two centuries of the American missionary movement, Christians of all traditions have been involved in a struggle to discover, communicate, and live out Christian values over against the values of their own culture and those of the cultures in which they have served.

In what follows we will trace the trajectories of three groups: Protestant missions, Catholic missions, and the relief and development agencies of both.

The Protestant Missionary Movement

The roots of the American Protestant missionary movement lay in the Puritan experiment and in the religious awakenings that occurred in the

Paul E. Pierson is dean emeritus and senior professor of history of mission and Latin American studies at Fuller Theological Seminary's School of World Mission, where he has taught since 1980. Previously he spent fourteen years in Brazil as a Presbyterian missionary, serving as a seminary professor and president and as a pastor. He is the author of *A Younger Church in Search of Maturity: Presbyterianism in Brazil, 1910–1959*.

mid-eighteenth and early nineteenth centuries. Common to all three were the convictions that (a) a new age was about to dawn in which God's redemption would be taken to every land, (b) American Protestants would play the most important role in this movement, which would lead to the consummation of history, and (c) the American political and social experiment was the highest and best the world had yet seen, and would serve as a model to other nations.

Puritans and other Protestants had worked among Native Americans since the middle of the seventeenth century, and two former slaves had gone to Jamaica and Sierra Leone after the Revolution, but the first American foreign-mission agency was the American Board of Commissioners for Foreign Missions (ABCFM), organized by New England Congregationalists in 1810. The board also served Presbyterians. Among its first missionaries, appointed in 1812, were Adoniram Judson and his wife, who sailed for India as Congregationalists but became Baptists en route. This led to the formation of the Baptist mission board in 1814. Indicative of the complex relationship between colonialism and missions is the fact that the Judsons, who hoped to go to Calcutta, were refused permission to reside there by the East India Company, which had also fought to exclude the pioneer English missionary William Carey. They therefore went to Burma.

The other major Protestant denominations soon organized their own boards, the Methodists in 1820, the Episcopalians in 1821, the Presbyterians in 1837, and the Lutherans in 1842. The goal of the early missionaries was to communicate the Christian faith, win converts, and establish churches, which, in the thought of Rufus Anderson, the greatest leader of the ABCFM, should be "self-governing, self-supporting, and self-propagating." An important assumption was that the planting of the Church would lead to positive changes in the receptor societies as Christian values were accepted. Naturally, in the minds of the missionaries those changes would involve Western-style education, literacy, and health care, and better treatment of women.

At times their goals brought them into conflict with other Westerners. The mission to Hawaii is an interesting case. When the native chiefs, under the tutelage of the missionaries, adopted a system of laws based on the Ten Commandments that prohibited, among other things, prostitution, the American and British consuls protested, and when American naval and whaling vessels arrived in port and were denied the services of women aboard the ships, riots ensued in which missionaries were attacked and threatened with death.[1]

The missionaries devised a system of writing the Hawaiian language using Roman characters, and they produced translations of the Bible and various textbooks. By 1826 there were sixty-nine schools in the islands with sixty-six native teachers and 20,000 students,[2] and by 1873 the mission had published more than 150 different works in the local language.[3]

Although Anderson and others insisted that evangelization, not civilization, was the goal of missions, most of the changes encouraged by the missionaries looked very Western. That was certainly not all negative. In India, Carey had worked to prohibit infanticide and suttee, the practice of burning widows on the funeral pyres of their husbands, and Scottish Presbyterians would speak out against female genital mutilation in Kenya. American missionaries began to open schools and even universities for girls, previously thought to be uneducatable, to provide health care for women, and eventually to train some of them in the medical professions, especially in India and China. And while most missionaries usually painted a negative picture of Asian and African religions and cultures, they were the first Westerners to study those religions and cultures seriously.

The relationship with colonialism was complex. American missionaries, espousing the separation of church and state, saw themselves as nonpolitical. Often they were naïve in doing so. Explicitly or implicitly they supported American policies, and in colonial lands they often encouraged the aspirations of nationals for independence. American missionaries in British India had to sign a pledge promising no involvement in Indian political affairs.[4] But most missionaries welcomed the opening to China made by the Opium War of 1839–1842, which granted them residence in the five treaty ports, and after the War of 1856 most welcomed the treaty that gave Christians access to all of China.[5] In contrast, at the turn of the century two American Presbyterians published articles condemning the exploitation of African rubber workers in the Congo as "twentieth century slavery." The case drew international attention and created tension between the Belgian and U.S. governments.[6] The missionaries themselves were sued for libel, though the suit was finally dismissed.

Missions were a subversive influence in ways that went beyond their interaction with colonialism. For instance, when women's interest in missionary service met no response from men, they formed their own societies, reaching out to neglected groups especially in Asia. This had a significant effect both on the receptor societies and in the United States. R. Pierce Beaver gave the second edition of his book *American Protestant Women in World Mission* the subtitle *A History of the First Feminist Movement in North America*.[7]

The Consensus Wavers

Two religious awakenings, before and after the Civil War, brought major changes to the American religious scene and the missionary movement. The first was led primarily by Charles Finney, who stressed social reform along with evangelism. The social activism of a number of Finney's followers—the Tappan brothers, Theodore D. Weld, the Grimke sisters—is well known. Yet Finney made it dear that he was primarily an evangelist, not a social reformer. The second awakening began in 1858 and had as its major figure the layman Dwight L. Moody.

Timothy Smith suggests that much of the social gospel had its origins in these movements, which stressed both social and personal holiness.[8] But a bifurcation began in the last third of the century. Among the factors that contributed to it were Darwinism, the "higher criticism" of the Bible, the study of comparative religions, the growth of cities and industrialization, and the growth of confidence in progress and "manifest destiny." By the 1920s the consensus in American Protestantism and the missionary movement was at an end. That consensus had included four broad points: (1) the assertion that the supreme aim of missions was to make Jesus Christ known, to persuade persons to become Christ's disciples, and to gather them into churches; (2) allegiance to the uniquely divine nature of Jesus Christ; (3) willingness to defend the social dimensions of missions; and (4) a pragmatic ecumenism.

For Moody and his followers, the focus was narrowed exclusively to evangelism, while theological liberals began to concentrate on the problems of urbanization and industrialization. While liberals were optimistic about human nature and stressed the perfectibility of humankind, the movement that would become fundamentalism adopted a "premillennial" outlook according to which, since the ideal human society would come only after the return of Christ, evangelism and the salvation of souls were of paramount importance. Yet both groups maintained confidence in the unique role of America in world history, and indeed, in the plan of divine redemption.

The Second Phase

The Student Volunteer Movement for Foreign Missions (SVM) arose among college students at a conference led by Moody in 1886 and ushered in the second phase of the American Protestant missionary movement. At a time when confidence about the role of America in world history, belief in the superiority of Western culture, and religious enthusiasm were on the increase, the volunteer movement caught the attention of thousands of college students. In 1890 there were 934 American Protestant missionaries serving in foreign lands. Twenty-five years later there were nearly ten times as many (9,072), largely as a result of the SVM.[9] Before its decline in the 1920s, more than 20,000 young people, the great majority American, had gone as missionaries to Asia and Africa, and a smaller number to Latin America.

Most of these missionaries served under the older denominational boards. By 1910, when the landmark Edinburgh Missionary Conference was held, there were 120 American mission boards; just over twenty of these were responsible for 65 percent of the missionaries and 80 percent of the funds. The four largest—the ABCFM, plus the agencies of the northern Presbyterians, the northern Methodists, and the northern Baptists—had more than 500 missionaries each. Other major agencies were those of the southern branches of the Baptists, Presbyterians, and Methodists, and those of the Episcopalians and Disciples of Christ, each with between 100 and 225 missionaries.[10]

A century had passed since the founding of the first American foreign-mission agency, the ABCFM, and the accomplishments of this first hundred years were impressive. While the churches established were still small, foundations had been laid for significant growth in many areas. Equally important in the opinion of many were the Western-style institutions that had been established, many of which brought greater opportunity to the poor and marginalized, especially women. These included primary and secondary schools, the first colleges for Asian women, and Western medicine and health care.

The "Faith Missions"

By the turn of the century a new type of mission agency had developed, the nondenominational "faith mission." The first was the China Inland Mission, established in England in 1865, which soon came to the United States and Canada. Others that were founded before the end of the century included the Africa Inland Mission, the Sudan Interior Mission, and the Central American Mission. The faith missions were nondenominational, supported by laypersons in the older churches, and fundamentalist in their theology. Most of their personnel were graduates of the newly established "Bible institutes," and they tended to be suspicious of the theology of the older denominational missions. In 1936, more than 1,400 missionaries, or nearly 12 percent of the American missionary force, were alumni of Moody Bible Institute.[11] The faith missions formed the Interdenominational Foreign Mission Association (IFMA) in 1917.

While the consensus in American Protestantism and its missionary movement was breaking down, an event that would have far-reaching significance began in 1906 in a former Methodist chapel on Azusa Street in Los Angeles. Under the leadership of black pastor William Seymour, blacks and whites who eventually numbered in the thousands engaged in expressive worship and praise that included speaking in tongues. The Azusa Street revival marked the beginning of Pentecostalism and its derivative, the charismatic movement, which after mid-century would play an important role in the missionary movement and in world Christianity.

Meanwhile, the greatest symbol of the loss of consensus was the 1932 Hocking Report, entitled *Rethinking Missions*. The report, funded by John D. Rockefeller Jr., a liberal Baptist, called for Christians to approach other faiths with sympathetic understanding, seeking to discover kindred elements within them. Missionaries should be co-workers with the forces for righteousness in every religious system. The goal would be "unity in the completest religious truth." The ABCFM sent copies to all its mission stations with a positive evaluation attached. Most denominational boards, led by Presbyterian Robert E. Speer, rejected the report, as did the faith missions. But it called attention to undeniably growing differences. And by 1935, while missionaries from the older "mainline" boards numbered 7,400, the American missionary force now included 1,200 Seventh-day Adventists and 3,500 others who would be considered fundamentalists or evangelicals.[12]

After the War

The postwar period saw great changes in Protestant missions. First came a period of optimism about mission and about America's role in the world. General MacArthur asked for "missionaries and more missionaries" to be sent to Japan, and wrote to the president of the Southern Baptist Convention, "Christianity now has an opportunity without counterpart in the Far East."[13] An article in the magazine *Moody Monthly* spoke of a "Christian America" that now occupied the position of "a moral and spiritual leader in world affairs," adding, "We must make sure the message of Christ, with its transforming power, is carried to those who are starving for the Bread of Life."[14] Fundamentalism and its evangelical allies began to move toward numerical parity with the Protestant mission establishment. Formed in 1945 was the Evangelical Foreign Missions Association (EFMA), a coalition of agencies somewhat broader than the IFMA, which excluded Pentecostals. A number of new missions were formed by former members of the armed forces, all of them conservative in their theology. These included the Greater Europe Mission, Far Eastern Gospel Crusade, and Mission Aviation Fellowship.

By mid-century the optimism that had fueled the missionary movement had broken down, especially in the older groups. Max Warren, leader of the Anglican Church Missionary Society, spoke for most of these older Protestant mission groups in 1952: "We know . . . that the most testing days of the Christian mission in our generation lie just ahead. . . . We have to be ready to see the day of missions, as we have known them, as having already come to an end."[15] Among the factors leading to this uncertainty about the future of missions were the beginning of the end of colonialism, the rise of nationalism, the resurgence of non-Christian religions, and movements away from missionary paternalism to partnership with the "younger churches." Also, by the sixties, social and racial turmoil in the United States caused many to focus on this country instead of the overseas mission.

While those associated with the missionary thrust of the previous century lost momentum, the more conservative groups surged forward. But in the words of one observer, the conservative missions "often acted as if they were still living in the nineteenth century. They treated sociopolitical issues simplistically and interpreted the missionary call as the simple and unambiguous action of saving souls."[16] As time passed, however, many were drawn into ministries of compassion. An earlier example was Susan Strachan, cofounder in 1922 of the Latin America Mission (LAM), which began as the Latin American Evangelistic Crusade. While her husband was holding evangelistic campaigns, Susan Strachan started a medical clinic that has become one of the most modern hospitals in Costa Rica, a child-care facility that has become a model for Central America, and a training school that became a theological seminary, some of whose graduates have taken radical positions on socioeconomic and political issues. A contemporary daughter mission of the LAM, besides engaging in evangelism and pastoral training, currently works with street children and battered women, has established a medical and dental clinic for Nicaraguan refugees, and has encouraged small business development.[17]

Such activities reflect theological changes in the conservative missionary community. In a study of forty years of evangelical theology of mission, Charles Van Engen asserted that as North American evangelicals "experienced new sociocultural strength and confidence, changes in ecumenical theology of mission, and developments in evangelical partner churches in the Third World," their theology of mission "became less reactionary and more holistic without compromising the initial evangelical élan of the 'spirit of Edinburgh, 1910.'"[18] A 1982 publication representing a broad coalition of evangelicals left no doubt that Christians were called both to evangelism and to social action, even though it was ambivalent about the role of the institutional church in the latter.[19]

Other significant features in the latter part of this century include: mission activity in previously closed areas of the world as a result of the end of the Cold War, the new relationship with China, and the breakup of the USSR; the rapid growth of short-term missions; and the growth of the Pentecostal and charismatic churches, many of which are strongly focused on mission. While some of the Pentecostal and charismatic churches, including the Assemblies of God, are members of the Evangelical Foreign Mission Association, most are unaffiliated.

What the Numbers Show

Perhaps the simplest way to see the changes is through numbers. Table 7.1 shows the sizes of the various categories of American Protestant missionaries from 1918 to 1996.[20]

About 450 new mission organizations have been formed in the last thirty years, nearly a hundred of those in the last ten. Many are small, but some are growing rapidly. For example, Frontiers was established in 1982 as "a sending agency of evangelical tradition engaged in church planting, evangelism, and mobilization for mission"; in 1996 it had 220 career personnel overseas and an income of $4.5 million.[21] By 2000 it had grown to over 600.[22] Campus Crusade for Christ, established in 1951, in 1996 had 665 persons serving four or more years and 367 serving one to four years in 137 countries; its income was $54 million.[23]

Among the older boards that were dominant up to mid-century, Presbyterians (northern and southern) showed 354 persons serving over four years and 421 serving one to four years, with expenditures of $40 million; the United Methodists, 246 and 62, $30 million; and the American Baptists (whose mission board was founded in 1814), 107 and 8, $14 million. The successor to the ABCFM, the United Church Board for World Ministries (combined with the former Disciples of Christ board), had 15 persons serving four years or more and 84 for shorter periods.

In contrast with two of these parent groups: the conservative Presbyterian Church of America, established in 1973, had 438 and 130 persons serving in the two categories, while five conservative Baptist groups (not including the Southern Baptists) had a total of 2,513 persons serving four years or more.

TABLE 7.1   U.S. Protestant Missionaries, 1918–1996

	1918	1935	1952	1968	1980	1996
Mainline Churches	8,900	7,400	8,800	8,700	4,000	2,600
Seventh-day Adventist	700	1,200	1,100	1,500	1,000	700
IFMA	800	900	3,000	5,700	5,800	5,700
EFMA*	400	1,700	2,100	6,800	8,400	10,800
Unaffiliated		900	3,600	11,600	16,400	23,800
TOTAL	10,800	12,100	18,600	34,300	35,600	43,600

*Not established until 1945; the earlier numbers represent missionaries in agencies that later became part of the EFMA.

The largest Pentecostal denomination, the Assemblies of God, had 1,569 persons serving four years or more and 192 for shorter terms, in approximately 100 countries, with expenditures of $113 million.

Of the three largest unaffiliated groups, the Southern Baptists had 3,482 persons in the first category and 689 in the second, with an income of $221 million, working in more than 100 countries; Wycliffe Bible Translators, 2,483 persons serving over four years; and the New Tribes Mission 1,434 persons serving over four years.[24] When Protestant missionaries are kidnapped or killed, they are likely to be from Wycliffe or New Tribes, whose workers usually live in the most remote areas.

Short-term mission service has grown remarkably in the last two decades, though accurate statistics are difficult if not impossible to obtain. The 1998–2000 Mission Handbook lists 64,000 short-term workers for 1996, defining short-term as from two weeks to one year. If those who go for less than two weeks—usually as part of a local church work group—are included, the number rises markedly. One additional category is that of "tentmaker," usually a self-supporting Christian professional who goes to a country of difficult access for the purpose of witness and service. "Tentmakers" probably number a few hundred.

As the Student Volunteer Movement declined in the twenties and thirties and eventually disappeared, a new student mission movement arose, parallel to the newer mission agencies. The Student Foreign Missions Fellowship was established in 1936, functioning in the more conservative Christian colleges and Bible institutes. In 1946 it joined forces with the Inter Varsity Christian Fellowship, which was of English origin and had entered from Canada. Two years later it moved to the campus of the University of Illinois, where now its triennial conferences normally draw 20,000 students for a week of focus on missions.

There have also been changes in the countries of service. Up to World War II, China received by far the greatest number of missionaries, with India in second place. For the American Baptists, Burma was an important field; that of course has changed. Today 25 percent of the missionaries serve in Latin America and the Caribbean, 17 percent in Africa, and, somewhat surprisingly, at least 10 percent in Europe, mostly in the west.

The Protestant missionary movement from the United States has grown enormously during its nearly two centuries of existence. Major shifts have taken place in its ideology or theology and in the areas in which missionaries serve. At the same time, large and vigorous churches have arisen in many nations formerly seen as "mission fields," and American missions are increasingly called to work alongside such churches in new relationships of partnership. But that is another story.

The Roman Catholic Missionary Movement

During the nineteenth century the Roman Catholic Church in the United States concentrated almost all its attention on the care and nurture of the millions of immigrants who had come from Catholic areas of Europe. Its accomplishments were impressive in forming parishes and building churches, schools, colleges, and universities. A few American Catholic missionaries went to St. Thomas in the Danish Virgin Islands in 1858, and some others went to Mexico, Argentina, Chile, and Jamaica. Catholic sisters went to the Hawaiian Islands in 1883 and were joined by a priest in 1886. By 1893 twenty-seven American sisters were teaching children in Jamaica. That same year ten Jesuit priests and two brothers began work in British Honduras (Belize), where they concentrated on planting the church, working to stabilize family life by encouraging men to marry the mothers of their children, and educating the "elites" for leadership in church and society. Near the end of the century, two sisters and two priests were sent to China, where they worked under the supervision of European congregations.

The Spanish-American War acted as a spur to missions as Catholics discovered to their dismay that Protestant missionaries were entering the traditionally Catholic countries of Cuba, Puerto Rico, and the Philippines. In 1903, four American priests were appointed to head Filipino dioceses. When Puerto Rico was annexed to the United States, the American church became responsible for a million more Catholics, and an American succeeded the Spanish bishop of San Juan. Several religious orders sent missionaries to teach and direct institutions in the Philippines and Puerto Rico. Even so, as late as 1906 there were fewer than fourteen American Catholic foreign missionaries. In 1909 a mission training school was opened at Techny, Illinois, and two years later the bishops approved the founding of the Catholic Foreign Missionary Society of America, with headquarters at Maryknoll, New York.[25] One of its prime movers was James Anthony Walsh, a Bostonian priest whose interest had been stimulated in part by his reading of Protestant missionary literature.

The Catholic concept of the priesthood and the sacraments meant that clergy were essential in planting the Church in a way that was not true for most Protestants. And while some Protestant missionary women worked as evangelists and did pastoral work, Catholic sisters could not do that. But Walsh left open the possibility when he wrote to Maryknoll sisters, "As you think of your work . . . keep in mind the thought that where you can take the place of a priest, you will do it. You will be . . . the handmaids of the priestly service. This is the apostolate, and as far as you can, you should exercise it. That is more or less a modern idea."[26]

Aware of the Protestant Student Volunteer Movement, seminarians in Techny encouraged the formation of the Catholic Students Mission Crusade in 1918. Seminarian John Considine, a future missions leader, was one of its officers. Its two goals were the support and promotion of home and foreign missions and the development of leadership skills in young Catholics. Before its demise in 1971 the group held twenty-four biennial conferences that attracted as many as 4,000 students to hear mission speakers and interact with students from other countries. From the beginning it used military terminology, harking back to the Crusades. The spirit of Peter the Hermit and St. Bernard was invoked to urge a twentieth-century crusade. By 1937 American Catholics were working in twelve countries.

As some Latin American nations adopted constitutions separating church and state, the church had to contend with persecution, anticlericalism, and the appropriation of church property. In 1924 the U.S. bishops declared solidarity with Catholics experiencing persecution in Guatemala. Two years later the National Catholic Welfare Council worked with the State Department and the Mexican consulate to negotiate for religious tolerance in Mexico, and in 1934 the bishops urged Catholics to pressure the American government to take action.[27] While some American Catholics called for social reform in Latin America following the principles of Catholic social action, the Latin American bishops insisted that the southern hemisphere was not a mission field, even though there was a severe shortage of priests. Consequently by 1940 American Catholics had only 154 missionaries in South America, 68 in Central America, and none in Mexico.

A significant new venture was initiated in medical missions. Missionaries saw the terrible plight of women, especially in India, where neither Hindu nor Muslim women could be treated by male doctors. The rates of infant mortality and death in childbirth were high. However, the Vatican did not permit the sisters to act as obstetricians. Dr. Anna Dengel and others lobbied to have the prohibition lifted, and when they were successful in 1936, the Society of Catholic Medical Missionaries was formed. Dengel, who had read widely about Protestant medical missions, served as the superior general as the society grew to include more than 700 sisters working in forty countries.

The two countries that received the most Catholic missionary attention in the 1920s were India and China, the latter becoming the major focus of interest, money, and personnel. From 1918 to 1949 Catholics entered China in great numbers. They faced great turmoil, terrible poverty, warlords and bandits, floods, disease and famine, nationalism and antiforeign sentiment, and eventually the Japanese invasion, war, and then the Communist revolution. But at the beginning of the period there was great optimism. In 1920 a Maryknoller wrote, "The acceptable time to convert the world has come. . . . The marvelous development of practical science and inventions has multiplied the individual missioner's efficiency many times over. . . . The heathen, too, are more favorably disposed than ever before."[28] Like many early Protestants, Catholics saw an essential link between Christianity and civilization. Another writer stated, "We Catholics . . . must become in deed what we are in name, the connecting link of the ancient and modern civilization."[29]

There was a growing emphasis on the need for lay missionaries. Several worked as physicians and nurses. Both lay and clergy missionaries pioneered in forming agricultural cooperatives, setting up rice, pig, and cow banks, and offering basic health care.

A major issue for Catholics as well as Protestants was how best to approach the Chinese people. Some worked directly in evangelization accompanied by work with the poor, women, and children. This involved setting up and operating clinics and schools and eventually seminaries. Others favored evangelization among the more cultured and educated persons, hoping they would have an impact on Chinese society and make it more open to conversion. In 1925 American Benedictines opened the first Catholic college in China. Four years later it included colleges of liberal arts, education, and natural sciences and was named Fu Jen University, and in 1930 Benedictine sisters arrived to establish an affiliated women's college. The university was reestablished in Taiwan in 1959.

Catholic sisters saw women as the foundation of the family and worked to free them from some of the restrictions of traditional life. The low social status of women was indicated by the numbers of baby girls who were either abandoned to die or left on the sisters' doorsteps. Orphanages were established, and American Catholics were encouraged to support the children. This became one of the most widely known missionary works in China.

The mission to China led many middle-class American Catholics to see the United States and the Catholic Church in global terms, even before World War II. As the Japanese invasion progressed after 1937, many missionaries had remained to serve the victims of the war. Their letters along with reports in missionary publications helped Americans realize the extent of the suffering. While Catholic missionaries attempted to work with the Communist government after 1949, soon they were imprisoned or expelled, just as the Protestants were.

With China now closed to mission, Africa called for attention. In 1945 there were only 197 American Catholic missionaries in Africa, but by 1960 there were 781, working in pastoral, medical, and educational ministries.

Missions in Latin America

Disputing the Latin American bishops' contention that Latin America was not a mission field, the Maryknoll leader John Considine in 1946 published a "Call for Forty Thousand," a bold request for that number of missionary priests in Latin America. This was accompanied by a Vatican emphasis on the need for the "rehabilitation" or renovation of the Latin American church. By 1958 one-third of the American Catholic missionary force was serving in the area, 807 in South America and 392 in Central America.[30] After the regional conference of Latin American bishops (CELAM) was formed in 1955, a Chilean bishop asserted, "Shocking social inequality . . . masses living in inhuman conditions, and the monopoly of land ownership all show how urgent it is for us to take a definite stand in this regard. With us or without us, social reform is going to take place."[31] The countries believed to be in greatest danger were Brazil, Chile, Cuba, Haiti, Nicaragua, Honduras, and Guatemala. In 1969 more than a hundred volunteers signed up to work for the reconstruction of social structures through Catholic social principles. They went to Latin America and worked in education, health care, community and agricultural development, and the organization of credit unions.

But soon another note was sounded. At the second meeting of the Catholic Inter-American Cooperation Program (CICOP) in 1965, a speaker talked about the social confrontation between Latin America and the United States. Several bishops, including Marcos McGrath of Panama, described the religious and social conditions in Latin America in a manner that produced alarm among both church members and U.S. State Department officials in attendance. Participants heard from the bishops, for the first time, an uncensored view of the role of the United States in Latin America. Now, as one analyst has put it, "social justice and disclosure of socioeconomic inequalities were on the front burner of what CICOP saw to be the missionary agenda."[32] This would soon bring conflict and, for some, a redefinition of the nature of the mission and the Church.

In the 1960s development was still the hope, and the United Nations declared the period the "decade of development." The 1967 encyclical of Pope Paul VI entitled *Popularum Progressio* (On the Development of Peoples) dealt with economic development, and the 1970 Bishops' Synod stated, "Action on behalf of justice is a constitutive element of the gospel." Slowly there developed a new understanding of mission, focusing on the response to human need, and some reformers began to urge complete and swift structural changes. This led to tensions. The National Conference of Catholic Bishops stated in 1971, "Salvation for some today means meeting people's needs in the temporal order. For others it cannot be found this side of eternity. The meeting of these two points of view constitutes the alleged conflict as to which is primary in the missionary effort, the development or the evangelization of people."[33]

Thus, although Latin America was not seen as a mission field in the thirties, after the war it became the major focus of American Catholic missions. In 1968, when the missionary effort was at its peak, 1,026 missionaries served in Oceania, 1,471 in Asia, 1,157 in Africa, 2,455 in South America, and 936 in Central America.[34]

A major shift occurred in the direction of Catholic missions in the 1970s. Among the contributing factors were: the growing study and interpretation of the documents of Vatican II; the 1968 conference of the Latin American bishops in Medellín, Colombia, and its adoption of the "preferential option for the poor"; the publication of A Theology of Liberation by the Peruvian priest Gustavo Gutiérrez; growing study of the problems of Latin America, often using Marxist categories of analysis; and the continuing political turmoil and military rule in the region. By the 1970s Maryknoll was the major publisher of works in English presenting Latin American viewpoints, often seen as radical by North Americans.

While missions had often targeted those on the social and economic fringe, a change in emphasis came with the study of the structural reasons for poverty. The "option for the poor" for some came to mean a commitment to radical changes in church and society. Archbishop McGrath of Panama supported more lay leadership and worked for the development of a social conscience among all. Fr. Leo Mahon worked in the barrios around Panama City, living at a subsistence level, working with small groups, using the Scriptures for communal reflection on the people's social and economic problems. Mahon was twice brought to trial for heresy. Some considered this the first attempt to practice liberation theology. The Panamanian government ordered him expelled three times, but the protests of the people overcame the attempts.

Traditional medical, educational, and parish work began in Nicaragua and El Salvador in 1939. There missionaries found poverty in its worst form. The 1960s saw the formation of the Alliance for Progress—an economic development partnership between the United States and twenty-two Latin American countries—and missionaries helped distribute surplus American food. After a few years they began to reconsider this participation, noting that such programs tended to encourage passivity and dependence. Increasingly missionaries worked with the poor, seeking to form Christian communities, making the poor aware of their own personal worth and that of their neighbors. "Consciousness raising" became in important conceptual tool of mission. With the overthrow of Nicaragua's Somoza government by the Sandinistas in 1979 and the subsequent sponsorship of the anti-Sandinista *contras* by the U.S. government, missionaries faced dilemmas. They carried with them American presuppositions about human rights, justice, and respect for the dignity of all, but many felt that their own government supported groups in Central America and elsewhere that violated those principles.

By the mid-seventies, younger, socially activist missionaries, now unsympathetic to anti-Communist rhetoric, drew attention to the results of U.S. intervention in Latin America. It was alleged that the CIA had used American missionaries to get information about "subversive" movements and that CIA actions had caused fear, hatred, oppression, and even death. In October 1974, U.S. Protestant and Catholic mission leaders met to protest CIA attempts to use missionaries, but CIA director William Colby told Senator Hatfield that the agency had indeed used missionaries for intelligence gathering and would do so again. After Hatfield pushed for legislation against the practice, George Bush, the new CIA director, issued a regulation in 1976 prohibiting contractual relationships between the CIA and American missionaries.[35]

In the struggle between the Sandinistas and the *contras*, missionaries cared for the wounded on both sides, often at great risk. Between 1959 and 1990 eleven American Catholic missionaries were killed, most of them in Central America. The deaths that received the most attention and especially affected public opinion were of four women in El Salvador in 1980, apparently killed by government soldiers. Many groups, Catholic and Protestant, called for an investigation. The tragic event increased skepticism about the purity of U.S. foreign policy. As missionaries returned home they spoke of the importance of educating American Catholics on Third World problems and U.S. foreign policy.

Thus the Latin American experience brought radical change to the Roman Catholic concept of missions. Evangelization was defined more and more as work with and for the poor to seek transformation of social, economic, and political systems.

After an initial increase in U.S. Catholic missionaries after Vatican II, the number dropped sharply. The statistics in table 7.2 tell the story.

Behind the decrease is a significant theological reformulation. The Vatican II document *Ad Gentes* stated the traditional view: "The reason for missionary activity lies in the will of God, who wishes all men to be saved and to come to the knowledge of the truth. Everyone, therefore, ought to be converted to Christ . . . and incorporated into him and into the Church."[36] But by the late sixties some Catholic theologians were advocating a very different view. Avery Dulles, for example, stressed the Church as servant, "helping to build up a

TABLE 7.2   U.S. Catholic Missionaries, 1960–1996

	Africa	Far East	Oceania	Caribbean	L. America	Total*
1960	781	1,959	986	991	1,424	6,782
1964	1,025	2,332	846	1,056	2,456	8,126
1968	1,157	2,470	1,027	1,198	3,392	9,655
1972	1,107	1,955	826	819	2,617	7,656
1980	909	1,576	711	5,482	255	6,393
1996	799	965	213	360	1,573	4,164

*Totals are not the sums of the numbers given here, since some areas of the world, such as the Near East, Europe, and the United States, were omitted from this table.
Source: Angelyn Dries, The Missionary Movement in American Catholic History (Maryknoll, N.Y.: Orbis, 1998), 273.

stronger human community in this world," while Ronan Hoffman called the goal of converting all men a "missiology of the past" that should now give way to "religionless Christianity" and "service in the development of the world."[37]

It is clear that Roman Catholics and mainline Protestant missions face similar questions regarding the essential nature of the Christian mission and the balance to be sought between evangelization and social transformation. The missionary movements in both groups have declined greatly in numbers and will probably continue to do so without the recovery of a more compelling theology of mission. Meanwhile, the tendency is for the newer post-denominational, charismatic, and evangelical churches to continue to increase their missionary efforts.

Christian Humanitarian Organizations

Most Christian relief and development organizations began during or shortly after World War II. The major exceptions are the Salvation Army, which came to the United States in 1880, and the Mennonite Central Committee, established in 1920. (Although the Salvation Army does not fit completely into this category, it is greatly involved in such ministries.) Ten major organizations with current annual incomes ranging from $6 million to $210 million were established between 1943 and 1956, motivated by the suffering caused by World War II and the Korean conflict. Among them are both denominational and ecumenical agencies such as Catholic Relief Services (1943), Church World Service of the National Council of Churches (1946), and Lutheran World Relief (1945), and large evangelical agencies such as World Vision (1950) and Compassion International (1952). Another group of agencies, most with evangelical roots, was established in the 1970s. These include Samaritan's Purse led by Franklin Graham (1970), Food for the Hungry (1971), World Concerns (1973), and Habitat for Humanity (1976). In addition, there are specialized groups such as the Christian Medical and Dental Society, which placed a thousand persons in short-term mission in 1996, and Flying Doctors, which reported 204 medical personnel involved in short-term mission that same year.

Some of the ministries concentrate on children (Holt International Children's Services and Compassion International), or on the construction of houses (Habitat for Humanity), or on medical work and health care (MAP International). However, most provide disaster relief and also promote long-term, sustainable improvement by helping the people develop water resources, improve their land management and agricultural techniques, develop small businesses, and so on.

The relief and development organizations work on every continent. Samaritan's Purse lists forty countries of service, Mennonite Central Committee fifty-two, World Vision seventy. Total income of these agencies in 1996 was approximately $600 million in cash and $280 million in kind. Personnel overseas numbered approximately 500 long-term (defined as four or more years) and 1,000 for shorter terms.

In any given year, the roster of faith-based organizations will show approximately 50,000 Americans serving overseas on a long-term basis and 100,000 short-term. Many more will go for brief (less than two-week) stints. Total expenditures for the more traditional mission organizations total over $1.5 billion annually. (This figure is separate from the figures given for relief and development agencies.) The growth is in the groups that are more conservative theologically and, usually, politically. But sometimes the political conservativism changes as missionaries experience first hand the poverty, injustice, and oppression that exist in many areas of the world. That may be a subject for future study.

Notes

1. Joseph Tracy, *History of the American Board of Commissioners for Foreign Missions* (New York: M. W. Dodd, 1842), 182 ff.

2. Tracy, *History of the American Board of Commissioners*, 187.

3. M. Tate, "The Sandwich Islands Mission Creates a Literature," *Church History* 31: 182–202.

4. W. R. Hogg, "The Role of American Protestantism in World Mission," in R. P. Beaver, ed., *American Missions in Bicentennial Perspective* (Pasadena, Calif.: William Carey Library, 1976), 374.

5. Hogg, "Role of American Protestantism," 375.

6. Stanley Sholoff, "Presbyterians and Belgian Congo Exploitation: The Companie du Kasia v. Morrison and Sheppard," *Journal of Presbyterian History* 47: 173–94.

7. R. P. Beaver, *American Protestant Women in World Mission: A History of the First Feminist Movement in North America* (Grand Rapids, Mich.: Eerdmans, 1980).

8. Timothy Smith, *Revivalism and Social Reform* (New York: Harper and Row, 1957).

9. Hogg, "Role of American Protestantism," 384.

10. W. R. Hutchison, *Errand to the World* (Chicago: University of Chicago Press, 1987), 127.

11. Joel Carpenter, "Propagating the Faith Once Delivered: The Fundamentalist Missionary Enterprise," in J. Carpenter and W. Shenk, eds., *Earthen Vessels: American Evangelicals and Foreign Missions, 1880–1980* (Grand Rapids, Mich.: Eerdmans, 1990), 105.

12. R. Coote, "Twentieth-Century Shifts in the North American Protestant Missionary Community," *International Bulletin of Missionary Research* 22, no. 4 (October 1998): 152.

13. R. V. Pierod, "Pax Americana and the Evangelical Missionary Advance," in Carpenter and Shenk, *Earthen Vessels*, 174 f.

14. Pierod, "Pax Americana and the Evangelical Missionary Advance," 156.

15. Pierod, "Pax Americana and the Evangelical Missionary Advance," 157.

16. Pierod, "Pax Americana and the Evangelical Missionary Advance," 159.

17. Christ for the City, "Costa Rica Ministry Report," October 1998, unpublished.

18. C. Van Engen, "A Broadening Vision: Forty Years of Evangelical Theology of Mission, 1946–1986," in Carpenter and Shenk, *Earthen Vessels*, 204 f.

19. Lausanne Committee for World Evangelization, "Evangelism and Social Responsibility," 1982, 43 ff.

20. Coote, "Twentieth-Century Shifts," 152 f.

21. J. A. Siewart and E. G. Valdez, eds., *Mission Handbook* (Monrovia, Calif.: MARC [World Vision], 1997), 164.

22. Conversation with the Director, Dr. Douglas McConnell, April 19, 2000.

23. Conversation with the Director, Dr. Douglas McConnell, April 19, 2000, 128 f.

24. Conversation with the Director, Dr. Douglas McConnell, April 19, 2000, 108–253.

25. J. T. Ellis, *American Catholicism* (Chicago: University of Chicago Press, 1956), 130.

26. Angelyn Dries, *The Missionary Movement in American Catholic History* (Maryknoll, N.Y.: Orbis, 1998), 84. I am indebted to this comprehensive account for information on the Catholic missionary movement in the twentieth century.

27. Dries, *The Missionary Movement*, 95 f.

28. Dries, *The Missionary Movement*, 116.

29. Dries, *The Missionary Movement*, 122.

30. Dries, *The Missionary Movement*, 186.

31. Dries, *The Missionary Movement*.

32. Dries, *The Missionary Movement*, 202.

33. Dries, *The Missionary Movement*.

34. Dries, *The Missionary Movement*, 213.

35. Dries, *The Missionary Movement*, 230 ff.

36. P. E. Pierson, "Roman Catholic Missions since Vatican II: An Evangelical Assessment," *International Bulletin of Missionary Research* 9, no. 4 (October 1985): 165.

37. Pierson, "Roman Catholic Missions since Vatican II," 219 ff.

~

Comment by Gerald H. Anderson

Paul Pierson has given us a remarkably comprehensive overview of the historical development of American mission and relief and development agencies, both Protestant and Catholic, over nearly two hundred years. I want to highlight a couple of what I would call defining moments he mentions that indicate the shifting attitudes toward church-and-state and foreign-policy issues.

First, the victory of Admiral Dewey in Manila Bay during the Spanish-American War of 1898 presented the United States with its first opportunity for colonial expansion in Asia. In the national debate that ensued over what to do with the Philippine Islands, now liberated from Spanish rule, Protestants were overwhelmingly in favor of keeping the islands a U.S. colony. Motivated by a compelling sense of America's manifest destiny and the white man's burden, as well as by anti-Catholicism and by the "Great Commission" of Christ ("Go ye into all the world and preach the gospel"), Protestants saw this as a providential opportunity for extending the blessings of American democracy and Protestant Christianity to other peoples.

President William McKinley, who once said, "I am a Methodist and nothing but a Methodist," was not indifferent to this sentiment. To a delegation from the Methodist board of missions that called on him in his office on November 1899, the President described how he had arrived at his decision to retain the Philippines as a mission of what he called "benevolent assimilation." "I walked the floor of the White House night after night until mid-

Gerald H. Anderson, now retired, was director of the Overseas Ministries Study Center in New Haven, Connecticut, and editor of the *International Bulletin of Missionary Research*.

night," he said, "and I am not ashamed to tell you, gentlemen, that I went down on my knees and prayed Almighty God for light and guidance more than one night. And one night late it came to me . . . that there was nothing left for us to do but to take them all, and to educate the Filipinos, and uplift and civilize and Christianize them, and by God's grace do the very best we could by them, as our fellow men for whom Christ died." Here was an early bonding of the American missionary enterprise with U.S. foreign policy.

There were always critics of this alliance, of course, especially as the twentieth century wore on. After World War II, critics within the churches, both Protestant and Catholic, formed a new alliance to challenge U.S. foreign policy over the Cold War, Vietnam, and Latin America.

A second defining moment mentioned by Dr. Pierson that had a profound impact on many American Christians occurred in 1980. Following the murder of Archbishop Oscar Romero in San Salvador in March 1980, a call went out for missionary volunteers to help in El Salvador in the midst of repression and violence. Among those who offered themselves for service were four American Catholic women—two Maryknoll sisters, an Ursuline sister, and a laywoman. The four women helped to set up refugee camps for the poor who were being driven from their land. They would guide refugees to the camps and try to provide food, clothing, and shelter for them. They would search out the missing, pray with the families of prisoners, and bury the dead, always in the midst of poverty and violence. What they did was right out of the gospel of Matthew—feeding the hungry, clothing the naked, ministering to the sick, visiting the prisoners.

The story of their brutal murder in 1980 is well known. These women had been in El Salvador only a short time and had perhaps accomplished little in human terms, but in their powerlessness, suffering, and death they are remembered today in a very special way. The U.S. secretary of state at that time commented coldly, "If those women had not been involved in political activities, they would not have been harmed." More than any other single event, this tragedy made American Christians realize that all humanitarian efforts have political implications. Giving bread to refugees in the midst of persecution and oppression is a political act. Refugees are in fact an intensely political issue. Their existence affects both foreign and domestic policy, exacerbates interstate conflicts, and influences international attitudes.

~

Comment by Leo P. Ribuffo

Early in his account of the history of American missions abroad, Paul Pierson points to a problem area. The Christian Church, he says, "is inextricably entangled with the values and suppositions of its society; it must constantly try to distinguish the essentials of its faith and action from values and assumptions that are simply a part of its culture." I would amend that slightly to say that Christian *churches*, plural, must constantly try to distinguish the essentials of their *faiths* and *actions*, plural, from values and assumptions that are simply part of their diverse *cultures*, plural, within the larger American society. This process has involved a great deal of intra-Christian shouting, sometimes fistfights and occasionally even gunshots. Pierson shows some of this: Protestants and Catholics clashing over the right way to "Christianize" the largely Christian Philippines; theologically liberal and theologically conservative Protestants increasingly differing on the propriety of missionary work; Roman Catholic traditionalists taking issue with advocates of liberation theology.

We need a deeper sense of these historical conflicts, for two reasons. The first is that to some degree they are still going on, despite ecumenical references to the Judeo-Christian tradition, a catch phrase since the fifties, or to the more recent formulation "people of faith." In the 1950s, the Catholic theologian John Courtney Murray wrote that immense hostility between religious groups lay beneath the surface civility and celebration of "religion-in-

---

Leo P. Ribuffo is Society of the Cincinnati Distinguished Professor of History at George Washington University, Washington, D.C., and the author of *The Old Christian Right* and *Right Center Left*.

general, whatever that is." To the secular eye, Mormon missionaries and Jerry Falwell are zealots of a feather flocking together. But Falwell used to say, and may still believe, that Mormons are not true Christians and are likely to burn in hell for their error. To be sure, we are not, repeat *not*, involved in a culture war. We haven't had a culture war since before the Civil War, when Catholics and Protestants shouted out on election day and President James Buchanan dispatched troops to suppress the Mormons. But we *are* involved in a shouting match, much of it concerning the proper place of religious faith in American life and the proper degree of separation of church and state. Since we Americans have not settled these issues for ourselves, we—including missionaries and their supporters—should offer our tentative answers to the world with more humility than usually seems to be the case.

Indeed, the second reason why we need a deeper understanding of the conflicts among American people of faith is to appreciate how long it has taken us to reach our current level of civility. If this is the case in a prosperous nation with a broadly liberal polity, then we should certainly be wary of expecting quick virtue in nations we are trying to convert to various religious or secular political and economic faiths.

CHAPTER EIGHT

~

Faith-Based NGOs
and U.S. Foreign Policy

Mark R. Amstutz

Throughout the post–World War II era, conventional wisdom has held that U.S. foreign policy should avoid entanglement with religion. This view is rooted in a secular realism that has de-emphasized moral reasoning in foreign affairs. Edward Luttwak attributes the neglect of religion in postwar statecraft to the "Enlightenment prejudice," which has led scholars and decision makers to analyze international relations solely from strategic perspectives. Too many have erroneously assumed, he says, that "the progress of knowledge and the influence of religion were mutually exclusive, making the latter a waning force."[1]

But the prediction that religion would decline has not been borne out. Religion continues to be a potent force in national cultural life, especially in the Third World. Even in Western societies, religion and religious institutions still play a vital role, not only in many people's private lives but also in defining and interpreting moral values and worldviews for the larger society.

Religion remains salient, then, but does it influence foreign policy? More specifically, do churches and faith-based nongovernmental organizations (NGOs) affect the conduct of U.S. foreign relations? My answer would be that they play only a modest, indirect role in the development and implementation of foreign policy. But as moral teachers and the bearers of ethical traditions, religious communities can help to structure debate and illuminate

Mark R. Amstutz has been a professor of political science at Wheaton College in Illinois since 1972. He is the author of several books, including *International Conflict and Cooperation: An Introduction to World Politics* and *International Ethics: Concepts, Theories, and Cases in Global Politics.*

relevant moral norms. Although religious organizations may become involved in the political process from time to time, supporting or challenging particular policies, their main contribution to international affairs and U.S. foreign policy is not political but ethical. They help to develop and sustain political morality by promoting moral reasoning and by exemplifying values and behaviors that are conducive to human dignity. In what follows we will consider three avenues through which churches and faith-based NGOs might have an influence upon U.S. foreign policy: as *institutions*, through *ideas*, and through *service*.

The Influence of Institutions

Nearly 70 percent of American adults are members of a church or synagogue.[2] Though their involvement varies greatly, this religiosity is noteworthy when compared to that of other industrial states. A 1996 study suggests, moreover, that religion is "a strong and growing force in the way Americans think about politics." This conclusion is based in part on the fact that church members express increasing support for political action by churches and religious institutions. While in the 1960s only 40 percent of Christian congregations said that churches should participate in the political process, this percentage had increased to 54 by the 1990s.[3]

The thousands of faith-based nonprofit organizations active in representing, organizing, and articulating religiously based concerns attest to the religious vitality that exists in the United States. Some of these NGOs—denominational headquarters, for instance, or such groups as the National Association of Evangelicals (NAE)[4] and the National Council of Churches (NCC)[5]—deal primarily with theological and ecclesiastical matters. Others, like Focus on the Family and the Southern Baptist Convention's Christian Life Commission, are concerned with moral questions affecting family and society, such as abortion, juvenile delinquency, and drug abuse. Religious institutions of a third type provide a wide range of social, medical, educational, and humanitarian services, both domestically and internationally. Some of these organizations, such as Catholic Relief Services and the NAE's World Relief, sponsor domestic refugee resettlement and provide significant humanitarian assistance in complex emergencies in foreign countries.[6]

Because of the wide diversity of their ecclesiastical traditions, theological convictions, and political views, churches and religious NGOs vary significantly in their political engagement. Historically, *mainline Protestant churches* have been active in public affairs, expressing their views on many domestic and international questions through denominational resolutions and joint declarations. The more centralized *Catholic Church* has been similarly active. Through papal encyclicals, such as *Pacem in Terris* (1963) and *Centesimus Annus* (1991), it has defined the church's perspectives on matters of human rights, international justice, and the global common good. In addition, the U.S. Catholic Conference, which is the public-policy agency of the American Catholic bishops, has frequently spoken about specific foreign and domestic issues in pastoral letters and policy statements.[7] Finally, since the 1970s, *evangelical and fundamentalist Christians* have moved out of their previous restraint and become as active politically as mainline Christians.

Not surprisingly, mainline Protestant political action has typically supported more progressive positions, while evangelical and fundamentalist groups have tended to advocate more conservative ones. In recent years, for example, mainline Protestants have supported environmental initiatives aimed at reducing industrial pollution and slowing global warming. The NCC spearheaded a public campaign in support of the UN's Kyoto Protocol on limiting greenhouse gas emissions. Evangelicals, by contrast, have supported Israel in the Middle East peace process[8] and have called attention to religious persecution in foreign countries.

Influence through Ideas

Perhaps the most significant contribution churches and religious institutions make to U.S. foreign policy is at the level of ideas. Concerned with ultimate questions about the nature and destiny of human beings, they offer a rich repository of teaching on such matters as the fundamental equality of persons, the priority of freedom, just war doctrine, and subsidiarity. While the foreign-policy establishment cannot directly appropriate religious morality, this does not mean, as George Kennan has alleged, that moral values have no place in the conduct of American foreign relations.[9] Rather, it means that religious values and moral norms play an indirect rather than direct role. As John C. Bennett noted some four decades ago, they "offer ultimate perspectives, broad criteria, motives, inspirations, sensitivities, warnings, [and] moral limits."[10] Churches and faith-based organizations can help to clarify and refine conceptions of the national interest and to structure moral discourse on foreign-policy issues.

Judith Goldstein has argued that major policy ideas perform two important roles in foreign-policy decision making. First, ideas serve as road maps, providing guidance to leaders. As Henry Kissinger once observed, "it is not possible to conduct a foreign policy without a vision of the world that one wants to bring about, some definition of what one means by peace, and by justice and by order and by stability and by progress."[11] Second, as ideas become widely accepted and institutionalized, they result in rules and norms that structure future foreign-policy debates.[12] By disseminating relevant ethical perspectives and moral values, churches and religious NGOs help draw the foreign-policy "road map." Churches and religious NGOs articulate and publicize their ideas in three general ways: through policy statements and teaching documents; through the preaching and teaching of the clergy, missionaries, and NGO staffs; and by the individual witness of believers as they personally model religious and moral convictions.

1. *Policy Statements and Teaching Documents.* Church bodies and faith-based NGOs periodically issue reports, studies, teaching documents, and policy statements on a wide array of public-policy concerns. The most influential document of this sort produced by an American church body is the U.S. Catholic bishops' 1983 pastoral letter on nuclear strategy, *The Challenge of Peace.* The letter—the result of multiple published drafts and more than three years of private and public deliberations with theologians, ethicists, and national-security specialists—was a carefully crafted document that called into question the long-term moral legitimacy of the U.S. policy of nuclear deterrence.[13] Although this pastoral letter provided a number of policy recommendations, its major contribution to the debate on nuclear strategy was its assessment of strategic doctrine in light of theological and moral perspectives.[14]

Because of its influence, *The Challenge of Peace* has become for many the standard by which religious bodies should seek to influence public-policy discourse. Indeed, Robert Bellah suggests that this letter and the bishops' subsequent pastoral letter on the U.S. economy (*Economic Justice for All,* 1986) constitute a watershed in the evolution of religion and public life in the United States. Before that, he says, the missionary enterprise was the major method of spiritual and social witness for American churches. From the early nineteenth through the mid-twentieth century, churches and religious institutions contributed to foreign affairs indirectly by personally modeling social, political, and economic values common in America. But with the issuing of the pastoral letters in the 1980s, Bellah contends, a new paradigm arose, one that calls attention to the intersection of biblical and theological reflection with political, social, and economic analysis.[15]

With the exception of a few pastoral letters by the U.S. Catholic bishops, however, the documents of Christian churches have rarely had much impact, either on public opinion or on policy-making institutions, largely because they usually are neither technically competent nor morally authoritative. For the most part they fail to integrate sophisticated biblical and theological reflection with a comprehensive understanding of the relevant policy issues. Most denominational pronouncements tend to be prudential policy judgments for which clergy and religious workers have no particular competence. Thus mainline Protestant policy statements on the nuclear dilemma and the Strategic Defense Initiative (SDI) in the mid-1980s, the Middle East peace process in the late 1980s and early 1990s, and the Persian Gulf conflict in 1991 had little impact on the decision-making process. Indeed, such documents may have hurt the churches themselves, as informed parishioners called into question the theological and technical competence of the professional staffs who had written them.[16]

2. *Preaching and Teaching.* Religious groups also propagate ideas and values through preaching and teaching. Although Protestants and Catholics have historically regarded the spiritual reformation of humankind as the Church's fundamental task, theological differences have led to sharply divergent views of the relationship between Christ and culture, church and society.[17] Evangelicals and fundamentalists have emphasized the radical dichotomy between the demands of the Heavenly Kingdom and those of the Earthly Kingdom and have tended to minimize temporal obligations to society and state. Mainline Protestants and Catholics, in contrast, have stressed the Church's responsibility to promote justice in the world.

In the 1960s, under the prodding of evangelist Billy Graham and theologian Carl F. H. Henry, among others, evangelicals began calling for greater social and political involvement. The National Association of Evangelicals had established a government-affairs office in Washington, D.C., in the late 1950s, and evangelicals slowly began to increase their political engagement, both domestically and internationally. In the 1970s, fundamentalists followed suit; at the urging of Jerry Falwell, Pat Robertson, and others, they expanded their political participation in the hope of halting the perceived moral decay of society. And so, whereas political engagement had been limited chiefly to Catholics and mainline Protestants during much of the Cold War, by the 1970s evangelicals and fundamentalists had become more active in political affairs. According to one 1996 public-opinion survey, current politicking from the pulpit is reported more often by white evangelical Protestants (20 percent) than by white Catholics (12 percent) or white mainline Protestants (12 percent).[18] And although priests and preachers from different denominations may express quite different opinions, the rate at which they address global topics such as hunger, poverty, and the world's trouble spots tends to be roughly the same regardless of whether the church is white mainline Protestant, white evangelical Protestant, Catholic, or black Christian.[19]

While the clergy can help to illuminate biblical and moral principles that may be relevant to global issues, they may undermine the Church's moral authority if they advocate specific policies. The late Paul Ramsey argued that, in confronting political issues, the Church should act as "theoretician." If the churches have any special wisdom in public affairs, he said, "it is in cultivating the political ethos of a nation and informing the conscience of the statesman. The church's business is not policy formation."[20]

3. *Personal Witness*. Finally, individuals informed by religious values model and propagate those values and moral ideals at home and overseas through their religious and humanitarian service. The international presence of American missionaries and religious NGO personnel is significant, involving a work force that is larger than the total civilian staff working for the U.S. government abroad. In 1997 nearly 45,000 Americans were serving as Protestant or Catholic missionaries or as relief and development workers. The income supporting this missionary and humanitarian enterprise exceeded $2.6 billion.[21] American religious organizations are active in most foreign countries, carrying out a vast array of services, including disaster relief, refugee assistance, and development aid. Many of the largest humanitarian NGOs are religious, and more than a third of the 159 members of InterAction, the principal association of development and refugee agencies, are religiously affiliated.[22]

The witness of missionaries and religious workers continues to be a vital means by which widely shared American cultural, political, and social values are disseminated abroad. Many of these values help to reinforce ideals of democratic rule, human rights, economic modernization, and political freedom. To the extent that U.S. citizens serving in religious organizations in foreign countries are engaged in public affairs, their words and actions have the potential either to reinforce or to undermine U.S. national interests and particular foreign-policy objectives. This was especially evident during the 1980s in Central America. Some mainline Protestant and Catholic groups working in Nicaragua espoused interests and ideals that contradicted U.S. foreign-policy goals, while some American evangelical groups reinforced official U.S. policies by criticizing the Sandinista government in Nicaragua and warning against Marxism in El Salvador.

Influence through Service

Humanitarianism has long been regarded as authentic religious expression. Today Christians and members of other religious groups continue to offer tangible evidence of their religious beliefs by providing many kinds of assistance to the poor, the sick, the weak, and the hungry. Many religious NGOs—including such Christian organizations as Catholic Relief Services, Food for the Hungry International, World Vision Relief and Development, and World Relief Corporation—use spiritual terminology to define their goals and purposes.[23]

In 1995, Christian NGOs channeled more than $2 billion in humanitarian relief to foreign countries. Evangelical Protestants, represented chiefly by some forty member organizations of the Association of Evangelical Relief and Development Organizations (AERDO), were responsible for roughly half of this amount.[24] Mainline Protestant and Catholic NGOs—led by Catholic Relief Services, the National Council of Churches, Church World Service, Lutheran World Relief, and the United Methodist Committee on Relief—gave more than $600 million.[25]

Alternative Theological Approaches

The work of faith-based humanitarian NGOs is inspired by religious commitments, and theological perspectives affect their approach to relief and development. Though it is an oversimplification to do so, Christian humanitarian NGOs can be differentiated into two groups: evangelicals, who give priority to individual religious transformation, and mainline Protestants and Catholics, who stress the social and political dimensions of justice.

Evangelicals emphasize biblical authority, personal conversion, evangelism, and personal witness.[26] As a result, evangelical Protestant humanitarian NGOs—the largest group of American faith-based relief organizations—focus on spiritual motivations and give less attention to structural change through social and political justice. Because their theological perspective minimizes politics, evangelical groups have generally worked in a complementary, cooperative manner not only with U.S. government officials but also with host governmental institutions. During the Vietnam War, for example, evangelical mission groups and humanitarian organizations continued their work in a largely apolitical manner. And during the Central American wars of the 1980s, evangelical groups maintained their evangelistic and humanitarian ministries despite the profound divisions that existed among U.S. citizens over the nature of the Central American political crisis.

Mainline Protestant and Catholic groups stress communal dimensions of justice rather than personal reformation. While acknowledging that believers owe their ultimate allegiance to the Heavenly Kingdom, such groups in practice emphasize the social and political implications of religion. In the early 1970s, for example, some mainline Protestant missionary groups in Chile eagerly identified with the radical socioeconomic reforms instituted by the government of Salvador Allende. As a result, when a military coup brought down the Allende regime in September 1973, some of these faith-based groups were forced to leave the country or to reduce their work.

During humanitarian emergencies, of course, all shades of religious and secular NGOs are concerned alike with meeting the basic material needs of people suffering from natural or man-made disasters. But in carrying out medium- and long-term development projects, Christians with a more holistic view of religion tend to link development to structural issues, while groups that emphasize human spiritual needs see progress in terms of individual transformations.

U.S. Government–Religious NGO Cooperation

Historically, faith-based NGOs and the U.S. government have cooperated in overseas humanitarian work, especially in refugee services, humanitarian relief, and economic development. Their partnership is rooted in shared interests. While the government did channel some resources through faith-based NGOs during the early postwar era, since the 1980s the "privatization" of U.S. foreign aid has accelerated. Government officials have come to recognize the advantages of cooperating with religious as well as secular NGOs in meeting humanitarian objectives.

In his fine study on refugees, J. Bruce Nichols shows that religious NGOs have carried the major burden of providing assistance to refugees around the world. Not only have they provided specific humanitarian services, he says, but they have also helped to define "America's ties with the rest of the world."[27] More recently, religious NGOs have played a vital role in the development of microenterprise. Funded in part by U.S. government grants, such organizations as Catholic Relief Services, Food for the Hungry, and World Relief have established community banks that provide small, short-term loans to foster job creation. For example, from 1995 to 2000 Opportunity International, a pioneer in microenterprise development, created 771,000 jobs in Third World countries. In 1999 alone it lent nearly $44 million that resulted in 276,000 jobs.

While many religious NGOs refuse government money, for fear of compromising their religious purposes or organizational independence, this kind of church-state cooperation is widespread and expanding. Table 8.1 shows that government funds constitute a substantial part of the budget of faith-based NGOs across the spectrum—Catholic, mainline Protestant, and evangelical.

Several developments have fostered the increasing "privatization" of foreign aid and humanitarian relief. First, the number of U.S. government offi-

Table 8.1   Major Faith-Based NGO Budgets, 1998

Organization	1998 Budget (millions of dollars)	U.S. Government Funds (percentage of budget)
Adventist Development and Relief Agency	70.1	60.0
Catholic Relief Services	276.0	47.1
Church World Service	57.9	20.8
Food for the Hungry	45.5	22.5
Lutheran World Relief	22.6	5.6
Mercy Corps International	93.2	32.9
Opportunity International	14.3	35.7
Salvation Army World Service Office	24.8	24.1
United Methodist Committee on Relief	44.9	35.6
World Relief Corporation	23.3	59.1
World Vision Relief and Development	358.4	16.1

Source: Adapted from Shanta M. Bryant and Tienne McKenzie, eds., *InterAction Member Profiles, 2000–2001* (Washington, D.C.: American Council for Voluntary International Action, 2000), passim.

cials working overseas in economic and community development and in humanitarian relief has declined dramatically since the 1960s. In 1972, in Vietnam alone the U.S. government had more than three thousand persons working on development and humanitarian projects; by 1998, however, the total worldwide staff of the U.S. Agency for International Development had been reduced to about a thousand.[28] Because of reduced staff, the U.S. government has increasingly relied on multilateral organizations and NGOs to implement economic and humanitarian goals. Second, private voluntary organizations are playing a more active role because they are considered more efficient and more effective in meeting local humanitarian needs. Their staffs generally have more knowledge of local needs, community structures, and environmental constraints. Also, NGOs typically face fewer bureaucratic regulations than governmental agencies. NGOs provide, in the words of one NGO official, "more bang for the buck" than U.S. agencies.[29] A third reason for the growing reliance on NGOs is the evolution in development paradigms—from centralized, government-initiated projects in the 1960s and 1970s to decentralized, market-based projects in the 1980s and 1990s.

Organizational competence is an important requirement in providing humanitarian relief. To the extent that disaster relief is essentially a managerial task, religious NGOs are no more effective in providing it than secular NGOs or government institutions. Religious organizations possess, however, distinct institutional advantages. They maintain closer associations with the people they are serving; they frequently work through churches and religious communities that can reinforce accountability; and they promote moral values—such as fidelity, integrity, thrift, and personal responsibility—that contribute to both human dignity and human enterprise.

Faith-based NGOs use public resources for humanitarian relief in accordance with widely accepted ethical norms: they focus on existing needs, whether these result from man-made political disasters or natural catastrophes; they abide by the prohibition against using aid for political purposes; and they do not discriminate in the distribution of relief. Religious NGOs do not make aid contingent on church membership or religious belief, nor do they use humanitarian supplies for proselytization. This does not mean, however, that religious NGOs keep religion out of their humanitarian work; religious perspectives and values are integrally related to the work of many faith-based NGOs.

Of course, minimizing religious elements is much more feasible in short-term humanitarian relief than in long-term development projects. Indeed, religious NGOs have been especially effective in microenterprise development precisely because religious and communal structures help to reinforce behaviors that are essential for sustaining enterprise. The advantage of faith-based NGOs in promoting small-scale enterprise is that they maintain close ties to local churches and encourage personal accountability. In a study of economic development in Guatemala, Amy Sherman shows that religion has significant social, economic, and political consequences. She argues, on the basis of opinion survey findings, that Christian conversion is conducive both to improved standards of living and to beliefs and behavioral patterns that enhance human dignity.[30] Sherman's study reinforces the view that religion can foster economic enterprise.

Although the overseas partnership between religious NGOs and the U.S. government creates fewer tensions than a similar domestic involvement would do, it is not problem-free. In this "uneasy alliance," the religious and temporal spheres cannot be clearly demarcated. Inevitably, faith-based NGOs fear governmental encroachment on the religious character of their work, and government institutions fear the misuse of public funds for religious purposes. Not surprisingly, government agencies institute regulations and restrictions to assure accountability over humanitarian projects funded by public revenues, and Stephen Monsma, for one, thinks that "all is not necessarily well in terms of the religious autonomy of religious nonprofit organizations receiving public money."[31] But, as one evangelical NGO official noted, government officials also tend to "turn the other way" in dealing with religion, provided NGOs fulfill their contractual obligations.[32]

Concluding Observations. While Leo Ribuffo is correct to say, as he does in his chapter in this book, that no major foreign-policy decision has turned on religious issues alone, religious organizations do have a legitimate role to play in the democratic development of policy. That role is modest and indirect. They provide broad perspectives, ethical traditions, and moral values that can help to shape conceptions of the national interest and of major policy ideals. Through their teachings, churches and religious NGOs can influence policy makers, and through their international services, they model values and behaviors that help to define America's relations with the world.

Notes

1. Edward Luttwak, "The Missing Dimension," in Douglas Johnston and Cynthia Sampson, eds., *Religion: The Missing Dimension of Statecraft* (New York: Oxford University Press, 1994), 9.

2. More than 80 percent of the American people are Christians, with 58 percent of the adults professing Protestantism and 25 percent professing Catholicism. Jews, the third largest religious group, make up roughly 2 percent of the adult population.

3. Pew Research Center for the People and the Press, "The Diminishing Divide: American Churches and American Politics," 1996, 1 and 6.

4. The National Association of Evangelicals encompasses nearly fifty evangelical denominations, with more than 8 million members. The Southern Baptist Convention, with its 15.8 million members, is not part of the NAE.

5. The National Council of Churches, the major association of Protestant churches in the United States, includes more than thirty denominations with nearly 40 million members.

6. As of 1999, World Relief alone has resettled more than 160,000 refugees in the United States.

7. For an overview of the Catholic Church's approach to international affairs, see John Langan, S.J., "The Catholic Vision of World Affairs," *Orbis* 42 (spring 1998): 241–61.

8. For a brief overview of the close connection between evangelicals and Israel, see Timothy P. Weber, "How Evangelicals Became Israel's Best Friend," *Christianity Today*, October 5, 1998, 39–49.

9. George F. Kennan, "Morality and Foreign Policy," *Foreign Affairs*, winter 1985–1986, 205–18.

10. John C. Bennett, *Foreign Policy in Christian Perspective* (New York: Scribners, 1966), 36.

11. Henry Kissinger, "The Realities of Security," *AEI Foreign Policy and Defense Review* 3, no. 6 (1982):11.

12. Judith Goldstein, *Ideas, Interests, and American Trade Policy* (Ithaca, N.Y.: Cornell University Press, 1993), 1–4.

13. The bishops argued that, in light of the significant military challenge posed by the Soviet Union, the U.S. strategy of deterrence was morally justified only as a temporary solution while the United States pursued a vigorous policy of mutual disarmament.

14. It is significant that the bishops emphasized the *authoritative* nature of the pastoral letter's biblical and moral analysis but the *prudential* nature of the specific policy recommendations.

15. Robert Bellah, "Religious Influences on United States Foreign Policy," in Michael P. Hamilton, ed., *American Character and Foreign Policy* (Grand Rapids, Mich.: Eerdmans, 1986), 53–55.

16. Two church documents that illustrate the problematic nature of ill-conceived policy documents are *Presbyterians and Peacemaking: Are We Now Called to Resistance?*, a study report issued in 1985 by the Presbyterian Church (USA), and *In Defense of Creation*, issued in 1986 by the United Methodist Church. Instead of providing an authoritative analysis of biblical and theological principles relevant to the nuclear dilemma, these documents simply provide a political and humanistic critique of U.S. strategic policy.

17. Although dated, the classic statement on the principal approaches to religion and culture is H. Richard Niebuhr, *Christ and Culture*.

18. Pew Research Center, "The Diminishing Divide," 2.

19. Pew Research Center, "The Diminishing Divide," 5. According to the Pew report, the following percentages of survey respondents indicated that clergy expressed views on (a) hunger and poverty and (b) world trouble spots, respectively, in their churches: white mainline Protestant, 91 percent and 68 percent; white evangelical Protestant, 86 percent and 55 percent; Catholic, 90 percent and 59 percent; and black Christian, 93 percent and 69 percent.

20. Paul Ramsey, *Who Speaks for the Church?* (New York: Abingdon, 1967), 149.

21. This is an estimate, based on the fact that revenue for Protestant missions groups totaled about $2.3 billion. John A. Siewert and Edna G. Valdez, eds., *Mission Handbook: U.S. and Canadian Christian Ministries Overseas, 1998–2000* (Monrovia, Calif.: MARC, 1998), 74, 481–502.

22. Tracy Geoghegan and Kristen Allen, eds., *InterAction Member Profiles, 1997–1998* (Washington, D.C.: American Council for Voluntary International Action, 1997), passim.

23. For example, World Vision, the largest evangelical relief and development organization with an annual budget of more than $300 million, states its mission as follows: "World Vision is an international partnership of Christians whose mission is to follow our Lord and Savior Jesus Christ in working with the poor and oppressed to promote human transformation, seek justice, and bear witness to the good news of the Kingdom of God." Catholic Relief Services, the major relief and development organization of the U.S. Catholic Church, defines its major motivating force as "the Gospel of Jesus Christ as it pertains to the alleviation of human suffering, the development of people, and the fostering of charity and justice in the world."

24. Estimate based on Carrene G. Rosser, ed., *Member Directory: Association of Evangelical Relief and Development Organizations* (Washington, D.C.: AERD, 1998). The largest

AERD organizations include the Adventist Development and Relief Agency, Compassion International, Feed the Children, Food for the Hungry, International Aid, Map International, Operation Blessing, Salvation Army, Samaritan's Purse, World Relief (the relief arm of the National Association of Evangelicals), and World Vision.

25. Estimate based on Tracy Geoghegan and Kristen Allen, eds., *InterAction Member Profiles, 1997–1998* (Washington, D.C.: American Council for Voluntary International Action, 1997).

26. For evangelicals, personal conversion entails a "born again" experience based on the belief that Jesus is the only way to salvation.

27. J. Bruce Nichols, *The Uneasy Alliance: Religion, Refugee Work, and U.S. Foreign Policy* (New York: Oxford University Press, 1988), 3.

28. Interview with a midlevel USAID official, September 1998.

29. Interview with a senior executive of a faith-based NGO, September 1998.

30. Amy L. Sherman, *The Soul of Development: Biblical Christianity and Economic Transformation in Guatemala* (New York: Oxford University Press, 1997), 4–18.

31. Stephen V. Monsma, *When Sacred and Secular Mix: Religious Nonprofit Organizations and Public Money* (Lanham, Md.: Rowman & Littlefield, 1996), 98.

32. Interview with evangelical missionary involved in relief and development work, September 1998.

~

Faith-Based NGOs
and U.S. Foreign Policy

Andrew S. Natsios

The reaction of the foreign-policy establishment in the United States to the rise in the visibility and influence of nongovernmental organizations has been one of either naïve infatuation or cynical disdain. Those infatuated with NGOs seem to believe they are part of the New Age wave of the future: people-centered organizations devoid of the fallen institutional imperatives of the traditional foreign-policy establishment. For theorists devoted to a foreign policy based on a rigorous definition of American national interest devoid of sentimentality (and ethical norms), nongovernmental organizations represent a threat to hard realism. But NGOs are more complex and varied in their internal dynamics than is commonly understood. The humanitarian assistance they provide in former Soviet states and in the Third World may serve the worldviews of both the idealists and the realists simultaneously or of neither, depending on circumstances. They are neither as idealistic nor as impractical as their enthusiasts or detractors suppose.

Faith-based NGOs (FNGOs) as a unique manifestation of the NGO spirit are even less studied than NGOs generally. Their roots reach back into the ancient religious traditions out of which they come even if their registration

Andrew S. Natsios was selected by President George W. Bush to head USAID. Previously he was chairman of the Massachusetts Turnpike Authority, responsible for the Big Dig, the largest public construction project in U.S. history. From 1993 to 1998 he was vice president of World Vision U.S. and executive director of World Vision Relief and Development. Previous to that he served with US-AID, first as director of the Office of Foreign Disaster Assistance and then as assistant administrator of the Bureau of Food and Humanitarian Assistance. In the latter post he was appointed by President Bush to manage U.S. government relief efforts in the Somalia famine.

with the United Nations and the U.S. government dates to the World War II period and its immediate aftermath. While there are in the United States a half dozen Jewish NGOs of some size and several more recently formed Muslim ones, I will be looking in this essay at Christian faith-based NGOs, both because I am most familiar with them and because their size, worldwide scope, and influence on a wide range of issues is so substantial.

Of the 150 members of InterAction, the NGO trade association, more than forty can be classified as faith-based. FNGOs behave differently than secular NGOs, particularly in the public-policy arena. This difference is not widely appreciated even among FNGOs, in part because institutional rivalries, organizational competition for scarce donor resources, and theological disputes among them have obscured their similarities to one another.

In December 1996, sixteen NGOs concerned with the unfolding famine in North Korea met in Georgia at the Musgrove Plantation of the R. J. Reynolds family, whose foundation funded the event. The meeting was called by Mercy Corps International, a faith-based group from Portland, Oregon, that started as a Protestant evangelical NGO but now has strong Roman Catholic representation on its board (its founder and president, a scholar and writer of some note, converted from Pentecostalism to Catholicism). All groups that had begun some sort of assistance program to the North were invited to the meeting. Of the sixteen NGOs that attended, thirteen were faith-based. An outsider might interpret this disproportionate interest in North Korea by Christian NGOs as motivated by the longer-term interest in evangelizing the country, if and when the current government falls or becomes more tolerant of religion. But a majority of the FNGOs represented at the meeting do not evangelize or proselytize in any form in any of their programs. Their interest, I suggest, may have had more to do with moral theology than with denominational competition. That meeting led to an aggressive NGO campaign to change U.S. policy on food aid in a famine, a campaign I shall say more about later.

Types of FNGOs

How are faith-based NGOs different from their secular counterparts? Some of the greatest present-day NGOs were founded as faith-based groups or by people of faith but for various reasons have evolved into entirely secular institutions. OXFAM, the largest British NGO, was founded by an Anglican priest, a Methodist minister, and a rabbi to respond to the Greek famine of 1942–1943, caused by the German Occupation forces when they stripped the country of food in order to provision Rommel's army in North Africa. CARE, the largest NGO in the world, was founded by a group of American Quakers to deal with the humanitarian needs of World War II. These groups are no longer considered faith-based, having clearly chosen to go the secular route. Also excluded from the category are NGOs such as Christian Children's Fund and the YMCA/YWCA that, while they retain in their names evidence of their religious roots, are not guided by any theological statement or denominational commitment in hiring staff and carrying out their work.

Faith-based NGOs as we will consider them here are groups that (1) in their articles of incorporation or mission statement make an overt statement of religious faith as the motivating force behind their work, (2) are associated with some religious hierarchy or theological tradition, and (3) hire all or some of their staff based on a creed or faith statement. Within this general grouping there are several categories. First, some FNGOs are appendages of particular denominations. Often their relationship with the church hierarchy is contentious for any of several reasons. Their staff members are professional relief and development managers, not theologians; they serve a somewhat different donor base within the church or among donors outside the church; their institutional objectives are quite different (while the church hierarchy serves parishioners and may seek converts, the FNGO serves the poor, usually regardless of denomination); often the denomination and its NGO are competitors for a limited pool of parishioner funding; and finally, the church by its nature is locally focused no matter how internationally minded, while FNGOs focus their attention almost entirely abroad. These differences make for conflict and rivalry.

A second category consists of FNGOs that are unattached to specific denominations; most of their donors belong to churches that have no FNGO or are not part of any denomination or hierarchical structure at all, as is the case with many evangelical and Pentecostal churches. Also, some mainline Protestant churches that are theologically more conservative than their denominational structure choose to give to Christian humanitarian work abroad through an evangelical FNGO rather than a more liberal denominational body. There are perhaps forty evangelical relief and development NGOs in the United States, of which only ten are of any substantial size. (There are probably another 50–100 very small evangelical NGOs, frequently associated with missionary-sending denominations or missions agencies, that engage in some sort of humanitarian activity.) The largest of these by a factor of five is World Vision; the income of its U.S. office alone (there are fifteen more fund-raising offices in other countries) was $410 million in 1999. By comparison, the next largest in income in 1999 was Compassion International, with a budget of $80 million. Nearly all belong to the Association of Evangelical Relief and Development Organizations, or AERDO, a loose confederation of theologically conservative and more justice-oriented FNGOs.

A third category of FNGOs consists of cross-denominational consortiums and coalitions, either permanent or temporary. An example of a permanent group is Bread for the World, formed in 1974 with Roman Catholic, mainline Protestant, and evangelical Protestant support from individual donors and some churches to lobby in Washington on issues related to hunger. Its first board chairman was the president of Catholic University, the treasurer was from World Vision, and its two presidents have been Lutheran clergymen. Other coalitions are created for a specific purpose and then end as the purpose is accomplished; an example is the Stop the [North Korean] Famine Committee, whose eighteen members—all but four of which were faith-based—included AERDO, the National Conference of Catholic Bishops, and the National Council of Churches.

The Internationalization of FNGOs

Most larger FNGOs have internationalized over the past two decades; they raise funds in more than one wealthy country, sometimes dozens of countries, to support their work in poor countries. Behind internationalization lies a complex set of sometimes contradictory motives. Growth has been justified in order to achieve theoretical economies of scale (though few of these have been realized by any NGO I am aware of). Larger NGOs can do more good in more countries by having more resources. Boards of directors tend to judge the success of their executives on organizational income each year: internationalization increases the number of donor governments from which public-sector funding can be claimed, the number of corporations and foundations that can contribute, and the number of individual donors that can be recruited. Perhaps an unspoken motivation in this expansion has been the notion that the larger an international NGO, the more powerful it would be in promoting its own international policies and expanding its field programs; senior executives want to be visible players in the NGO world, and expanding helps them reach this objective.

The three largest FNGO confederations, representing mainline Protestants, evangelical Protestants, and Roman Catholics, have become huge international organizations with staffs of 5,000 to 10,000, a program presence in most poor countries, and huge budgets that in the aggregate exceed a billion dollars annually. Mainline Protestant denominations work through national councils of churches that are coordinated in Geneva by the World Council of Churches. The evangelical agency World Vision has sixteen offices in wealthy northern countries, each with its own staff and independent board, which raise money for field programs in eighty countries in the developing world and former Soviet states. Its international secretariat, called World Vision International, is located in California and reports to an international board of directors that is only 20 percent American. Catholic Relief Services, an agency of the U.S. Catholic Bishops' conference, is part of the international Caritas network with an international secretariat in Rome; the bishops in each country sit as the board of directors for their national office.

Very few FNGOs have anything like a single hierarchy with some international chief executive officer who has the authority to make policy decisions for all the affiliates. Most are more decentralized and confederal in structure; they work by consensus, with many chief executive officers negotiating with one another.

Decolonialization in FNGOs

A second trend in international governance among NGOs is decolonialization. Until the 1970s NGOs had been managed and led by western European, Canadian, and American staff—not surprisingly, since it was from these three regions that most resources came. But the same Third World nationalism that led the great imperial powers to relinquish colonial empires also led NGOs to turn over control of field programs to people in the beneficiary countries. FNGOs were well ahead of secular NGOs in making these changes, perhaps because the indigenous churches to which the FNGOs were attached demanded it, and because these churches displayed an energy and vibrancy (though not necessarily the desirable managerial and technical capacity) that northern churches lacked. No such indigenous power base for decolonialization existed for secular NGOs. Part of the reason for this decolonialization is a reflection of the central Christian theological principle that all men and women are equal in God's sight.

The decolonialization movement among FNGOs has not been free of complications. In contrast to NGOs, multilateral corporations have skillfully built into their personnel systems mechanisms to curb or diminish the more destructive nationalist sentiments of their multinational staff, and yet still allow the corporation a worldwide presence to expand corporate markets and to recruit talented and motivated people from every country. Few NGOs have taken similar measures, and as a result many suffer a certain degree of paralysis as ethnic and national frictions complicate management.

Although it is customary to see this conflict in terms of the wealthy northern countries versus poor southern countries, the reality is much less simple. The simmering national and ethnic rivalries among states in Africa, for example, do spill into FNGO governance issues and the creation of international policy. Rivalries among European countries, or between English-speaking countries and continental countries, or between Canadian and American FNGO structures, are more common than most FNGOs publicly admit.

The internationalization and decolonialization of FNGOs has greatly complicated the design and implementation of their policy on a host of issues. What few FNGO boards of directors considered when they insisted on expansion and internationalization were the unintended consequences of size and complexity: much higher overhead costs, decision-making complications, cultural conflict among the national staffs that spills over into policy making, and policy statement ambiguity.

Some FNGOs have established guidelines for the development of policy to ensure some consistency and coherence. World Vision designed some ground rules for member offices engaging in international policy work. One rule is that a national office may not advocate, with its own government, policies affecting another country unless that country's national director approves them. This means, for example, that the World Vision U.S. office may not issue a statement about the U.S. government's policy in Sudan unless the World Vision director in Sudan has approved it. This effectively places the burden of ensuring consistency, accuracy, and coherence on the national director of the field office. A second ground rule is that all policies, regardless of who approves them, must be consistent with the principles set forth in World Vision's general statement of orthodox Christian theology. These principles focus on the role of the Church and of World Vision in dealing with the poor in the developing world; they are somewhat akin to Catholic social teaching, though not as developed intellectually or rooted historically. Finally, World Vision policy making must focus on those issues about which it has direct knowledge and some ground presence. This rule significantly constrains a national office's inclination to comment on such issues as international narcotics, nuclear proliferation, or international trade agreements, issues on which World Vision personnel can claim no particular expertise. Given the confederal structure of the World Vision partnership, as it is called, these rules can occasionally be broken, since there is no effective mechanism to ensure compliance. The system relies on the good faith of the national offices and the fear that if one office breaks the rules, another might follow and compromise other offices.

How FNGOs Influence Foreign Policy

The techniques used by FNGOs to influence the design and execution of the foreign policy of national governments are neither particularly innovative nor unusual. Faith-based groups mobilize their constituencies much as other interest groups do; though they may claim a superior moral purpose over other interest groups in doing this, the techniques are no different.

Nearly all FNGOs have regular newsletters and magazines to inform donors about their work. Frequently these publications explain why a particular problem or crisis has occurred. For example, the fall 1998 issue of World Vision's magazine, which goes to 700,000 donors, described the Sudanese famine, the suffering it had caused, its roots in the civil war, and what could be done about it. Occasionally donors may be told how to write or call elected officials about a particular crisis, but this is done infrequently, as most FNGO (and NGO) fund-raising managers object to using donor lists to carry on advocacy campaigns. A sizable number of Americans probably get their most trusted news about the Third World not from *Time* or *Newsweek* or the *New York Times* but from their favorite FNGO publications. When a crisis occurs in, say, Bosnia, or Somalia, or North Korea, information about the situation and fund-raising appeals are sent to donor lists. These appeals, like the magazines and newsletters, raise public awareness and thereby influence public opinion about foreign-policy issues.

Most larger FNGOs have Washington offices from which they run some form of public advocacy campaigns on international issues. They do this through letters and visits to influential persons in Congress, the White House, the Pentagon, the Agency for International Development (USAID), and the State Department. Like all lobbying, this may or may not be effective. I recall that during the Rwandan genocide in 1994, representatives of Catholic Relief Services, World Vision, and Africares visited Dick Clark, the National Security Council's director of peacekeeping operations, to urge military intervention to stop the slaughter. The meeting became quite heated, for the Administration had no intention of intervening except to provide military equipment to other African countries that were sending troops. Even this provision of support was lethargic; the NGO group challenged the Administration on it, though apparently to little effect. A few weeks later, InterAction held its annual conference at which a letter was circulated urging then UN ambassador Madeleine Albright to support the continuation of a UN peacekeeping presence in Rwanda. A vote on this was to take place in the Security Council the next day. Most of the membership of InterAction, including forty FNGOs, signed the letter, but with little effect: Ambassador Albright voted to withdraw the troops.

FNGOs—more often, proportionately, than NGOs generally, I suspect—sometimes appeal to the public through the American news media for support on a foreign-policy issue. For example, for six months during 1998 the members of the Stop the [North Korean] Famine Committee sent opinion pieces to local newspapers, sent mass mailings to Congress, and appeared on radio and television. In what was a first in NGO history, they even used TV advertisements to criticize the U.S. government's denial of food aid to North Korea on the basis of geostrategic calculations. Their efforts appeared to have been successful: on July 11, President Clinton announced a large increase in food aid for North Korea.

But then, in reaction, Republican Congressman Christopher Cox of California proposed an amendment to end all food aid to North Korea. The Stop the Famine coalition decided on several actions to fight the measure. A newly formed Korean American NGO called the Korean American Sharing Movement (KASM) began mobilizing Korean Americans across the country to contact their congressional representatives. Although KASM was not explicitly faith-based, much of its board membership and funding came from Korean American churches. In addition, World Vision asked the Rev. Ben Soong, pastor of a Korean American church outside Seattle, to mobilize his fellow pastors in California to call Congressman Cox's office and oppose the amendment. Soong and the other pastors contacted nearly 300 churches within three days. As a World Vision representative I myself appeared on a Korean American Christian radio station in Los Angeles to explain what the amendment would do and why it had to be stopped. Calls flooded Cox's office, and he backed down and agreed to innocuous compromise language proposed by Congressman Tony Hall of Ohio. This concerted effort was successful.

In at least one instance FNGOs were used to make controversial policies more acceptable to conservative congressmen suspicious of Clinton administration policy. USAID announced that a consortium of five NGOs (CARE, Catholic Relief Services, World Vision, Mercy Corps International, and Amigos Internationales), all but one of which were faith-based, would monitor the distribution of food aid in North Korea by the UN's World Food Program (WFP). Unlike WFP, these NGOs had a sizable constituency among the American people. During House Republican debates over the food-aid program, objections were quickly silenced when the consortium membership was announced. Many Republicans had been elected with evangelical Christian support, and World Vision's participation in the consortium reportedly enhanced the acceptability of the food-aid program. Food aid played a central role in getting the North Korean regime to the negotiating table with the United States and South Korea, despite claims by the State Department and National Security Council that the food issue was separate from the geostrategic negotiations.

A final and in some ways the most significant way in which NGOs affect the formulation of foreign policy is through the collection and analysis of information on conditions on the ground in a crisis or on chronic problems facing poor countries. This use of NGOs appears to be generally appreciated by makers of foreign policy, regardless of their worldview. Embassy reporting, CIA analysis, and military intelligence all lack one characteristic that NGO information possesses: it derives from a relatively permanent presence on the ground with a large number of staff who speak to a great many local people. They have access to people in their homes and workplaces and marketplaces, and they are likely to have dependable and up-to-date information on such matters as changes in public mood toward political leaders, the formation of political movements, the viability of central government authority, and economic conditions. Sometimes NGO workers will witness military battles or atrocities or population movements, or will see the onset of drought or famine, before anyone in the capital city.

The role of FNGOs in this process is qualitatively different from that of secular NGOs in one central respect: local religious institutions with which FNGOs work provide a permanent source of information that, since it is not limited to the area in which the FNGO is working, may have more national scope. The indigenous church working with its related FNGO may also serve as a mechanism for mobilizing popular discontent in order to address some of the problems in the society. In Zambia it was primarily the church that monitored elections to ensure free and fair voting when longtime president Kenneth Kaunda was pressed—also by the church—into holding elections. After he lost, it was church leaders who convinced him to retire gracefully when he was considering voiding the election.

Because of this unique view of events, NGOs are sometimes asked to White House, State Department, and USAID meetings during major crises to share information and also to give advice on policy options for U.S. action. This occurred during the refugee crisis in western Zaire in 1995 and then again as the refugee camps were being shut down by Rwandan troops in 1996, and in Bosnia after the Serbian attack on the marketplace in Sarajevo in 1995. In 1997, after former InterAction president Julia Taft was confirmed as assistant secretary of state for population, refugees, and migration, and Roy Williams, former director of operations for the International Rescue Committee, was appointed director of USAID's Office of Foreign Disaster Assistance, they arranged to meet monthly with NGO leaders for a continuing exchange of information and views.

Do FNGOs Have a Foreign Policy?

While the increasing role of FNGOs in the design and implementation of foreign policy can be documented, this does not necessarily mean that the actions of FNGOs are based on a coherent set of doctrines that might qualify as international policy. But if we take a more Burkean and less ideological view of policy making, we can say that FNGOs show certain consistent patterns of reaction to world events. FNGOs directly or through their churches do have an established set of doctrines that are published in policy papers (some kept private and some released to the public) and in books by their in-house experts. For example, in 1997 the National Conference of Catholic Bishops in the United States published under the title *Peacemaking* a thoughtful set of essays by Catholic intellectuals, both clerical and lay, that applied Catholic social teaching to issues facing the post–Cold War world. Catholic social teaching formally began in 1891 with the encyclical by Pope Leo XIII entitled *Rerum Novarum* and has been extended by subsequent papal encyclicals, declarations of the Second Vatican Council, and other authoritative documents. It is rooted in the ancient church, particularly in the just war principles and other teachings of Saint Augustine and Saint Thomas Aquinas. When Catholic Relief Services takes international policy positions, those positions are constructed within the context of this rich tradition of social teaching.

World Vision has a publishing arm called MARC that has produced a number of useful books on the theological justification of World Vision development policy among the poor, though most are focused not on international policy in a general sense but on program-specific approaches. World Vision national offices in the United States, Canada, and the United Kingdom have produced policy papers on the Sudanese civil war, the international convention banning land mines, economic sanctions as an instrument of foreign policy, and the exploitation of children; all recommend international policy options for addressing these problems.

The National Council of Churches and its NGO arm, Church World Service, have an elaborate network of committees working on a wide range of foreign-policy issues.

Most FNGOs are interventionist, which is to say they believe that Western countries should intervene in crises to reduce the loss of human life and stabilize deteriorating situations. The degree and quality of intervention they are willing to tolerate depends on the theology of their tradition. The Mennonite and Quaker FNGOs come out of a pacifist tradition and oppose the use of U.S. military force in nearly all conflicts; their initial endorsement of military intervention in Somalia in the fall of 1992 was a rare exception. Most FNGOs are generally reluctant to advocate the use of force by the United States or other powers even if carried out under a UN banner; if force is used, they want constraints and limits put on the rules of engagement of the military force. The Roman Catholic Church generally opposes the use of economic sanctions as a tool of American diplomacy against rogue regimes, as it believes that sanctions harm the poor and not the elites responsible for the abuses.

Virtually all FNGOs, regardless of their denominational roots, focus their efforts on the problems facing the poor in poor countries. The Catholic Church, joined by some Protestant denominations, undertook a campaign to persuade developed countries and international institutions to forgive a vast amount of the debt of Third World countries on the two thousandth anniversary of Christ's birth; the custom has precedent in ancient Israel, where debts were forgiven at the beginning of each century. The effort had some noteworthy successes.

While it may be possible to find some economists in FNGOs, they are not likely to advertise their professional credentials much, as the international marketplace is held suspect by the theological culture of FNGOs. Free trade, structural economic reform, international economic institutions and multinational corporations, and liberal economic policy—these things are regarded as wolves in sheep's clothing. FNGOs generally wish to see constraints placed on the expansion of this sort of economic policy and have been critical of the failure of international institutions such as the World Bank, the International Monetary Fund, and regional development banks to improve the lot of the poor. While some FNGOs have modified their criticism of these institutions and of market economics, my own experience has been that the rank-and-file staff harbor serious reservations about market economics even when church leaders support it. Pope John Paul II in his 1991 encyclical *Centesimus Annus*, which marked the hundredth anniversary of Pope Leo XIII's *Rerum Novarum*, makes a powerful theological argument for democratic capitalism, though always in subordination to God's justice and providential will, but his statement has not been greeted with universal acceptance within the Church or church charities. (See the 1992 book *Doing Well and Doing Good: The Challenge to the Christian Capitalist*, by Richard John Neuhaus.)

FNGOs as Policy Makers

That FNGOs make recommendations on international policy matters is not in doubt; how competent they are at doing this is another matter. Perhaps their greatest weakness as policy makers is that they not accountable for the outcome of the policies they advocate, either to their donors, to the people they serve, or to the governments they are trying to influence. (This absence of accountability systems led in 1996 to the publication of a book on the subject by British NGO intellectuals: *Beyond the Magic Bullet*, edited by Michael Edwards and David Hulme.) It is easy enough to tell a diplomat or military officer what to do, but if the policy recommended proves to be either disastrous or entirely ineffective, the FNGO will not be held responsible; the government agency that carries it out will. FNGOs seldom consider the effects of a U.S. policy action in one country on U.S. policy in other countries. Like most interest groups with a limited agenda, they tend to be narrowly focused on the local and regional over the national and international, on the humanitarian over the military, economic, and political. They lack a sense of the possible unintended consequences of what they propose. Despite or perhaps because of their theology, FNGOs sometimes seem naïve in dealing with malicious political leaders and at other times tend to demonize those groups that oppose the people they are serving, people whom they seem willing to accept uncritically. Much of their advocacy implies that they represent the opinions of their constituencies, when in fact they make no systematic effort to determine what those opinions are (and might not reflect such views even if they knew them). Finally, the quarrels and rivalries among FNGOs not infrequently undermine any policy influence they might have had.

On the more positive side, FNGOs do bring the moral dimension to the foreign-policy debate, which is usually dominated by political calculations that may ignore a policy's cost in human life. They also provide a unique knowledge of true conditions (though sometimes they exaggerate in order to press their policies on resistant governments). More than secular NGOs, FNGOs will take risks and innovate in policy making and programming, which can be helpful in situations where geostrategic options have run out. They can accomplish tasks in chaotic circumstances that no other organizations can do effectively. Sometimes, when they reflect the views of their constituencies accurately, they can mobilize their local church constituencies to sustain a foreign-policy initiative by the U.S. government or in the countries they work in. Finally, they perform a powerful educational function, alerting their donors and constituencies to what is happening in certain parts of the world. And they have easy access to the national news media, which they sometimes employ skillfully to bring issues to public attention.

To the degree that FNGOs can overcome their inherent weaknesses and build on their very considerable strengths they will become increasingly formidable players in the foreign-policy establishment. While most American and European foreign-policy elites may hold a secular worldview, much of the rest of the world lives in one of the great religious traditions. FNGOs have much more in common with the rest of the world and thus may understand ethnic and religious conflicts, political movements driven by religious devotion, and the way in which the religious mind functions, better than secularized foreign-policy practitioners.

Comment by Allen D. Hertzke

Since I was asked to comment on both the Mark Amstutz and the Andrew Natsios chapters, I will mostly address points of common interest. First, I think we should note the difference between what churches do to form the ethical norms, mores, and habits of the heart and what their NGOs or denominational offices or church lobbies do in promoting particular agendas. Second, I would call for more prudential reasoning or calculation on the part of some faith-based NGOs. I have heard, for instance, that NGOs may have kept some refugees in the Rwandan refugee camps longer than necessary because they were running the camps and were raising money from the fact that they were performing that service. Third, I would also like to know more about how theological reflection by churches undergirds their relief and development work. As one of the writers points out, the development agencies of even the conservative evangelical churches can sometimes become quite progressive—as we use that term politically—abroad, whereas their lobby offices here may not be taking the same positions.

Another thing I'd like to hear more about is the extent to which NGOs use U.S. government funds. Mark Amstutz gives a very interesting table showing the 1998 budgets of the major faith-based organizations that accept government funding, including Lutheran World Relief at $22.6 million, Catholic Relief Services at $276 million, and World Vision at $358.4 million. In that year, 47 percent of the Catholic budget came from U.S. federal

Allen D. Hertzke is the Noble Foundation Presidential Professor of Political Science at the University of Oklahoma.

dollars, in contrast to 16 percent for World Vision and less than 6 percent for Lutheran World Relief. What is the explanation for this great range? Do some organizations have self-imposed limits? Does the amount of government money available depend on such things as what geographical areas the NGO is working in and what kinds of projects it is doing? This whole question is fascinating, and I'd welcome more information.

These religious NGOs are implementers of U.S. foreign policy in that they receive huge amounts of U.S. money to carry out refugee resettlement, famine relief, development projects, and the like. They are not, however, solely American, a development that reflects a profound demographic shift. Although we don't have really good numbers on this, I think it is safe to say that at least 60 percent of the world's practicing Christians are in Asia, Latin America, and Africa. There are probably more actively engaged Christians in Africa than in northern Europe. What does it mean for NGOs to be implementers of U.S. foreign policy when they are no longer "U.S." or even Western organizations?

Finally, what needs to be sorted out is the complex relationship between church bodies, missions, and faith-based relief and development NGOs. In a study of the growth of Pentecostalism in Central America, *Beyond Missionaries*, Anne Hallum suggests that a kind of Weberian uplift is really happening there. As enough people experience personal conversion, society is transformed. Thrift, industry, sobriety, and other such virtues taught in the Pentecostal churches are actually having an impact on families and communities and the overall culture of these developing countries. Thus, while I am a firm supporter of NGOs that do relief and development work, I think we should be careful not to slight the importance of traditional missionary work as well.

CHAPTER NINE

~

Faith-Based NGOs and the Government Embrace

Stephen V. Monsma

In March 1997 Andrew Natsios, then vice president of the evangelical Protestant relief and development agency World Vision, testified before the House Committee on International Relations that World Vision welcomed "a renewed partnership with the U.S. government in international assistance programming":

> This partnership has allowed us to influence how USAID does some of its work, by showing how our approach to relief and development works. In turn, World Vision has learned much from USAID in how to measure impact, conduct rigorous evaluations on our programs, and ensure high standards of accountability. Partnership means both sides learn from the other.[1]

Natsios painted an idealistic picture in which faith-based NGOs and the government work together in partnership. Each partner gives and takes, and each partner learns from the other; each is more effective in carrying out its mission because of the other.

In contrast, Bruce Nichols, after an exhaustive study of government funding of faith-based international development and relief agencies, sounded a cautionary note: "Financial cooperation between religious bodies and the government inevitably results in a loss of religious freedom. . . . Religious institutions are allowed to expand through such funding arrangements but

---

Stephen V. Monsma is a professor of political science at Pepperdine University in Malibu, California. From 1972 to 1982 he served in the Michigan House of Representatives and Senate. He is the author of *When Sacred and Secular Mix: Religious Nonprofit Organizations and Public Money*.

their specifically and distinctively religious functions are then restricted by law."[2] Similarly, Thomas Jeavons, though not referring specifically to international aid agencies, has written that "in most cases, accepting government funds to support the work of Christian service organizations requires compromising the character of that work."[3]

Although opinions vary sharply over its desirability and its effects, no one can deny the existence of a long-standing, ongoing relationship between faith-based NGOs (FNGOs) and the U.S. government. My purpose here is, first, to explore the nature of that relationship; next, to consider how FNGOs are affected by it; and lastly, to suggest some steps by which FNGOs that receive government funds can protect their religious autonomy.

The Relationship

The basic financial facts tell the story. Table 9.1 lists eight faith-based international relief and development agencies and the amounts they received from the U.S. government in 1996. From 1992 to 1996 the total amount of USAID funds going to NGOs increased from $900 million to $1.2 billion.[4] The Clinton administration was fully supportive of this partnership. In fact, in 1995 Vice President Al Gore reported that the administration intended to increase the portion of USAID's budget going to NGOs from 13 to 50 percent.[5]

In 1993–1994, I sent a survey questionnaire to the heads of 174 international relief and development agencies, and nearly ninety completed it.[6] In the questionnaire I asked extensive questions about the nature of the agencies, whether religious or nonreligious, and about their receipt of government funding. Table 9.2 shows the amounts that these agency heads—fifty-three secular and thirty-three religious—reported receiving. Among the faith-

TABLE 9.1   Government Funds to Faith-Based International Aid Agencies, 1996*

Adventist Development and Relief Agency International	$ 37.2 million
Catholic Relief Services	128.2 million
Christian Reformed World Relief Committee	0.7 million
Hadassah, the Women's Zionist Organization of America	1.6 million
Lutheran World Services	1.6 million
Salvation Army World Service Office	6.0 million
World Relief Corporation [National Association of Evangelicals]	11.7 million
World Vision Relief and Development	37.7 million

*Includes USAID freight, P.L. 480 freight, P.L. 480 donated food, USAID grants, USAID contracts, and other U.S. government grants.

Source: Voluntary Foreign Aid Programs, 1998 (Washington, D.C.: U.S. Agency for International Development, Office of Private and Voluntary Cooperation, 1998), 84–105.

TABLE 9.2   International Aid Agency Budgets and Government Funds

Portion of budget from public funds	Secular agencies* (percentage; N=53)	Religious agencies (percentage; N=33)
None	36	30
1 to 19%	15	39
20 to 39%	13	6
40% or more	36	24

*Agencies that have no religious base or history or that once had a religious orientation but now are largely secular.

based agencies, nearly 70 percent reported receiving some of their budget from government sources, compared to 64 percent for the secular agencies. Those that received public funds included Jewish, Roman Catholic, mainline Protestant, and conservative or evangelical Protestant agencies.

This study also showed that the faith-based agencies were religious in more than name. The questionnaire listed nine religiously based practices and asked directors of the faith-based agencies which ones their agencies engaged in. Table 9.3 gives the results. One thing it reveals is that the religious agencies receiving public funds did not seem to vary much from those not

TABLE 9.3   Religious Practices of Faith-Based Aid Agencies

Religious practice	All religious agencies (percentage; N=33)	Religious agencies receiving public funds (percentage; N=23)
1. Spirit of service/love	85	78
2. Religious orientation reflected in name or logo	79	83
3. Informal references to religious ideas by staff to persons served	52	52
4. Voluntary religious activities	30	30
5. Staff hiring: preference given to persons in agreement with religious orientation	24	22
6. Overt religious activities by an associated organization	21	26
7. Staff hiring: only persons in agreement with religious orientation	21	22
8. Religious commitments by persons served encouraged	21	22
9. Help in the construction of religious centers	15	9

receiving public funds in the religious practices they pursued. Notably, of the agencies receiving public funds, significant minorities engaged in such activities as proselytizing (encouraging religious commitments by the persons being served) and favoring persons from their religious tradition in the hiring of staff. More than half of both groups reported that their staff make informal references to religious ideas among the persons they serve.

Many faith-based NGOs receiving public funds are apparently able to maintain a significant religious dimension while delivering humanitarian services.

Effects of the Government Embrace

The FNGO-government embrace appears to be alive and well, but what does it do to the religious partners? Can faith-based international aid agencies that receive government funds maintain their religious integrity? Can they avoid becoming in effect arms of USAID, reflecting its priorities?

There is no shortage of voices arguing that with government funds inevitably come pressures to secularize. We have already noted the assertions of Nichols and Jeavons. Another cautionary note comes from the Norwegian analyst Terje Tvedt: "The mission organizations studied face—and their leaders often seem to acknowledge this—a dilemma between being organizations formed to spread the gospel and at the same time being heavily funded by public institutions."[7]

Adding to the case that the government embrace inevitably leads to the loss or serious diminution of religious autonomy are the church–state theories under which faith-based NGOs receive government funds. At first blush it seems surprising that such agencies are able to receive public tax dollars at all. After all, in the case of faith-based elementary and secondary schools the Supreme Court has again and again ruled in sweeping language that public funds may not directly support them or their programs. The baseline from which deviations are sometimes allowed was established in the Supreme Court's 1947 *Everson* decision:

> No tax in any amount, large or small, can be levied to support any religious activities or institutions, whatever they may be called, or whatever form they may adopt to teach or practice religion. . . . In the words of Jefferson, the clause against establishment of religion by law was intended to erect "a wall of separation between church and state." . . . That wall must be kept high and impregnable.[8]

Nonetheless, hundreds of millions of tax dollars flow every year not only to faith-based international aid and development agencies but to faith-based hospitals, family-service agencies, drug treatment centers, homeless shelters, and the like.

Two Legal Theories

This flow of tax dollars to FNGOs is made possible by two legal theories. The first is the *secular-sacred distinction*, which holds that as long as the secular and religious activities of a faith-based organization are separable, government may fund the secular activities. In a case allowing government funds to go to faith-based colleges, the Supreme Court noted that "the secular and sectarian activities of the colleges were easily separated."[9] Another decision observed that the challenged program of aid "was carefully drafted to ensure that the federally subsidized facilities would be devoted to the secular and not the religious function of the recipient institutions."[10] In 1899—in one of only two cases to come before the Supreme Court dealing directly with government financial aid to faith-based service organizations—the Court approved a program of aid to a Catholic hospital in the District of Columbia on this same basis.[11]

Closely related to the sacred-secular distinction is the *pervasively sectarian standard*. This is the key means by which the Supreme Court has distinguished between faith-based elementary and secondary schools (for which most forms of public funding have been found unconstitutional) and colleges, universities, and social-service agencies (for which, in the six cases to come before the Supreme Court, public funding has been found constitutional). The Court has held that K–12 faith-based schools are pervasively sectarian and that therefore it is impossible to separate the religious and the secular and fund only the secular, but that this not true of religiously based colleges and universities. In one of these cases the Court said: "Aid normally may be thought to have a primary effect of advancing religion when it flows to an institution in which religion is so pervasive that a substantial portion of its functions are subsumed in the religious mission."[12] It then went on to observe that the colleges whose receiving of government funds was under challenge were not marked by a pervasively religious nature such as this.

In 1988—in the second of the two Supreme Court cases dealing directly with government funding of religious social-service agencies—the Court upheld a program of government aid to centers that counseled young people on matters of sexuality and unwanted pregnancies. Religiously based agencies were explicitly included by Congress in the program. Key to the Court's decision was its conclusion that nothing "indicates that a significant proportion of the federal funds will be disbursed to 'pervasively sectarian' institutions."[13]

But the exact characteristics of a "pervasively sectarian"—or nonpervasively sectarian—institution or agency are far from clear. The plurality opinion by Justice Harry Blackmun in the 1976 case *Roemer v. Maryland Public Works Board* contains the fullest attempt at defining the term. Justice Blackmun outlines six indications that the four Catholic colleges whose receiving of public funds was under challenge were not pervasively sectarian: (1) they were not under direct church control, (2) religious indoctrination was not common, (3) normal liberal arts courses were offered and academic freedom prevailed, (4) normal academic standards prevailed, (5) religion was not a factor in the hiring of faculty, and (6) religion was not a factor in the admitting of students.[14] Yet these six ought not to be taken as essential criteria, all or even most of which must be present if an organization is to avoid the "pervasively sectarian" label. Blackmun himself later acknowledged that the "pervasively sectarian" standard is "a vaguely defined work of art."[15]

The result is that faith-based agencies are left in legal uncertainty. No case involving faith-based international aid agencies' receipt of public money has been litigated up to the Supreme Court. While it does seem clear that they must not be pervasively sectarian and that only their secular activities can be funded, the exact meaning of "pervasively sectarian" is not known. It seems to say they may be religious but not too religious—or that religion must not permeate their programming to too great an extent.

Two Vulnerable Areas

The danger, as I see it, is not that these agencies will suddenly be denied public funding—no one seems particularly interested in blocking it—but that their religious autonomy is threatened. More specifically, I think there are two areas in which religiously based NGOs receiving public funds have been left legally vulnerable. The first is their hiring policies. If a faith-based NGO could not limit its hiring to persons of its own faith, its religious nature would be severely compromised. Employees and their religious commitments virtually define an agency. Being within a religious tradition means more than simply having some sentimental or traditional ties to that tradition or having some religious elements tacked onto an otherwise secular program. It usually will mean a commitment to a certain worldview, a certain set of values and perspectives that deeply affect how the agency approaches the needs of those it serves. If an agency were forced to hire persons who do not share those values and perspectives, its position as a faith-based agency would be undermined. Yet one of the marks of a nonpervasively sectarian college outlined by Justice Blackmun was a hiring policy that did not discriminate in favor of that college's religious tradition. Does this mean that a faith-based international aid agency receiving public funds may not restrict its hiring to persons from its own faith tradition? The Supreme Court has never decided this issue. Some lower courts have ruled, though not in relation to international aid agencies, that religious agencies receiving federal funds may not have a shared-faith criterion for hiring, and bureaucratic officials have forced some agencies to broaden their hiring policies.[16]

A second area in which FNGOs that accept government funds have been left legally vulnerable lies in the extent to which they can integrate religious aspects into their service programs. Some deeply religious agencies working in sustainable development believe that their work will be effective only if it has a religious dimension. If sustainable development efforts are to succeed, they believe, the power of religion to change attitudes and values and to help people overcome disappointments and setbacks must be utilized. They are committed to a holistic approach that includes the spiritual dimension of human beings. But to integrate spiritual elements into "secular" development programs flies in the face of the Supreme Court's sacred-secular distinction. Public funds may support only the secular activities of an agency. Yet to require an agency to give up the religious aspects of its programming or to carefully segregate them from "secular" aspects may limit the agency's effectiveness as well as violating its religious beliefs.

May an agency that receives public funds limit its hiring to persons from its own religious tradition? May it integrate religious elements into its relief and development efforts? No one can answer these questions with any real assurance. The Supreme Court has not heard a single case dealing with faith-based NGOs that receive public funds. What precedents there are are drawn from the related areas of religiously based schools and colleges. And those precedents are not promising. They are rooted in legal principles that are unclear at best and destructive of religious autonomy at worst.

If a religiously based agency cannot follow policies dictated by its faith commitment, its religious autonomy has effectively been destroyed. Let no one underestimate the depth of the religious-freedom issue at stake here.

The Testimony of Experience

But in what is admittedly a complex, confused area, there is another story to be told. We must listen to the testimony of the faith-based NGOs themselves whose officials time and time again insist that their receipt of government funds has not led to the compromise of their religious missions. The previously quoted statement made by Andrew Natsios when he was a vice president of World Vision is a case in point. Similarly, Michael Wiest, deputy executive director of Catholic Relief Services, spoke positively before a House Appropriations subcommittee in March 1997 of "the public/private partnership" that is "critical to the success of food aid programs."[17] Wiest spoke for the Coalition for Food Aid, which includes, in addition to Catholic Relief Services, the Adventist Development and Relief Agency and World Vision Relief and Development.

In several interviews with executives of faith-based NGOs I have repeatedly been assured that their receipt of government funds has not caused them to water down their religious emphasis. A high-level official with an evangelical Protestant NGO, for example, assured me that his agency has had only very minor problems with government officials over its religiously motivated practices. USAID officials have repeatedly told him, he said, that they like to work with faith-based NGOs since they respect the FNGOs' moral framework, feel they can trust them, and know they deliver. A former official with an FNGO that received government funds told me that when he asked a USAID official whether the religious character of his agency posed any problems, she replied that there was no problem as long as his agency delivered the humanitarian services for which USAID was granting it funds.

It strains credulity to conclude that faith-based agencies that report positive working relationships with the government are either so naïve that they have been hoodwinked by government officials into thinking that their religious independence has not been seriously compromised when in fact it has, or so wedded to government money that they will proclaim their religious independence even when they realize it has been seriously compromised.

My study—which included twenty-three FNGOs that accept public money—offers further support for the position that such agencies are able to receive public funds and also maintain their religious practices. My questionnaire asked, "Are there any other religious practices [in addition to several listed] you feel you have had to curtail or eliminate because you receive government funds?" and "Have any government officials ever questioned any of your religiously based practices or brought pressure to bear on you to change any of them?" In response to these two open-ended questions, five of the twenty-three agencies (22 percent) reported some sort of a problem or limitation. The problems the five reported had to do with (1) a building constructed in part with government funds that was being used for "voluntary services on Sunday" (the problem was resolved so that the building could continue to be used for worship services), (2) questions raised about a fundraising letter, (3) questions about the use of overtly religious language in some technical publications, (4) alleged proselytizing efforts, and (5) sexual behavior standards in an overseas foster-care program. There was no pattern to the five issues. More significant was the fact that eighteen of the twenty-three agencies receiving government funds said they had experienced no problems or limitations at all. Even when the study focused on the nine agencies that engaged in many religious practices, seven reported no problems or limitations.

The study also presented the agency directors with a list of nine potential effects—four positive, two neutral, and three negative—of receiving public funds and asked which ones their agencies had experienced. Here is what the twenty-three directors reported:

1. Expanded services and programs: 87 percent
2. Hired staff with higher levels of education: 39 percent
3. Provided more effective services: 39 percent
4. Avoided having to shut down: 0 percent
5. Became involved in lobbying legislators and government agencies: 39 percent
6. Used fewer volunteers and more professional staffing: 13 percent
7. Put more time and effort into paperwork than necessary: 57 percent
8. Became more bureaucratic and less flexible and creative: 17 percent
9. Received fewer private gifts and volunteer hours: 4 percent

The positive effects were claimed more often than the negative ones. In fact, the only negative effect cited by a majority of the agencies was the common one about too much paperwork. Only four of the twenty-three agencies felt they had become more bureaucratic and less flexible and creative as a result of receiving government funds, and only one reported receiving fewer private gifts and volunteer hours. Twenty of the agency directors indicated that government funds have allowed them to expand their services and programs, and a significant minority (nine) said government funds had enabled them to hire staff with higher levels of education and to provide more effective services. The overall picture that emerges is one of satisfaction with the effects of receiving government funds.

In summary, my study of twenty-three faith-based international aid agencies, public statements made by leaders of FNGOs, and my own interviews with a number of officials of FNGOs leave the impression that the faith-based NGOs believe they have been able to work with government in such a way that their ability to fulfill their missions has been increased without undue constraints on their religious character. In fact, table 9.3 shows that agencies that accepted government money did not report fewer religiously based practices than those that did not. They seemed able to mix significant religious elements into publicly funded activities and programs. How is this possible?

How Religion Stays In

One part of the answer lies in the fact that watchdog groups—such as Americans United for the Separation of Church and State and the American Civil Liberties Union—that snap to attention at the smallest forms of public assistance to faith-based elementary and secondary schools, or at the slightest nod to religion in public schools, pay no attention to public funding of faith-based international aid agencies. It is simply a nonissue for them. Not one case dealing with this question has ever reached the Supreme Court. In fact, after almost ten years of paying close attention to church-state issues, I have yet to come across even a lower-court case challenging the funneling of millions of dollars of USAID funds through faith-based NGOs. As noted earlier, the Clinton administration, which appointed two strict church-state separationists to the Supreme Court (Ruth Bader Ginsburg and Stephen Breyer), also indicated its intention to increase the NGO share of USAID funds from 13 to 50 percent, with much of that going to religiously based NGOs. In my study, of the forty-four directors of international aid agencies who opposed public funding for K–12 schools, thirty-three (75 percent) favored public funding for religiously based international aid agencies.[18] It is clear that while we as a society have deep misgivings about religion in schools, we do not have such concerns about government and religion in other areas—and surely not in the area of international relief and development. Thus a high level of cooperation between government and FNGOs is possible.

Faith-based international aid agencies are largely doing work that no one else is eager to do. Working under difficult and sometimes dangerous conditions with some of the poorest of the poor in little-known areas of the world does not lead to a great deal of competition from other societal groups or government agencies. In fact, often overseas government agencies need NGOs as much as or more than the NGOs need them. In a typical scenario, there is famine or a natural disaster in a far-off part of the world. Television cameras have brought graphic photos of the horror to the public. Politicians demand that USAID or other government agencies do something. Often it is only the NGOs that have an infrastructure in place to distribute food and medical supplies. Michael Wiest of Catholic Relief Services has pointed out that "AID does not have offices in some of the most food-insecure countries in West Africa—such as Togo, Cape Verde, Mauritania, Chad, Burkina Faso and Sierre Leone," but Catholic Relief Services has "established linkages with communities in eighty poor and less developed countries."[19] Realities of this sort encourage a genuine partnership in which both government and the NGO must give and take, rather than a lopsided relationship in which those with the money call all the shots.

Sometimes there is even an interchange of personnel between USAID and NGOs. For instance, Andrew Natsios, whom I quoted earlier in his former capacity as vice president of World Vision, was previous to that a US-AID official. An executive in one faith-based NGO told me that this is not an unusual pattern. In his experience, he said, it was not unusual for USAID officials to be motivated by the same religious-humanitarian impulses as officials at FNGOs. This helps to make the working relationship cooperative rather than adversarial.

What can we conclude about the effect on faith-based international aid and development agencies of their accepting government money? The answer, I am convinced, is a mixed one. Both the danger and the positive potential in the relationship are real and large. The danger is in the ever-present threat that with government funds will come a dictation of priorities, limiting regulations, and pressures to tone down religious mission or practices. The latter danger is enhanced by the shaky constitutional grounds on which faith-based NGOs currently receive public funds. Nevertheless, many FNGOs seem to have successfully avoided the pitfalls and have used government funds to extend their healing reach without compromising their religious mission. In doing so they have been helped by a long tradition of non-concern over the sort of church-state separation issues prominent in other areas, by the difficult nature of their work and the networks they often have in place in remote parts of the world, and, to at least some extent, by a sharing of their sense of mission by some government officials.

A Strategy for Partnership

While there may be some circumstances under which some agencies would be well advised to refuse government money, as a general rule I believe faith-based NGOs should avail themselves of available government funds. In this section I will explain why I think this, offering two practical and then three more theoretical reasons.

Practical Considerations

First, in most fields of overseas relief and development, millions of government dollars are available. In 1996 USAID funneled some $1.2 *billion* through NGOs, many of which were faith-based.[20] A financially hard-pressed FNGO that cuts itself off from this funding should have firm reasons for making such a choice; it owes this much to its supporters, its employees, and the needy persons it is seeking to serve. If it turns down public funds, it will need to approach its supporters for even more money. Perhaps it will need to lay off employees eager to be of service to those in need; perhaps it can serve fewer persons, thereby fulfilling its own mission less fully.

A second practical consideration is that if faith-based NGOs refuse government funds, that money will then be spent either by secular NGOs or directly by USAID or other government agencies. Faith-based NGOs have a long and distinguished history of conducting effective, efficient relief and development work.[21] They often have an infrastructure of schools, health clinics, and churches (either their own or those of cooperating indigenous agencies) that government agencies and even secular NGOs cannot match. For this and other reasons, faith-based NGOs are usually more effective channels of assistance than government agencies and sometimes than secular NGOs. In some countries FNGOs are almost the only means available to get assistance to a population in peril from drought, floods, war, or other disasters. Thus when they turn down government funds, the very real effect may well be that needy, suffering people are not helped as quickly and as effectively as they could be.

Theoretical Considerations

The first of my three more theoretical considerations in favor of accepting government money is that when government funds are channeled through a faith-based NGO, government is not thereby "aiding" that NGO. When Catholic Relief Services, for example, receives a million dollars in USAID funds for famine relief in the Horn of Africa, the beneficiary of these funds is not Catholic Relief Services but the hungry and dying in the Horn of Africa. If such funds are thought of as "aid" to the recipient organization, both the government officials and the organization may take the wrong approach. The government officials may feel they have a right and perhaps a duty to establish certain priorities and to demand that certain religious elements be removed from the program, and the FNGO may agree that the officials have the right to do this. A better approach is to see the funding as the government's purchase of certain desired development or relief services.

A second theoretical consideration is that the government obtains its money from American taxpayers, including the millions of deeply religious Americans, and so the funds it channels through faith-based agencies have in part been collected from persons who are supportive of the religious missions of those agencies. There is a fairness issue here. In accepting government funds, an FNGO helps to ensure that the proportion of tax dollars paid by religious citizens will better correspond to the proportion of tax dollars going to faith-based rather than secular organizations.

A third theoretical consideration is more complex but also more fundamental than the first two. We noted previously that the Supreme Court has approved the funding of religiously based colleges and social-service organizations on the legal theory that they are not pervasively sectarian and that their religious and secular aspects can be separated. This legal theory creates an uncertain foundation on which to defend the religious autonomy of faith-based NGOs. Their receipt of public funds seems to require that they not be "too religious" and that they neatly segregate their religious and secular efforts. My recent study demonstrated that not only in faith-based international aid agencies but also in faith-based colleges and family-services agencies, the segregation of religious from secular facets is often not much more than a thinly disguised fiction.[22] As long as this remains the legal basis on which such agencies receive public funds, they remain vulnerable to lawsuits from church-state separationist watchdog groups, disgruntled employees, and others. And the mindset this approach fosters among faith-based agencies causes them perhaps even unconsciously to soft-pedal their religious mission.

Yet there is an alternative legal basis on which faith-based agencies can receive public funds in keeping with the First Amendment. It is one to which the Supreme Court has given some support, and one that would do much to safeguard the religious independence of the agencies receiving public funds. I refer to the neutrality or equal-treatment doctrine, which says that the demands of the First Amendment are met when public funds are made available to religiously based organizations providing certain social, health, or educational services, as long as those funds are available equally to religious and nonreligious organizations.

In 1995 the Supreme Court held that when the University of Virginia decided to help fund a wide range of student publications, it could not exclude a Christian student publication from funding. "The guarantee of neutrality is respected, not offended, when the government, following neutral criteria and evenhanded policies, extends benefits to recipients whose ideologies and viewpoints, including religious ones, are broad and diverse."[23] Similarly, in a 1997 case dealing with public-school instructors placed in religiously based K–12 schools to offer remedial instruction, the Supreme Court held that such a program was constitutional since "the aid is allocated on the basis of neutral, secular criteria that neither favor nor disfavor religion, and is made available to both religious and secular beneficiaries on a nondiscriminatory basis."[24] The key point in these decisions—and some other recent Supreme Court decisions—is that the religiously based organizations were eligible to receive public funding, not because their religious practices were neither too overt nor too integrated into the services they were rendering, but because they as religious organizations were not being favored over their secular counterparts. They were not being given public funds *because* they were religious; they were merely sharing in funds that were generally available. Under this interpretation of the First Amendment, religious agencies may not be favored over nonreligious agencies, but neither may they be discriminated against.

This is a more solid basis for the participation of faith-based NGOs in the NGO-government partnership than the old legal theory that they are not pervasively sectarian and that the money they receive funds secular activities only. Under the neutrality doctrine, it is not the religious or nonreligious character of the NGO that is the issue but the NGO's effective provision of desired services and the evenhanded, neutral distribution of public funds to religious and nonreligious NGOs alike. It is *essential* for religious NGOs to insist that this is the basis on which they are constitutionally entitled to public funds. I cannot overemphasize this.

Protecting Religious Autonomy

Although the neutrality or equal-treatment doctrine is highly promising, it is not yet generally accepted in the courts and has never been applied directly to faith-based international relief and development agencies. Thus it is only prudent for the faith-based NGO to take certain steps to protect its religious autonomy in case it should ever be challenged.

First a faith-based NGO accepting government money needs to *be clear about the nature of its religious mission and what religious practices are and are not negotiable.* I have interviewed persons associated with FNGOs that receive government funds in three countries: the United States, Germany, and the Netherlands. Some of the agencies followed many religious practices, while others were only nominally religious. My observations have convinced me that the single most important factor in preserving a religious mission is a self-conscious, openly discussed, agreed-upon determination to do so.

The big danger for faith-based NGOs in accepting government funds under present conditions is not that suddenly the NGO will be told it must abandon all religious practices but that, over a period of years, it will end up compromising a little here and a little there. Luis Lugo of the Pew Charitable Trusts once spoke of "preemptive capitulation" as the policy too many agencies follow once they accept public funds. Fearing lawsuits or hassles by government officials, faith-based agencies may quietly abandon certain religious practices they fear will act as red flags. Sometimes agencies too quickly accept the complaint of some low-level official as the final word.

FNGOs receiving public dollars must not necessarily seek to retain all of their religiously based practices. There are certain practices—such as worship services and overt proselytization efforts—that no agency should expect government money to fund directly. This part of the work needs to be covered by private donations. Also, there may be some religious practices that are not crucial to an agency's mission and may even be counterproductive to that mission. What is important is that every agency accepting government funds must draw a line in the sand beyond which it will not go. The staff, board, and top management of the agency all need to be involved in determining what their essential, "nonnegotiable" religious practices are.

Also, faith-based NGOs need to realize that they are not without bargaining strength. They often provide services to needy persons that not many others are interested in providing. At the same time there would be a public outcry if the U.S. government failed to respond to critical humanitarian concerns. The prospect that starving children would no longer be helped because some low-level official stood in the way of using a faith-based NGO as a conduit for aid would constitute a public-relations problem that most policy makers would like to avoid. Also, there are increasing calls in the public-policy community for government to run fewer overseas assistance programs and instead to turn to private, nonprofit agencies. Often it will be easier for a busy, harried government official to give way to a faith-based NGO that objects to the official's latest directive than to insist on strict compliance and run the risk of the FNGO's dropping out of the program.

A second basic step a faith-based NGO can take to protect its religious integrity is to *maintain a significant financial base in addition to government funds*. There is a danger in becoming too dependent on government money. Once the government provides over half of an agency's funds, danger flags should start to fly. There are two factors in play here. One is that the threat to forgo government funds if some official insists on the removal of certain religious practices becomes less credible as the percentage of the budget from government funding increases. There is no way to escape this fact. A second and related factor is that as the percentage of an NGO's budget that comes from the government goes up, government officials will feel more justified in imposing restrictions on it—and the NGO's leaders may feel a greater obligation to accept those restrictions. The truth of the old adage about "he who pays the piper calls the tune" is rooted in economic realities, but it is also rooted in the *right* of the payer to call the tune. Every NGO that accepts government funds should place a limit on the proportion of its budget it will accept from government sources.

A third step is to *cultivate good relationships with the news media and elected officials*. Faith-based NGOs seeking to address persistent problems around the world tend to have strong support across the political spectrum. Political liberals—whether in public office, in the news media, or in other positions of community leadership—tend to admire and respect FNGOs that are actually seeking to do something about starvation, disease, illiteracy, and underdevelopment, while political conservatives tend to respect the religious commitments of FNGOs and to see them as good alternatives to ever more, ever bigger government programs. In terms of public perceptions, faith-based NGOs are in a strong position.

If positive relationships with the news media and members of Congress have been developed over the years, then if a strict-separationist group or a government bureaucrat should ever challenge an NGO's religiously based practices, the NGO will have a reservoir of good will and sympathetic understanding to draw upon. In short, while the current legal protections for a faith-based NGO may be weak, the potential political and public-relations protections are strong.

The nature of the FNGO-government embrace is not simple or one-dimensional. To see it either as problem-free or as necessarily fatal is naïve and unwarranted. On balance, in my judgment, the practical and theoretical reasons for faith-based NGOs to accept government funds clearly outweigh the risks, as long as the FNGOs approach this financial embrace carefully and thoughtfully.

Notes

1. Andrew S. Natsios, testimony before the House Committee on International Relations, March 13, 1997.

2. J. Bruce Nichols, *The Uneasy Alliance: Religion, Refugee Work, and U.S. Foreign Policy* (New York: Oxford University Press, 1988), 187.

3. Thomas H. Jeavons, *When the Bottom Line Is Faithfulness: Management of Christian Service Organizations* (Bloomington: Indiana University Press, 1994), 128.

4. See *Voluntary Foreign Aid Programs, 1993*, 86, and *Voluntary Foreign Aid Programs, 1998*, 104 (Washington, D.C.: U.S. Agency for International Development, Office of Private and Voluntary Cooperation, 1993 and 1998).

5. Cited in Terje Tvedt, *Angels of Mercy or Development Diplomats?* (Trenton, N.J.: Africa World Press, 1998), 1.

6. For a full report on the larger study of which this survey was a part, see Stephen V. Monsma, *When Sacred and Secular Mix: Religious Nonprofit Organizations and Public Money* (Lanham, Md.: Rowman & Littlefield, 1996).

7. Tvedt, *Angels of Mercy*, 217.

8. *Everson v. Board of Education*, 330 U.S. at 16 and 18 (1947).

9. *Roemer v. Maryland Public Works Board*, 426 U.S. at 764 (1976).

10. *Tilton v. Richardson*, 403 U.S. at 679 (1971).

11. See *Bradfield v. Roberts*, 175 U.S. at 291 (1899).

12. *Hunt v. McNair*, 413 U.S. at 743 (1973).

13. *Bowen v. Kendrick*, 487 U.S. at 610 (1988).

14. See *Roemer v. Maryland Public Works Board*, at 736.

15. From Blackmun's dissent in *Bowen v. Kendrick*, 487 U.S. at 631 (1988).

16. See, for example, *Dodge v. Salvation Army*, 1989 WL 43857 (S.D. Miss.). An official with an evangelical Protestant international aid agency acknowledged in an interview with the author that because of some pressures his agency has hired some lower-level employees who do not share its faith commitment.

17. Written testimony of Michael R. Wiest before the House Committee on Appropriations, Subcommittee on Agriculture, FDA, and Related Agencies, March 12, 1997.

18. See Monsma, *When Sacred and Secular Mix*, 49.

19. Wiest, testimony, March 12, 1997.

20. *Voluntary Foreign Aid Programs*, 1998,104.

21. See, for example, Nichols, *Uneasy Alliance*.

22. See Monsma, *When Secular and Sacred Mix*,120–31.

23. *Rosenberger v. Rector*, 515 U.S. at 839 (1995).

24. *Agostini v. Felton*, 1997 U.S. Lexis, 4000.

~

Comment by Michael R. Wiest

Professor Monsma has given us a useful review of the experience of NGOs that cooperate with the U.S. government in international relief and development work. Moreover, I found his conclusions sound: that faith-based NGOs should not shun government funding because of fears that such assistance will dilute their religious content, but that they need a clear sense of their identity and specific rules of engagement when they take such funding. We at Catholic Relief Services would endorse these conclusions on two grounds: theoretically, on the basis of Catholic social teaching, and practically, on the basis of deep and broad experience in working with government funding.

Catholic Relief Services (CRS) is an agency of the U.S. Catholic bishops. Its primary funding is supplied by the generosity of American Catholics, but for many years it also has received substantial funding from the U.S. government. Professor Monsma rightly asks faith-based agencies like ours, "What are the sources of your integrity? What makes you able to accept public funds without losing sight of your original mission and methods?" For CRS the answer lies with the long tradition of Catholic social teaching, which is addressed to Catholics as a community of faith, to all Catholic agencies that represent the Church, and to all in society who seek normative direction for public policy.

Michael R. Wiest is deputy executive director of Catholic Relief Services, with headquarters in Baltimore, and has had extensive experience with CRS in various parts of Africa.

Catholic social teaching provides the foundation for the purpose and mission of Catholic Relief Services. The Second Vatican Council in its document *The Church in the Modern World* said that it is the task of the Church to stand as a sign and safeguard of the transcendence of the human person. This means that the Church must publicly be engaged in a ministry of protecting human dignity and promoting human rights. Some Catholic agencies, like Catholic Charities USA and the Campaign for Human Development, are focused on issues of dignity and rights within the United States. Catholic Relief Services has the responsibility of addressing these questions in the more complex fabric of international relations.

Our identity and work as an agency are founded on the belief that human dignity is an attribute of every human person, that human rights are universal in scope and content, that a common human community exists in the moral order, and that the bonds of that community demand action to protect individuals when their lives or rights are threatened by natural catastrophe, economic collapse, war, or political oppression. CRS exists to provide institutional expression of these convictions. Whether U.S. government funding exists or not is a secondary question; we would undertake the same work of relief, development, and global justice without it.

A major purpose of the Church's social teaching has been to specify the moral responsibility of states, international organizations, and other international actors in three areas: the pursuit of peace, the achievement of international distributive justice, and the protection of human rights. There is an irreducible religious responsibility to address these questions. This means that from a Catholic perspective, even if CRS never took any government funding, we would as part of the larger Church urge the U.S. government to fulfill its moral responsibilities in such areas as debt relief for poor countries, sustainable development, famine relief, peace-keeping, and the creation of international institutions to foster the universal common good.

Both church and state, then, have responsibilities to promote human dignity, human rights, and international justice, and so the possibility for collaboration is clear. Of course, faith-based agencies need internal guidelines that will protect them from being co-opted by the state or simply being seen as an agent of the U.S. government. For us this means, among other things, that we must support needed programs that the government cannot fund because of legal restrictions; we must refuse to participate in some government undertakings, such as certain population-related programs; and we must be able to distinguish the CRS position from that of the U.S. government or other institutions, such as the IMF or the World Bank, if we believe their policies in a particular situation are counterproductive.

On a practical level, our collaboration with USAID and other government agencies enables us to expand our outreach to the poor and vulnerable, improve the quality of federally funded programs, and influence public policy related to America's responsibility in the world. Our partnership with the U.S. government dates from the closing years of World War II, when together with other American faith-based agencies Catholic Relief Services helped to provide government-funded humanitarian assistance to millions in Europe and Asia whose lives had been devastated by war.

Sometimes-competing public policies induce government agencies to do things that we, as faith-based constituencies, find reprehensible. For example, in 1983 AID removed a longstanding program of food assistance to Ethiopia from its congressional budget request although there was an impending famine; the belief was that hunger would help to bring down the Marxist government. CRS and other faith-based organizations were present to make the issue public, to lobby Congress, and eventually, with help from a visit by Mother Teresa to President Reagan, to see the reversal of an immoral policy. Certainly there are risks in this partnership, but we owe it to the poor and marginalized to manage these risks, not avoid them.

Index

About the Editor

Elliott Abrams is the president of the Ethics and Public Policy Center. In June 2000 he became chairman of the U.S. Commission on International Religious Freedom. During the 1980s he held three assistant secretary posts at the State Department: International Organization Affairs, Human Rights and Humanitarian Affairs, and Inter-American Affairs.